WHY the LEFT HATES AMERICA

WHY the LEFT HATES AMERICA

EXPOSING THE LIES THAT HAVE OBSCURED OUR NATION'S GREATNESS

DANIEL J. FLYNN

FORUM

An Imprint of Prima Publishing

Published by Prima Publishing, Roseville, California. Member of the Crown Publishing Group, a division of Random House, Inc., New York.

FORUM and colophon are trademarks of Random House, Inc. PRIMA PUBLISHING and colophon are trademarks of Random House, Inc., registered with the United States Patent and Trademark Office.

Library of Congress Cataloging-in-Publication Data
Flynn, Daniel J.
Why the left hates America : exposing the lies that have obscured our
nation's greatness / Daniel J. Flynn
p. cm
Includes bibliographical references and index.
ISBN 0-7615-6375-X
1. Anti-Americanism. 2. National characteristics, American. 3. September 11
Terrorist Attacks, 2001—Causes. 4. Radicalism—United States—
History—20th century. 5. Public opinion—United States. I. Title.

E169.12.F67   2002
306'0973—dc21   2002073377
02 03 04 QQ 10 9 8 7 6 5 4 3 2
Printed in the United States of America

First Edition

Visit us online at www.primapublishing.com

CONTENTS

ACKNOWLEDGMENTS

Why the Left Hates America is the culmination of nearly a decade's work in studying, writing about, and speaking on the American Left. While the need for this book became clear in the aftermath of September 11, 2001, its seeds were planted long before that tragic date. I greatly appreciate all of the people who helped me air my ideas on the peculiarity of the Left's contempt for America, particularly the many students who helped organize speaking events on campus even when it was clear that what they were doing was not popular with their professors or the administrators running their schools.

Many individuals aided me by making suggestions, reviewing portions of the manuscript, and offering help in researching various topics. Their assistance does not imply the endorsement of any of the ideas contained in the book, which are my own. Additionally, any errors or mistakes in these pages are my own. Undoubtedly, the input of the following individuals saved me from a greater number of errors that the book would've contained without their assistance.

I am forever grateful to my editor at Prima Forum, David Richardson. I am in David's debt not only for believing in the book but for providing direction to the project. I also thank Andi Reese Brady, who guided the production process. Their pleasantness made the task a happy process.

With an unmatched eye for grammatical errors and other mistakes, Joe St. George proofed several chapters. His expertise saved me from numerous embarrassing errors. Burt Folsom, a historian who truly makes the past come alive, reviewed several chapters as well. His suggestions, insights on history, and advice were invaluable. My friends Cormac Bordes, Morgan Knull, and Matthew Rarey all scoured portions of the manuscript too, steering me in the right direction when I drifted off course. Drawing on his own experiences, Dinesh D'Souza provided adept guidance to a neophyte author in his attempts to get his work published. Those aiding my efforts in researching various topics include Roger Aronoff, Ed Corrigan, Stan Evans, and Cliff Kincaid.

I greatly appreciate the freedom given to me at my job as executive director of Accuracy in Academia to write this book. Reed Irvine and his son Don deserve special thanks for this, and Sara Russo and Christopher Chow have my thanks for the prosperity of the organization during any absences while I was writing the book.

I also wish to thank the many Flynns—including Ryan, Dennis, Barry, Sean, Ronald, and honorary Flynn Eric Auciello—for their input and support in my efforts. The hard work of my mother, Janet Flynn, over the years provided me with a great example in my attempts to meet tight deadlines while juggling a full-time job and my duties as a sergeant in the United States Marine Reserves. Finally, the love and support of my wife, Molly, as well as her talents as an editor, aided me tremendously in bringing the project to completion.

INTRODUCTION

"THERE IS THE National flag. He must be cold, indeed, who can look upon its folds rippling in the breeze without pride of country."[1] So spoke Senator Charles Sumner during an 1867 address in New York City.

As the Stars and Stripes blanketed that very city one hundred and thirty-four years later, some indeed looked upon the flag, not with pride, but with contempt. Most conspicuously, Katha Pollitt, a writer for *The Nation*, penned a column lamenting the appeals of her 13-year-old daughter to fly an American flag outside their New York apartment. Pollitt reacted to her daughter's requests with the type of parental hurt normally reserved for such occasions as a child's arrest, unwanted pregnancy, or expulsion from school. Pollitt, as she noted in her column, admonished her daughter: "The flag stands for jingoism and vengeance and war." She resolved the generational dispute by settling on a compromise. "I tell her she can buy a flag with her own money and fly it out her bedroom window, because that's hers, but the living room is off-limits."[2]

If flying the American flag is condemned after a national event as tragic as 9-11, when is it deemed acceptable? For the Katha

Pollitts of the world, the answer is never. Expressions of patriotism are off-limits, according to this worldview, because Americans have nothing to be patriotic about. Tellingly, Pollitt's unusual view of America is not unusual among her fellow progressives. Hating America is de rigueur in left-of-center political circles. What's truly deserving of censure, leftists claim, is not the act of hating America, but pointing out that some Americans actually do hate their country. Questioning someone's patriotism, they hold, is anti-intellectual; or, as Samuel Johnson famously remarked, invoking patriotism is the last refuge of a scoundrel. Yet some Americans clearly hate their country. Simply acknowledging this is neither anti-intellectual nor the act of a scoundrel. Denying this reality, however, may make one both.

This is a book about people who hate America. More specifically, it explores the prevalence of anti-Americanism among those on the political Left. These pages seek to expose the strong undercurrent of reverse patriotism on the American Left, explain why so many leftists loathe the United States, and refute the arguments of those who hold their country in contempt.

Everywhere but in the United States, the Left is candid in its contempt for America. American leftists, quite aware of the political stupidity of tying their philosophy's fate so overtly with rhetorical tirades against the very people they're trying to win over, often seek to downplay the anti-Americanism inherent in their ideology. Increasingly, however, we see clear signs of domestic leftists dropping any pretense that their program is inspired by love of country. In the aftermath of 9-11, as shall be explored more comprehensively in chapter 1, examples of this national self-hatred have proliferated:

- Poet Bell Hooks* ranted that the U.S. military's response to the terrorist attacks was inspired "by the
imperialist, white supremacist, capitalist, patriarchal
hunger to show the planet our nation's force, to show
that this nation would commit absolute acts of violence
that will wipe out whole nations and worlds." She continued that the American government is devoted to
"violence" and "death" and operates in a "culture of
domination."[3]
- The vitriol against America was particularly harsh
on campus. One confused undergraduate reacted to
9-11 by maintaining, "sometimes it is our fault," while
another opined that "we had it coming."[4] A professor
in New Mexico told his students, "Anyone who can
blow up the Pentagon would get my vote."[5]
- America-haters torched U.S. flags in such diverse
locales as Fullerton, California; Amherst, Massachusetts; and Palm Harbor, Florida. The perpetrator in
the Palm Harbor incident burglarized cars that flew the
national colors, giving his criminality a political flavor
by burning the flags as the encore to his larceny. The
car burglar/flag burner explained his actions to police
by declaring that he was sick of "capitalists flying the
American flag," adding that he wished that he lived in
China and that the arresting officers had died in the

---

*Hooks regularly writes the name she gave herself in lowercase letters, ostensibly
to take attention away from herself and place it on her work. Like her usurpation
of her parents' privilege of naming her, Hooks's eschewal of capital letters is an
exercise in egotism. The tactic is a juvenile attention-grabbing scheme. The
author chooses not to indulge her silliness.

World Trade Center. When told about the man's flag-burning activities, his own brother remarked, "He might do that, yeah. He doesn't like America."[6]

This jaded view of the United States wasn't born on September 11, 2001. It merely revealed its true self to a larger audience in the ill-timed tirades against the nation. Juxtaposed with the heightened sense of country brought on by the national tragedy, the Left's rhetorical offensive seemed particularly ridiculous. As documented in chapter 2, the anti-American roots of today's Left stretch back more than a hundred years before 9-11.

For good reason, I do not use the terms "liberal" and "leftist" interchangeably. Liberal Al Gore and leftist Gore Vidal share a family name in common, but little else. Ideologically, Al Gore in fact has more in common with his 2000 election nemesis than he does with his distant cousin. This book is not called *Why Liberals Hate America*. It's called *Why the Left Hates America*. "Left" and "liberal" aren't merely semantic distinctions.

So who are the Left? They include the anticapitalist protestors who recently vandalized Seattle, Washington, and Genoa, Italy. Holdovers from Communist movements of an earlier age continue to find a welcoming home on the Left. Multiculturalists seeking to promote every culture save our own, zealous atheists who resent the central role religion has played in American life, socialists who despise the free market, and moral-anarchists seeking to overthrow the social conventions of the West all display great contempt for the culture that offers their offbeat views the greatest tolerance.

Taken together, these and other components of the contemporary Left constitute a very small portion of society. While

self-hating Americans make up but a fraction of the total population (certainly no more than 10%), their influence is great.
They are museum curators, journalists, college professors, li-
brarians, and movie stars. They may write the high school cur-
ricula our children learn from or direct the movies we see. This
numerical fragment concentrates itself in fields that influence
the way people think. Thus their slight numbers belie a massive
cultural influence affecting not just their ideological soul mates
but mainstream society as well. The Left does not operate in an
intellectual ghetto.

Nowhere is the impact of anti-Americanism as great as it is
on the campuses. I know this from experience. For the better
part of the past decade, working as a program officer for Young
America's Foundation and currently as executive director of
Accuracy in Academia, I have sought with some success to gain
a hearing for views that challenge the intellectual orthodoxy
that exists on campus. My efforts have included pamphleteer-
ing, lecturing at dozens of campuses, and organizing scores of
weekend conferences at such schools as Harvard University, the
University of Chicago, and Princeton University. On a great
number of occasions, the reaction of radicals to views that challenge their own is not spirited debate but censorship.

In the fall of 2000, I was invited by students at the University of California–Berkeley to speak on the guilt of convicted
murderer and anti-American propagandist Mumia Abu-Jamal.
Prior to the utterance of my first word, an angry mob began
an orchestrated campaign of shouting to prevent the audience
from hearing my remarks. "White motherf——er!" and "You're
a f——ing murderer!" were among the epithets hurled my
way. One hirsute young man "mooned" me and later tried to
rip the microphone cord out of the wall. Several other students

threatened harm against the event's organizers and me. After the anarchic event prematurely concluded, activists stole the remaining copies of my lengthy pamphlet *Cop Killer: How Mumia Abu-Jamal Conned Millions into Believing He Was Framed* and held a Nazi-style book burning. All the while, the book burners marched around the fire holding signs admonishing others to "Fight Racist Censorship."[7] The irony, apparently, was lost on them.

Two years earlier and 3,000 miles away, a similar scenario played out at a conference that I organized at Columbia University. After 150 activists protested a Friday evening lecture by Ward Connerly, the nation's leading opponent of racial preferences and quotas, administrators at Columbia acceded to the heckler's veto and banned Accuracy in Academia's event, "A Place at the Table: Conservative Ideas in Higher Education." Columbia's inventive form of censorship involved banning the audience rather than the speakers from the rented lecture hall. Thus a school official assured me when I arrived for the event on Saturday morning that the school was not engaging in censorship. As the conference was forced off campus into a nearby park, swarms of activists surrounded and shouted down author Dinesh D'Souza. The mob chanted, "Ha! Ha! You're Outside/ We Don't Want Your Racist Lies." They held up signs reading "There's No Place at the Table for Hate" and "I'd Throw a Rock If I Could, but I Know It Would Hurt Our Cause." "I'll do whatever needs to be done [to stop the conference], in order to make sure they know their sentiments are not shared," activist Franklin Amoo told the *Columbia Spectator*. Black Students' Association president Roxanne Smithers explained to the paper, "I thought it was great. They were entirely dislocated. The black people have been dislocated for years, and they were dislocated for a couple of hours. It doesn't equalize it, but it's a start."[8] Later, several of the protestors bragged to ABC News's John Stossel about their "accomplishment."

Despite paying a $70 registration fee and identifying myself as a journalist, I was ejected, along with a colleague, from the Black Panthers' 35-year anniversary conference at the University of the District of Columbia in April 2002.* When the event organizers learned that I was a conservative, they informed me that I was banned not only from that public event, but from all their future gatherings as well.[9] Two months earlier, a Georgia State University mob attempted to confiscate mass quantities of my booklet *Enemies Within*, which exposed anti-Americanism on campus in the wake of 9-11. The mob contended that by picturing a man dressed in Middle Eastern garb on its cover, the booklet unfairly stereotyped Arabs as terrorists—ignoring the fact that the man pictured was Osama bin Laden![10] While providing opposing views to the press at a February 2000 Mumia Abu-Jamal rally, I was physically attacked outside of the Supreme Court. Later, in a second

---

*I was merely kicked out of the conference. A colleague was not as fortunate. Christopher Chow questioned a Boston College course instructor about his remarks that denied widespread atrocities by Communists. Agitated at having to field the challenging query, the teacher asked what publication Chow wrote for. Upon hearing the answer (Accuracy in Academia's *Campus Report*), the instructor lost his poise. Despite taping the session himself, the BC teacher demanded Chow's audiotape. Chow refused and left the lecture hall. The Black-Panther-turned-university-instructor followed, shouting, "This guy's a conservative! This guy's with *Campus Report!*" Soon, Chow found himself amid an angry crowd and wisely decided to depart the campus. The former Black Panther and an accomplice followed Chow several city blocks, cornering him in an apartment building. The duo took Chow's bag and walked off with his tapes of the conference. While Chow persuaded the two to return his bag, the former Panther and his more youthful crony refused to return Chow's tape of the controversial session. A security camera caught the theft of the bag.

attack, the first attacker's female companion ripped a small chunk of skin from my hand via her untrimmed fingernails.[11] In 1999, a left-wing campus activist deliberately sent me computer viruses. It is certainly true that some of the attempts by radicals to silence my voice have been quite petty in nature. It is also true, however, that activists attempting to tackle me or rushing the stage to unplug my microphone are something more than a mild annoyance.

My experiences, unfortunately, are not abnormal. David Horowitz, Ann Coulter, and Reginald Jones are among the numerous conservative lecturers who've been shouted down or subjected to the heckler's veto by the self-appointed censors within the campus Left. Clearly, it is the Left that represents the greatest threat to free speech in America today.

At the same time progressives indignantly censor others, they confuse—deliberately, perhaps—any criticism of their program with censorship. To posit that books such as this attempt to "silence" the Left is a brazen reversal. It is the height of hypocrisy that the people who exercise their free speech rights to run down their country then cry censorship when they are criticized for their irresponsibility. Let no one mistake the warranted criticism contained in this book for censorship. The author does not seek any restrictions on any form of political speech, including flag burning and wartime dissent. This book is merely the author's use of the same free speech rights that the Left doggedly guards for itself but seeks to deny to its critics. In fact, the Left's affinity for crying censorship when their views are simply being criticized is itself an attempt to muzzle the speech of others.

There are many nations deserving of our contempt. America does not seem to be one of them. Why not focus a critical eye toward the Arab world, the five remaining Communist states, or the plethora of dictatorships polluting the African continent? Knowing what goes on in the world, why does the Left focus its animus almost exclusively on the United States?

Poverty, racism, discrimination against women, religious intolerance, imperialism, and environmental pollution are the most common reasons offered by leftists as to why hating America is a rational exercise. Yet these commonly cited problems are by no means peculiar to the United States. Not only are they found in every land, as we shall see in chapters four and five, but they are almost always found in greater abundance outside the West.

Look out America's window at the world beyond Western civilization* and you're likely to observe a very unpleasant picture. In Africa, one finds widespread female genital mutilation, race-based slavery, extreme poverty, land expropriation campaigns aimed at whites, and a paucity of rights. Democracy is absent from the entire Arab world. While self-government is nonexistent, one finds conversion by the sword, so-called honor killings, public enthusiasm for terrorism, and the veil in abundance. Parts of Asia boast dowry killings, forced abortions, and imprisonment for rape victims. Cultural sensitivity should not require us to don cultural blindfolds to the many discomforting scenes beyond our borders.

---

*"Western civilization" is an ambiguous phrase inclusive of such non-Western locales as Japan and Israel. At the same time, geographically western nations such as Mexico, Haiti, and Brazil are almost always excluded. By "western civilization"—a phrase used frequently throughout the book—this writer means the United States, Canada, Australia, New Zealand, and all of Europe save Russia and several of its former satellites. Despite the term's geographic implications, the author uses it to denote nations that hold cultural attributes—such as Christianity, the rule of law, and self-government—in common.

When Americans look in the mirror, a much more pleasant sight emerges. We see the country that serves as the model for many of the world's democracies. We see great freedom and, as a result, great wealth. We see unprecedented national generosity, the immigrant's most welcoming destination, and the primary defender of the freedoms of other nations. The mirror's reflection reveals the nation most responsible for the world's advances in technology, medicine, and scientific discoveries. Strangely, America's positive attributes are hard to swallow for domestic progressives. This nation's overlooked greatness will be the focus of the concluding chapter.

We find something noble in patriotism even when practiced by our enemies. There is the sense that something is not altogether right with someone who despises his country. Our reaction to this disloyalty is a visceral one akin to what a Red Sox fan might feel about a fellow Bostonian rooting for the Yankees or what society collectively feels when celebrities, such as LaToya Jackson, dish inside dirt on their famous families. Even the New York City–based Yankee fan, or the observer who agrees that there is indeed something strange about the Jacksons, views the turncoat with suspicion. There is something we find admirable about loyalty—be it loyalty to families, employers, regions, teams, institutions, or nations. Despite all this, there is truth behind the Left's criticism of blind patriotism. Was the "patriotic" German or Japanese during World War II serving the good of his countrymen? Commitment to something that is wrong or harmful ultimately is not in the best interest of any nation. Blind patriotism is no patriotism at all.

America, however, is a force for good as no nation has been. There is a rational basis for Americans to be patriotic. Contrary to the beliefs of countless intellectuals, it is the thinking American who loves his country. Anti-Americanism, on the other hand, is reactionary and reflexive. It is the automatic response of one who has been conditioned what to think.

Stephen Decatur, a naval hero of the War of 1812, famously toasted: "Our country! In her intercourse with foreign nations, may she always be in the right, but our country, right or wrong."[12] To this, the American Left mindlessly retorts: Our country, she is always wrong.

PART 1

ENEMIES WITHIN

CHAPTER 1

SEPTEMBER 11, 2001: "WE HAD IT COMING"

ON SEPTEMBER 11, 2001, Middle Eastern terrorists hijacked four cross-country flights originating from East Coast airports. The ensuing suicide bombings, which used the fuel-laden planes as explosives, killed more than 3,000 people. The World Trade Center's twin towers were leveled, and portions of the Pentagon lay in ruins.

Just as they have done in times of tragedy in the past, millions of Americans rallied behind their nation. American flags adorned front porches and hung from highway overpasses. Forgotten recordings, such as Whitney Houston's 1991 Super Bowl rendition of "The Star-Spangled Banner" and Lee Greenwood's "God Bless the USA," suddenly were in vogue again. Enormous amounts of money were generously given to relief funds. In Normal, Illinois, a five-gallon jug collecting donations in front of the local supermarket took in $5,000 an hour on September 11, netting $118,000.[1] Those who could give more gave more. General Electric, Pfizer, and DaimlerChrysler each pledged $10 million to relief funds in the days after the attacks, heading a list of corporations that ultimately donated hundreds of millions of dollars.[2] Blood donations skyrocketed. On that fateful Tuesday, typical was the scene at the Bonfills Blood Centers in Denver, which had collected 2,000 pints of blood in just a few hours.[3]

Divisions along political, economic, and racial lines had, at least temporarily, evaporated. We were all just Americans once again.

The reaction to the attacks was quite different elsewhere in the world. In Nablus, on the West Bank of the Jordan River, thousands took to the streets to express glee, chanting, "God is great!"[4] The chairman of the Syrian Arab Writers Association wrote that, on hearing the news of the attacks, "My lungs filled with air and I breathed in relief, as I have never breathed before."[5] The Egyptian newspaper *Al-Maydan* editorialized, "Millions across the world shouted in joy: 'America has been hit'! This call expressed the sentiments of millions whom the American master had treated with tyranny, arrogance, bullying, conceit, deceit and bad taste."[6] A columnist for another Egyptian paper wrote, "I am happy about the American dead," while a competing periodical's scribe boasted, "If Osama bin Laden is proven to be involved in the attacks on the U.S., I will make a statue of him and set it in my home."[7]

Intellectuals in the West joined the blame-America chorus. Italian Nobel laureate Dario Fo hypothesized, "The great speculators wallow in an economy that every year kills tens of millions of people with poverty—so what is 20,000 dead in New York?"[8] Sunera Thobani, a Canadian feminist and former leader of the National Action Committee on the Status of Women, decried U.S. international policy as being "soaked in blood." She asked, "[D]o we feel any pain for the victims of U.S. aggression?"[9]

The foreign anti-Americanism that greeted the September 11 attacks may have been disturbing, but it certainly was not a total shock. That the same societies that produced 19 men who eagerly gave up their lives to kill American civilians would also house countless others who share their hate is no surprise. The impulsively anti-American responses from the Western intellectual community, where hating the United States has long been an article of faith, wasn't totally unexpected, either.

Truly perplexing was a phenomenon within our own borders. A campaign by a small but influential group of Americans blamed the mass murder on the United States. The tragic occasion was seen not as a time of sorrow but as an ideal opportunity to cart out a list of past sins, both real and imagined, committed by America. These sins (racism, sexism, homophobia, classism, and so on), they said, were the real reasons we were targeted. Those exploiting the attacks to push these pet grievances were not immigrants, the poor, minorities, or members of some other group that might have cause to grumble. They were, for the most part, wealthy elites who called America's cultural institutions—such as the campuses, museums, and the media—home. Thus, September 11 revealed a second, less obvious, threat. Those entrusted with passing on our culture, traditions, and history frequently exhibit an extreme contempt for our culture, traditions, and history. What are the prospects for a nation taught to hate itself? The question answers itself.

Just as King Priam and his subjects awoke to a Trojan horse within the gates of their city, America is now waking up to the fact that it houses enemies within.

"WE HAD IT COMING"

AMERICA IS "an imperialist nation who exploits, starves and kills civilians around the world—daily."[10] "What has the United States done to make itself this kind of target?"[11] "This is a case of the chickens coming home to roost."[12]

Such misguided statements weren't uttered in Tehran or Baghdad but in American college towns with more familiar-sounding names—Madison, Morgantown, and Boulder. As the rest of America came together in the wake of the horrific terrorist attacks, some on campus exploited the tragedy to bash the United States and attribute the cause of the attacks to old grudges. Patriotic students and faculty were punished, and pro-America speech was stifled.

At Marquette University, undergraduates were blocked from holding a moment of silence around an American flag. The gesture, top officials worried, might alienate foreign students.[13] Florida Gulf Coast University's head librarian banned her underlings from wearing "I'm proud to be an American" stickers in the days following the attacks. The overbearing librarian maintained, "We're doing everything we can to meet FGCU's standards of civility and tolerance."[14] The sight of American flags on university buses so angered Lehigh's vice provost for student affairs that he initially reacted by banning Old Glory's display by school employees. "The message was supposed to be that we are sensitive to everyone," John Smeaton, the administrator responsible for the order, ironically claimed.[15]

Residence hall directors in Central Michigan University's Emmons dormitory scoured the halls in search of doors adorned with forbidden patriotic images and statements. Sophomore Don Pasco, who had pictures of an American eagle and the World Trade Center taken off his door, remarked, "It was the whole hall. American flags or pictures that were pro-American had to be taken down because they were offending people."[16] The overseers of a cafeteria at Arizona State University worried that an American flag hanging in the eatery might offend foreign students, so they had it removed.[17] Margaret Post, a secretary in Holy Cross College's sociology department, lost a friend—hero Todd Beamer, who is thought to have helped foil the hijackers' suicide mission—on United flight 93 and decided to honor him by hanging a flag outside her office. Incensed, professors called for its removal. She refused, so department head Royce Singleton took it down himself. Singleton refused to explain his actions to local media: "There is nothing I can say that will make anybody understand the social context in which this occurred."[18] Defenders of the flag burners at Amherst College implied that the act of burning the Stars and Stripes might in some way be patriotic.[19]

In the Orwellian world of academe, prohibiting the American flag is viewed as an act of sensitivity. A more civil libertarian view emerges when campus denizens seek to burn rather than ban the national colors. Tolerance, free speech, and sensitivity are one-way streets in higher education, particularly when those seeking to be heard are patriotic voices.

Professors were quick to preach from their lecterns and take to the pages of college newspapers to allege American culpability in the attacks. "Many commentators are describing the disasters in New York as terrorist attacks—the worst since Pearl Harbor 60 years ago," University of Massachusetts–Amherst journalism professor Bill Israel observed. "None I've seen call them what they are: the predictable result of American policy." Large corporations, President Bush, and the Supreme Court that sided with him in the election controversy, the professor informs us, are the real culprits.[20] "*The New York Times*' headline was 'U.S. Attacked,'" historian Chalmers Johnson remarked. "That's insane. In many ways," he told a group at Yale, the terrorists "rightly identify us as the leader of those who are trying to keep them down."[21] A professor at the University of Hawaii blamed the attacks on their victim. A few weeks after September 11, she asked, "Why should we support the United States, whose hands in history are soaked with blood?"[22]

Professor Robert Jensen of the University of Texas–Austin maintained, "my primary anger is directed at the leaders of this country." The attacks on the Pentagon and the World Trade Center are "no more despicable than the massive acts of terrorism—the deliberate killing of civilians for political purposes—that the U.S. government has committed in my lifetime." We are "just as guilty," he concluded.[23]

American University professor Peter Kuznick used his history course to blame the United States for the attacks and intimated that an American conspiracy was at work. Kuznick, who teaches a course on Oliver Stone's view of history, told his class, "this is very convenient, the Pentagon needs an enemy, and now they have one—very convenient that such opportunistic things happen." Kuznick then turned the class over to a number of critics of the United States. Berkeley professor Peter Dale Scott telephonically imparted to the students, "what goes around comes around," and defended the terrorists by proclaiming, "they aren't cowards, if nothing else, it surely isn't cowardly to ride the plane in for something you believe."[24]

University of New Mexico professor Richard Berthold bluntly declared to his students, "Anyone who can blow up the Pentagon would get my vote." Having time to think about it, he repeated his ridiculous assertion to his next class.[25]

The tolerance that administrators demanded for these anti-American voices was in short supply for those in support of the war against terrorism:

- Johns Hopkins University professor Charles Fairbanks was fired from his position at the school's Central Asia-Caucasus Institute for remarks in support of the war on terrorism. Fairbanks spoke at a forum in favor of waging war against states that harbor terrorism. He concluded by offering to "bet anyone here a Koran" that he was right. A dean at the school took offense and eliminated his position at the institute. Public outcry against the infringement on academic freedom forced Fairbanks's reinstatement.[26] The chilling effect on speech, however, remained.

- Tenured professor Kenneth Hearlson of Orange Coast College was suspended without a hearing for claiming in class that Muslims who condemn terrorism in the United States but not in Israel are inconsistent. Several Muslim students took offense at the discussion, which grew heated. They complained to administrators that the professor accused them of personally driving the planes into the World Trade Center and then threatened them with violence—a contention that the professor and other students in the class contested—and Hearlson was immediately removed from his teaching duties.[27] "It's not a free speech issue," school spokesman Bob Dees contended. "It's a teacher conduct issue."[28] The California school was given an audiotape of the shouting match that revealed the Muslim students' allegations to be lies. Hearlson neither threatened the students nor accused them of being terrorists.[29] Not until Professor Hearlson released the tape to the media did the school reinstate him. Orange Coast College contested the idea that the case hinged on the truth or falsity of the accusations. "It was a very, very complex situation," school spokesman Jim Carnett explained. "And there was a lot to go through."[30]

- Duke University removed a professor's Web site that linked to articles proposing a strong military response to terrorism. Public uproar compelled the embarrassed school to allow the silenced academic to repost his site, but not without a university disclaimer—something absent from other faculty Web sites advocating various causes.[31]

- University of North Carolina–Wilmington professor Mike Adams responded critically to a shrill e-mail sent to him that blamed the September 11 atrocities on America. For this, a student threatened him with a lawsuit, and the university launched an investigation that culminated with school officials reading Adams's personal e-mail. Rosa Fuller, the student who sent the original message, labeled the attacks "retribution." In the e-mail sent en masse to members of the university community, she wrote, "far from being 'the brightest beacon for freedom and opportunity in the world,' the U.S. is seen by tens of millions as the main enemy of their human and democratic rights, and the main source of their oppression." When Adams took Fuller up on her offer of having an "open" and "democratic discussion" on her angry missive, the ensuing discussion was a bit too "democratic" for Fuller's liking. She repeatedly demanded that the university give her access to her antagonist's e-mail account. Ultimately, the university acceded to her demands, invading Adams's privacy and providing Fuller with a printout that logged when and to whom Adams had sent messages.[32]

Students, who perhaps absorbed the noxious ideas imparted by faculty and administrators, joined the campus chorus of those blaming the victim. "We are kidding ourselves in thinking we have been 'wronged,'" Lisa Mann of Wake Forest University wrote, adding, "sometimes it is our fault." She continued, "I do not feel as though the 'safety' of Americans has been affected. It took these terrorists years to plan the kind of destruction we have wreaked on other countries in a matter of days to weeks. That is right; America is not a 'nice' country."[33]

After September 11, renditions of "God Bless America" and "The Star-Spangled Banner" brought listeners to tears. At the University of Wisconsin, protestors actually broke into an Iraqi song.[34]

"We sponsor dictators who maim, we defend corporations that enslave and then we have the arrogance to pretend we're safe and untouchable," professed West Virginia University's Joshua Greene.[35] In light of the "destructive" nationalism calling for war, a Duke University student opined, "the sight of the flag burning would be preferable to its display."[36] An article in New York University's student newspaper was bluntly titled "Take a Look in the Mirror, America, and Ask Why."[37] A University of Colorado student maintained, "we had it coming."[38]

If you hate your country, the campuses are indeed a very tolerant place. If you love America, the intellectual climate can be about as hospitable as Iran. Zewdalem Kebede found this out the hard way at San Diego State University, where he was harassed by the university simply for disagreeing with people who welcomed the killing of Americans.

On September 22, 2001, Zewdalem Kebede, an immigrant to America from Ethiopia, overheard a group of Saudi Arabian students discussing the suicide bombings of the Pentagon and the World Trade Center. "I was studying in the library. I was in a booth and [the Saudi students] were in a round table behind me," Kebede explained. "They entered a discussion about September 11. That discussion was totally for praising the courage and the preciseness of the hijackers, and also, the morality of bin Laden and his strengths and how he spreads his ideology."[39] The anti-American group, speaking in Arabic, presumably thought that no one would be able to hear what they were saying. Kebede, who speaks fluent Arabic, surprised the students by interrupting their conversation in their native tongue.

"Guys, what you are talking about is unfair. How do you feel happy when those five- to six-thousand people are buried in two or three buildings?" Kebede said to the students. "You are proud of [the terrorists]. You should have to feel shame."[40] Kebede claims that he addressed his fellow students in Arabic because he did not want to embarrass them in front of others. A Saudi student sitting at a nearby table then angrily confronted Kebede in English. The ensuing conversation grew contentious, with the Saudi accusing the recently naturalized American of objecting to students speaking Arabic. Shortly thereafter, Kebede and the Saudi students went their separate ways.[41]

Thirty minutes later, campus police came—for Kebede! They informed him that a complaint had been issued against him. Soon, the university's Center for Student Rights ordered him to attend a disciplinary meeting and threatened him with expulsion because, it was alleged, he had been "verbally abusive to other students." He received a letter ordering him to respond to his accusers or face sanctions. Outraged, the Ethiopian immigrant went public with his story in a class. The university subsequently backed off the charges and concluded the matter with an October 9 letter threatening disciplinary action against the senior. "You are admonished to conduct yourself as a responsible member of the campus community in the future," San Diego State's missive warned.[42] That's precisely what some would say that Kebede was doing on September 22, when he castigated those who celebrated the mass murder of thousands of Americans. For acting responsibly, the political science major had the police sent after him, a letter from his school threatening him with criminal charges and expulsion, a hearing held against him where he could neither confront his accusers nor have legal representation, and his name dragged through the mud by university public relations specialists.

All that he is guilty of, Kebede insists, is loving his adopted country. "Is that a crime?" he asks.[43] On campus, unfortunately, some people think that it should be.

Punishment was liberally meted out against people such as Kebede who had committed no offense. Professors were removed from the classroom, students were hauled before kangaroo courts, and campus organizations were threatened with disbandment. Many people who had committed actual crimes, however, were let off the hook. Unlike the unfortunate victims of the campuses' anti-American hysteria, those who were allowed to commit politically motivated crimes with impunity were against America's military response to the attacks.

A month after the carnage of September 11, a group of patriotic Tufts University students partook in a long-standing tradition at the Medford, Massachusetts, school. They painted the cannon that adorns their main quad with a message and guarded it overnight as hundreds of others had done in the past. The red, white, and blue design with the words "God Bless America" turned out to be so controversial to the school's Coalition for Social Justice and Nonviolence that members of the group abandoned their pacifistic stance and attacked the student guarding the freshly painted cannon. As two masked members of the group attacked Sam Dangremond, another painted over the patriotic message with the words "Violence has no peace." Dangremond struggled to prevent the group from vandalizing his work but was repeatedly thrown to the ground and restrained. Finally, Dangremond broke away. He summoned the police, who found his three attackers still at the scene and still wearing hooded sweatshirts and bandannas covering their faces.[44]

Dangremond filed charges against his attackers, who in turn claimed that they had been the victims of the attack and filed charges against him. The stories of each of the attackers contradicted one another. The attackers' numerical superiority and the fact that they were wearing masks might have seemed to make their charge implausible, yet Dangremond was brought before a tribunal along with his assailants. While common sense finally dictated that Dangremond be acquitted, his three attackers from the Coalition for Justice and Nonviolence got off practically scot-free. Assault normally merits a semester's suspension at Tufts. The trio, however, was given probation without punishment. A friend of Dangremond's noted that this was the same punishment given to students caught outside their dorm rooms with cans of beer. The dean overseeing the case excused the light sentence by euphemistically noting that the violent triumvirate had "practiced physical non-violent strategies prior to going to the cannon."[45]

Arizona State University refrained from punishing a student who had violently attacked an unlikely victim: himself. Ahmed Saad Nasim, a dedicated activist at the University of Arizona and Arizona State University, had long crusaded for left-wing causes. As a student at the University of Arizona, he claimed that hackers posted threatening racist language on his anti–death penalty Web site. Later, he told police that he received death threats on home and work voice mail, which had been erased prior to the investigation. He was active in student government and became a member of campus groups fighting against sweatshops and the death penalty. A serial author of letters to the editor, his published responses to student articles favored mandatory diversity training for police, called for public sensitivity toward hermaphrodites, demanded humanitarian aid for the people of Iraq, and blasted the FBI for detaining two Saudi Arabian men who attempted to open the cockpit door on a 1999 flight.[46] Nasim was obviously neither a stranger to controversy nor a stranger to hate crimes. So when he became the victim of racist attackers because of his Middle Eastern descent, he made the most of the assaults by attempting to raise awareness for the issues that he had publicly championed so many times in the past.

Just two days after the attacks on the Pentagon and the World Trade Center, Ahmed Saad Nasim was thrown to the concrete and pelted with eggs by attackers who shouted, "Die, Muslim! Die!"[47] Following the attack, there was a mass exodus from Arizona State of Arab students concerned for their own safety. The university increased the police presence on campus,[48] and the Arizona State community displayed an outpouring of support for the Muslim student activist.

"Many of you e-mailed to show your support, gave online get well cards and many kind messages that made me burst into tears," he explained. "My physical injuries will take time to whither away. But you Sun Devils have certainly taken care of the emotional pains I had."[49]

Then, two weeks after the first assault against him, Nasim was attacked again. He was found with a plastic bag tied around his head in a locked bathroom stall. His assailants had scribbled "die" on Nasim's face and body. Paper with a slur written on it had been stuffed in his mouth. If this all sounds too coincidental to be true, that's because it is. Nasim finally conceded that he was both victim and perpetrator of these two "hate" crimes.[50] Despite the media's strong interest in hate crimes, they had little interest in reporting this phony hate crime at Arizona State.

For its part, the university declared, "there's nothing the university would gain" by charging the student for engaging in the hoax.[51] Public outrage led more sensible heads to prevail outside the university. The political science major has since been charged with two misdemeanor counts of false reporting of a crime by the Maricopa County Police Department.[52]

When Berkeley's student newspaper ran a cartoon of the September 11 terrorists burning in hell while wondering if they had arrived in their promised paradise, students claimed that the sketch unfairly stereotyped Muslims. Copies of the offending issue were pulled from shelves, the offices of the *Daily Californian* were stormed, and the newspaper's Web site was hacked.[53]

A few weeks later, another mass confiscation of the *Daily Californian* occurred. An ad that ran in the paper blasted the past 10 U.S. presidents for failing to effectively fight terrorism and called for harsh measures against nations that harbor terrorists. "The behavior of such militants is that of the regimes which make them possible. Their atrocities are not crimes, but acts of war," the hawkish ad claimed. "The proper response, as the public now understands, is a war in self-defense. . . . A proper war in self-defense is one fought without self-crippling restrictions placed on our commanders in the field. It must be fought with the most effective weapons we possess. A few weeks ago, [Defense Secretary Donald] Rumsfeld refused, correctly, to rule out nuclear weapons."[54]

In response, thousands of copies of the paper were stolen. In their place, a flier was inserted. "We must take a stand against the continuation of a systematic policy of eliciting and reinforcing hatred and racism from our student newspaper," the flier explained. "We do not believe that hate speech, which advocates the killing of entire nations and the innocent people who live in them, is protected."[55] As is usually the case when Berkeley students refuse to let guest speakers talk, confiscate literature, hold book burnings, or steal newspapers, no punishment was issued against these newspaper thieves.

The campus double standard is clear. For patriotic students and faculty, merely offending someone can be sufficient cause for disciplinary actions as severe as expulsion or employment termination. Those against America, on the other hand, can commit actual crimes yet go unpunished.

Large numbers of young Americans are taught to hate their country. The impressionable minds that are fed a distorted picture of America will be our next generation of teachers, journalists, clergy, and government officials. Unless the prevailing negativism is countered, the kind of history, traditions, and government that is passed on to future generations will be adversely affected.

"AMERICA, WHAT DID YOU DO?"

ANTI-AMERICAN SENTIMENT may have been strongest on our nation's campuses; however, they were not the only places one could find self-hating Americans blaming the victim, justifying the terrorism, stifling patriotic sentiment, or in some extreme cases even celebrating the thousands of deaths. At the very time that one would expect domestic anti-Americanism to be in short supply, it was instead abundant.

Former San Francisco city supervisor Amos Brown asked, "America, America, what did you do—either intentionally or unintentionally—in the world order, in Central America, in

Africa where bombs are still blasting?" The remarks, which took place at a memorial event for the victims of the terrorist attacks, continued: "America, what did you do in the global warming conference when you did not embrace the smaller nations? America, what did you do two weeks ago when I stood at the world conference on racism, when you wouldn't show up? Ohhhh—America, what did you do?"[56]

The Madison, Wisconsin, school district initially barred its teachers from leading students in the Pledge of Allegiance.[57] The Boulder Public Library refused to hang a 10-foot-long American flag in its lobby, claiming that some of its patrons might be offended. While the U.S. flag was deemed too controversial, the library had no problem with an exhibit of ceramic penises, which it prominently displayed.[58] A teacher in Sacramento burned an American flag in front of his sixth-grade class.[59] The anti-Americanism at Berkeley was so great that the city ordered firemen to remove American flags from their trucks out of fear that locals would destroy the vehicles if they saw the flags.[60] Before a single bomb had been dropped on Afghanistan, other U.S. cities played host to "antiwar" protests that quickly degenerated into anti-American rallies.

Much of the entertainment community sacrificed to give America a helping hand in its time of need. Not all of Hollywood, though, caught the patriotic bug. "I've been an advocate of peace my whole life," claimed *Lethal Weapon* star Danny Glover. "One of the main purveyors of violence in this world has been this country, whether it's against Nicaragua, Vietnam, or wherever."[61] Congresswoman Barbara Lee's vote against a military response to the attacks on America motivated comedian Bill Cosby, actor Ossie Davis, and musician Bonnie Raitt to each make the maximum contribution allowed by law to the Bay Area

Democrat's reelection campaign.[62] Robert Altman, director of *Gosford Park* and *M.A.S.H.*, branded America's government "disgusting," adding, "We've got a war going on to protect their oil interests." The acclaimed filmmaker did not indicate who in the administration had oil interests in Afghanistan or why oil would drive a military campaign in one of the region's few countries without major oil reserves. He did, however, complain, "Wherever you go in America there is nothing but flags. The Americans are so full of it."[63]

The elusive Bobby Fischer broke years of silence to applaud the attacks. "This is all wonderful news," the chess grand master declared. "It is time to finish off the U.S. once and for all." Fischer felt so strongly about the hijackings that he phoned a radio station in the Philippines to air his views, proclaiming, "I was happy and could not believe what was happening. All the crimes the U.S. has committed in the world. This just shows, what goes around comes around, even to the U.S."[64]

The most extreme manifestation of homegrown anti-Americanism was the strange case of John Walker Lindh, the American al-Qaeda fighter. When a dirty, hirsute American stumbled from the basement of a Mazar-e Sharif fortress following a failed uprising that killed one American and many Northern Alliance soldiers, the nation was shocked. What was an American doing fighting for the Taliban? On examining the background of the unfortunate young man, his treasonous behavior became much easier to comprehend. Lindh grew up in Marin County, California, home to Berkeley, site of Angela Davis's flight from the law, and the constituency of the lone congressional voice against an American military response to the terrorist attacks. If simply by osmosis, John Walker Lindh could not help but absorb the trendy anti-Americanism that pervades his community. Sent to an "alternative" high school that did away with such antiquated schooling techniques as classes and a curriculum, Lindh was rudderless. Direction came, his parents say, when he read *The Autobiography of Malcolm X*. With his parents' blessing, Lindh dropped out of school and began to study the Koran at a local mosque. Unsatisfied with the instruction he received, he traveled to Yemen, then to Pakistan, and finally to Afghanistan in pursuit of pure Islam—all on his parents' dime. Along the way, he enthusiastically enlisted in the fighting forces of a group that sees the destruction of America and Christian civilization as its primary objective. When his journey ended amidst the uprising that claimed the life of American CIA agent Mike Spann, Lindh's father incredibly declared, "I don't think John was doing anything wrong."[65]

John Walker Lindh may have been the sole member of his generation to have picked up arms against his country, but one need only sit in on a college lecture or read a campus newspaper to know that he has many kindred spirits.

Even a former American president seemed to provide rationalizations for the attacks. In a speech at Georgetown University, former president Bill Clinton accused the United States of "arrogant self-righteousness" and seemed to suggest that slavery, the Crusades, and the displacement of American Indians caused the September 11 attacks. He proclaimed,

> Those of us who come from various European lineages are not blameless. Indeed, in the first Crusade, when the Christian soldiers took Jerusalem, they first burned a synagogue with 300 Jews in it, and proceeded to kill every woman and child who was Muslim on the Temple mound. The contemporaneous descriptions of the event describe soldiers walking on the Temple mound, a holy place to Christians, with blood running

up to their knees. I can tell you that story is still being told today in the Middle East and we are still paying for it. Here in the United States we were founded as a nation that practiced slavery and slaves were, quite frequently, killed even though they were innocent. This country once looked the other way when significant numbers of Native Americans were dispossessed and killed to get their land or their mineral rights or because they were thought of as less than fully human and we are still paying the price today. Even in the 20th century in America people were terrorized or killed because of their race.[66]

That a former president of the United States would mine the history of Western civilization to implicate America in the attacks demonstrates just how pervasive cultural self-hatred has become. While one might be inclined to dismiss the rant of a college professor as the product of a lone crank, Clinton's remarks are evidence that it is not just fringe figures who view our nation's history as shameful.

REFLEXIVE ANTI-AMERICANISM

THE SIGHT OF waving flags is enough to make many intellectuals cringe. What is most upsetting about patriotism to the intellectual is that he views it as an anti-intellectual exercise. It's emotive, not cognitive. Far from being cerebral, our learned men's response to patriotism has been a mirror image of the supposed mindlessness that they decry. For years, faculty and administrators have inundated students with a reflexive anti-Americanism whose want of intelligence is matched only by its predictability. Whatever the global misfortune—poverty, war, ecological catastrophe, terrorism—the fault is always America's. This single-bullet theory of history provides a preprogrammed stock answer to all the questions. It forgoes critical thinking in favor of the mental straitjacket of ideology and abandons the spirit of open-mindedness that should govern academic inquiry. Never has the utter stupidity of a dogma been exposed more unequivocally than chic anti-Americanism has been in the days following America's great tragedy. Lost on those kicking America when it is down is that we were attacked. No amount of mental gymnastics can erase this fact.

If the automatic assignment of fault to the United States no matter the circumstances bespeaks an irrationality inherent in the self-hating American, what does his projection on the terrorists of his own views say about him? Not only do the terrorists reject the principles he links them to, but he discredits the ideas he seeks to gain favor for. None of the hijackers cared about the Kyoto environmental treaty, the Durbin conference on racism, or hate crimes legislation in Congress. Yet the self-hating American insists the U.S. government's inaction on these and other issues caused the catastrophes in Tribeca, in rural Pennsylvania, and near the shores of the Potomac.

Homophobia, patriarchy, and the exploitation of workers are among the reasons given why America is hated. Does any thinking person believe that the hijackers had the eradication of these ills in mind when they hatched their nefarious plot?

Osama bin Laden and the Taliban government that harbored him represent all that many activists claim to be against. The oppression of women, outlawing homosexuals, the destruction of non-Islamic cultural relics, a wide chasm between rich and poor, and no separation of church and state were a few of the characteristics of the late Afghani state and, not coincidentally, the ideal community that the bin Ladens of the world seek to impose. Yet the Taliban and bin Laden were not considered the bad guys: We were. Hatred for America is so great that it blinds its adherents to the sins of our enemies.

America finds itself almost alone in the history of nations in its cultivation of an elite that hopes for its country's demise. Museums, libraries, art galleries, schools, colleges and universities, and other institutions charged with passing on our culture seek instead to destroy it. One finds in other nations a much more sugarcoated self-portrayal. To many Turks, the Ottoman Empire's genocide of Christian Armenians never occurred.[67] Open up a Japanese history textbook, and the Bataan Death March, the Rape of Nanking, and the cause of World War II evaporate from the record.[68] Inhabitants of the late Soviet Union were led to believe that their country invented the television, but their government's eight-figure body count was kept hidden from them.[69] In America, it is our sins that are exaggerated and our virtues suppressed.

The antidote to cultural self-hatred among American elites is not the blind jingoism that characterizes how other nations present themselves. This would simply be replacing one dishonesty with another. What is needed is an honest retelling of the facts.

Was slavery practiced in a large portion of the United States during the republic's first 89 years? Were the Indians who inhabited America before the Europeans arrived displaced, mistreated, and at times killed by the newcomers? Were some Americans forced to relocate and others placed into internment camps simply because of their ethnicity during World War II?

The answer to all these questions, unfortunately, is yes. But is this all that we should learn about our country? Doesn't teaching the good, the bad, and the ugly include teaching the good, too? There is much good about America that leads its citizens to love their country. Patriotism is not always obligatory. It is not always arrived at through blind devotion. Patriotism can be a well-reasoned conviction. Americans, more so than any other people, have strong reason to love their country.

America is the oldest republic in existence, shining as a beacon of freedom in a dark world for more than two centuries. Free elections have been held here for hundreds of years. The rule of law, not the rule of kings or numbers, reigns supreme. Trial by jury, unknown to most defendants outside the West, is every American's right. For more than a century, we have been the world's most prosperous nation. John D. Rockefeller, Ross Perot, Oprah Winfrey, and countless others prove that upward mobility, not entrenched nobility, is the reality here. The airplane, the lightbulb, the television, the Internet, the space shuttle, and the telephone were all invented in the United States. For more than half a century, we have been the most powerful military force in the world, using our might not to make an empire but to defeat the most murderous ideologies in human history: Nazism and Communism. We have given the rest of the world scientific inventions, our wealth when they needed it, medical cures, principles of self-governance, and the lives of our soldiers defending their freedoms.

The United States is a nation based on an idea, not an ethnicity or a religion. An American immigrating to Japan, for instance, could never become Japanese. Yet a citizen of any foreign country who immigrated here could one day be called an American. Andrew Carnegie, Alexander Hamilton, and Albert Einstein are just a few of those who escaped the poverty or oppression of their homelands to find success and to better mankind in America. So appealing is the idea of America that people continue to risk their lives on makeshift rafts to come across dangerous seas just to live here. They don't go to Saudi Arabia, or Madagascar, or Denmark, or Brazil. They come here. This is significant.

To the self-hating American, all this is irrelevant. What matters is the promulgation of the idea that America is a racist, sexist, and oppressive society. Anything that supports this view, even lies, is promoted. Anything that contradicts it, even truth, is suppressed. Their ends justify their means.

As striking as the smear campaign against America is the whitewashing of what goes on in other countries. Female genital mutilation, apostasy executions, ethnically based land expropriation, trial by ordeal, and even slavery are practices that currently exist outside the walls of Western civilization. Ironically, the self-hating American who blames the West for introducing the world to racism, sexism, and other forms of oppression could find no greater ally than America—the West's anchor nation—in the eradication of these ills. The focus on America's shortcomings on these issues—where it clearly outperforms the rest of the world—raises the question as to whether these critics are against racism, sexism, classism, and so on or whether they care about these issues only to the extent that they are useful in tarnishing their homeland.

September 11 presented America with a challenge unprecedented in its history. Terrorists loyal to an idea and not any single country killed thousands of Americans, damaged and destroyed two functioning symbols of American power, and vowed further attacks that would end America as we know it. America faced this challenge. Law enforcement rounded up suspects, seized funds supporting America's enemies, and prevented further attacks. Citizens gave their time, money, and blood to help the victims of terrorism. The military destroyed the capabilities of the enemy overseas and hunted down its ring-leaders. Al-Qaeda, it became apparent, would eventually join Nazi Germany, the Soviet Union, and other foes of the United States on Ronald Reagan's "ash heap of history." Another challenge, however, remains. Contempt for America, its history, and its traditions is imparted to increasing numbers of people in the United States. Anti-Americanism's presence outside our borders is not nearly as troubling as its advancement within them. Rising generations of Americans are taught that theirs is a racist, sexist, and exploitative country. No longer the dream destination of oppressed people, young people are taught that America is the source of Third World peoples' nightmarish oppression. To the self-hating American, ours is not a culture worth defending.

It is this internal rot rather than any foreign enemy that poses the greatest danger to the future of the United States of America. "We have met the enemy," Walt Kelly's Pogo famously declared, "and he is us."[70]

CHAPTER 2

THE ROOTS OF ANTI-AMERICANISM

ANTI-AMERICANISM IS, in a sense, as old as America itself. The words "Benedict Arnold" are now most often used as an insult, but they of course refer to the Revolutionary War general who turned traitor after shoddy treatment from the Continental Congress. The idea of the United States of America was so off-putting to a third of colonials that they cast their allegiance to England during the great fight. Later conflicts, such as the War of 1812 and the Mexican War, would test the loyalty of many Americans, particularly Northeasterners. The issue of slavery sparked hatred toward America from others. Abolitionists Frederick Douglass and William Lloyd Garrison thought that no nation was as sinful and tyrannical as the United States. Many Southerners valued slavery more than their nation, fighting a bloody war to leave the union mostly because they feared that their "peculiar institution" was threatened. The varieties of anti-Americanism that we find in the antebellum years cast no real genealogical lines that live today.

The anti-Americanism presently found in the United States has its roots in the industrial age of the late 19th century. Changes in the economy brought great inequalities, the wealth that allowed the formation of America's first real intellectual class, and immigrants to toil in newly created jobs. This trio of developments would have a major effect on America. Inequality was at the heart of our system, charged the partisans of the "have-nots" in the emerging economy. Therefore, our government needed to be overthrown and not merely reformed. With the massive waves of immigration came Old World ideas, such as Marxism, which found enthusiastic cheerleaders even on capitalism's home court. The prosperity created by the industrialized economy bred a leisured class that pondered intellectual questions without concern for their impact on the real world.

Despite the rise of an intellectual class contemptuous of the society that hastened its ascendancy, the nascent movement found difficulty articulating its message. Bombs and bullets, rather than soapboxes and pamphlets, commonly served as its megaphone of choice. On May 4, 1886, seven policemen were killed in Haymarket Square in Chicago when an anarchist hurled a bomb at a group of policemen. Fifteen years later, proto-Communist Leon Czolgosz assassinated President William McKinley. The tumultuous age would witness the murder of the governor of Idaho in 1905, the dynamiting of the *Los Angeles Times* headquarters in 1910, and more than 35 mail bombs sent to Supreme Court justices, U.S. senators, the U.S. attorney general, and various business leaders in the spring of 1919. In these last terrorist attempts, the bomber hoped to strike a blow against the ruling class. He succeeded only in blowing off the hands of a maid who opened one of the packages. Eighty-one Septembers before September 11, 2001, a bomb exploded on Wall Street, killing 40. As the anti-American Left developed, more mainstream methods of persuasion supplanted the guns-and-bombs approach. Coherent intellectual philosophies began to articulate the cynicism directed at America that violence had earlier expressed.

There are four movements that have had a major role in fostering anti-Americanism in the United States. It is worth pointing out that three of these movements were imported from abroad. At least 90% of the members of America's original Communist Party were foreign born, with the initial Communists printing eight daily newspapers in foreign languages but none in English.[1] Relativism, an intellectual rather than an activist movement, immigrated to America with its founder, Franz Boas. Cultural Marxism, which helped spawn the New Left of the 1960s, was a refugee from Nazi Germany. While these movements may have originated across an ocean, their success was contingent on the enthusiasm of the native-born Americans who embraced them. Multiculturalism, the final ideology that we will examine, is the lone movement of the four to have indigenous origins.

So how did we arrive at the point where Americans would rejoice at the slaughter of 3,000 of their fellow countrymen? The answer can be found via a road that travels back through multiculturalism, Cultural Marxism and the New Left, relativism, and Communism.

"TWENTIETH-CENTURY AMERICANISM"

IT IS ESTIMATED that from 1917 to 1989 Communist governments murdered nearly 100 million human beings.[2] Many of the decimated met their demise through particularly barbaric acts. *The Black Book of Communism* details the mutilation of body parts by the Red Chinese: "Sometimes the pieces were cooked and eaten, or force-fed to members of the victim's family who were still alive and looking on."[3] In March 1919, thousands of Russian strikers were thrown into the Volga River with stones tied about their necks.[4] One Romanian reeducation jail, the last stop before death for many, was remembered by a former inmate: "Prisoners' whole bodies were burned with cigarettes; their buttocks would begin to rot, and their skin fell off as though they suffered from leprosy. Others were forced to swallow spoonfuls of excrement, and when they threw it back up, they were forced to eat their own vomit."[5] Cambodian "Ly Heng tells of a Khmer Rouge deserter who was forced to eat his own ears before being killed."[6] Most did not die so graphically. A bullet to the back of the head, the hangman's noose, and deliberate starvation were each far more common—and efficient—methods of eradication.

Heaven on Earth would not come without the requisite sacrifices. Thus, the American Left was willing to overlook the carnage. In fact, many leftists did more than remain passively silent about Communism's atrocities. They actively sought to import the same kind of totalitarian regimes that elsewhere promiscuously murdered their own citizens. Prominent leftists pledged their allegiance to the Soviet Union rather than the country of their birth.

The individual embodiment of evil for the Communist was the rich capitalist. As the world's richest nation and its most conspicuous enthusiast of free-market economics, the United States of America became the collective embodiment of evil for the Communist. Both the United States and the capitalist would have to be destroyed if Communism were to triumph. Thus, being a Communist and a patriotic American was incongruous.

Although special enmity was reserved for America, Communist ideology dictated disloyalty to any government that was not Communist. Lenin himself exemplified this tenet of Communism when he worked for his own country's defeat in World War I. Lenin's concept of "revolutionary defeatism" sought to "turn the imperialist war into a civil war."[7] In layman's terms, Lenin called for Communists to take advantage of wartime situations (or any crisis) by siding with their nation's enemies for the purposes of weakening the state and hastening the overthrow of the regime. American Communists followed Lenin's example. The aim of the Communist Party in America since its inception has been the violent overthrow of the U.S. government. Its 1921 constitution bluntly declares, "The Communist Party will systematically and persistently propagate the idea of the inevitability of and necessity for violent revolution, and will prepare the workers for armed insurrection as the only means of overthrowing the capitalist state."[8] Unlike czarist Russia, the United States of America was, and is, a democracy. Calling for revolution in such a country bespeaks the arrogance of self-anointed arbiters decreeing what's right for the rest of us. While the party was not always as candid in its aims as it was in 1921, the destruction of the United States has forever remained the improbable goal of American Communists.

One of the reasons that we know that American Communists were not loyal to the United States is that so many leading Communists openly said so. Party leader William Z. Foster spoke for his flock when he told a congressional committee that he would fight for the sickle and hammer against the "Red, White, and Blue" should the United States and Soviet Russia go to war.[9] In 1961, party member W. E. B. Du Bois renounced his American citizenship and emigrated to the Marxist cesspool that was Kwame Nkrumah's Ghana.[10] Journalist Lincoln Steffens declared, "I am a patriot for Russia; the Future is there; Russia will win out and it will save the world."[11]

Actions, not words, were how others sought to undermine America. Hundreds, perhaps thousands, of Americans engaged in espionage and acts of sabotage against their own country on behalf of the Soviet Union.

The Venona decrypts (to name just one source of information on espionage declassified after the fall of the Soviet Union) confirm that more than 300 Americans worked as agents for the USSR, with many of them working within the U.S. government.[12] Since the Venona program was able to translate only a tiny fraction of intelligence traffic to and from the Soviet Union over the course of just a few years, the actual number of Americans involved in espionage during the Cold War is certainly much higher. While many traitors worked anonymously in low-level posts, several dozen attained positions of tremendous influence. Top officials identified as Communist agents by the deciphered cables include Alger Hiss, the State Department official who presided as the first secretary-general of the United Nations at its founding; Harry Dexter White, the assistant secretary of the treasury who later served as the director of the International Monetary Fund; and prominent White House aide Lauchlin Currie.[13]

Influencing policy, as Hiss did at Yalta and during the founding of the United Nations, was the primary method employed by American turncoats to undermine their own nation. Handing over sensitive information was a secondary aim. Roosevelt confidant Lauchlin Currie and intelligence officer William Weisband were among those who snitched to Russian intelligence that America had broken the Soviets' code.[14] Harry Dexter White gave the Soviet Union the currency plates for printing money in the U.S. zone of occupation in postwar Germany.[15] And, most important, the Rosenbergs and their associates gave one of mankind's most prolific mass murderers the blueprints for the atomic bomb.[16] Clearly, the influence of Communist infiltrators was by no means minor.

Government was but one institution that Communists sought to subvert. Higher education, the arts, entertainment, labor unions, and journalism were additional fields that afforded Communists the opportunity to do Moscow's bidding at their own country's expense.

Some of America's most famous journalists betrayed their country, as well as their professional obligation to the truth, by intentionally distorting their articles to favor the Soviet Union. Whether their motivations were financial or ideological, their betrayal of their country was nevertheless the same. Walter Duranty, the British-born *New York Times* reporter who won the Pulitzer Prize for his articles denying Soviet atrocities, served as a propagandist for Stalin because of political sympathies and special treatment by the regime.[17] Michael Straight, editor of the *New Republic*, admitted in his 1983 biography that he was once an agent for the Soviet Union. Despite his direct knowledge that the Communist conspiracy was very real, Straight continued to tag anti-Communism as a witch-hunt long after he had left the party.[18] Soviet operatives clandestinely met with newspaper columnist and *Nation* editor I. F. Stone during the 1940s, seeking to use the writer as a pro-Soviet mouthpiece in the American press. Stone expressed a willingness to meet their request, but only for the right price.[19] A clue to whether Stone's relationship with the Soviets became formalized could be found in his later erroneous reports that the South had attacked the North to launch the Korean War and that the United States had used poison gas on the Vietnamese people. In the early 1990s, Soviet general Oleg Kalugin confirmed to no one's shock that Izzy Stone was indeed a paid agent of the Soviet Union.[20]

"We smuggled our ideology into all sorts of movies," screenwriter Paul Jarrico boasted years after he was blacklisted from Hollywood for his membership in the Communist Party.[21] Other than unions and academia, the entertainment industry was perhaps the area in which Communists found their strongest foothold. Attempts to inject Communist themes into movies ran the gamut from something as innocuous as party actor Lionel Stander whistling the "Internationale" in *No Time to Marry* to full-length propaganda pieces such as *Mission to Moscow, North Star,* and *Song of Russia.* The devotion to Communism among entertainers was particularly apparent during the Hitler-Stalin Pact. The Hollywood Anti-Nazi League was instantly transformed into the Hollywood League for Democratic Action because of Moscow's change in foreign policy.[22] The play *Meet the People* was changed to conform to party standards. A show tune called "Mr. Roosevelt, Won't You Please Run Again?" was pulled from the play after the Nazi-Soviet agreement made support for Roosevelt once again verboten. Insults directed at FDR were put in the song's place. The Communists working on the theatrical production also erased a scene equating Stalin with Hitler.[23] While such familiar faces as Paul Robeson and Charlie Chaplin were committed Stalinists, Communists most heavily populated the ranks of writers and directors. Writers Dalton Trumbo (*Spartacus, Roman Holiday*), Lillian Hellman (*The Children's Hour, The Little Foxes*), Clifford Odets (*None but the Lonely Heart*), Berthold Brecht (*The Three-Penny Opera*), and Ring Lardner (*Woman of the Year, M.A.S.H.*) were but a few of the influential figures working off camera and out of the theatergoer's eye. Most shared the attitude of playwright John Howard Lawson, who frankly proclaimed, "I do not hesitate to say that it is my aim to present the Communist position, and to do so in the most specific manner."[24]

The Screen Writers Guild was predictably one of the unions in which Communists played a major role. Others in-

cluded the Longshoreman's Union; the United Electrical,
Radio, and Machine Workers of America; and the National
Maritime Union. Mainstream labor's long-standing hostility to
Communism presented the extreme Left with great difficulties
in their drive to communize unions in the United States. In
spite of this hurdle, Communists found a degree of success. Between 20% and 25% of the unions in the Congress of Industrial Organizations (CIO)—representing more than a million
people—were Communist aligned, with members of the party
helping to lead 18 CIO member unions.[25] The editor of the
CIO's newspaper, for instance, was a Communist, as was the organization's general counsel.[26] Communist-led unions served
Moscow's purposes, not the American workingman's. During
the Hitler-Stalin Pact, Communist-run unions shut down fac-
tories supplying Britain with military aircraft at Allis-Chalmers
in Milwaukee and at California's North American Aircraft Company and Vultee Aircraft Company.[27] When Hitler turned on
Stalin and American industry became essential to the Soviet
Union's very survival, American Communists suddenly became
shills for their employers and vehemently opposed all strikes.[28]
What guided the leaders of these unions was not the needs of
dues-paying members but the demands of a foreign government
thousands of miles away.

"To the victors belong the spoils," the old axiom goes. These
"spoils" typically include telling the history of the times from the
winner's perspective. The Cold War is different. In this, the
longest struggle between good and evil in modern times, it is the
losers who write the history. In their version of reality, McCarthy
and not Stalin is the evil Joe of the Cold War. The Soviet Union
becomes a bulwark against Nazism rather than the country that
enabled Hitler to launch his most significant conquest. Communist governments, which banned organized labor and murdered

strikers, and their party admirers in the United States, who called for the destruction of unions, are portrayed as friends of the working class. The anti-Communist crusade is likened to a witch-hunt, an analogy that holds only if you buy into the idea that witches exist or that Communists do not.

The Communists were not the victims of the Cold War. They were its villains. The great irony of America's Communist Party is that it initially championed many of the institutions that were later used to dismantle it.

The House Committee on Un-American Activities was actually the creation of a far-left Democratic officeholder who would later become a paid agent of the Soviet Union.[29] In 1934, Samuel Dickstein, a congressman from New York City, called for Congress to investigate the un-American activities of anti-Semites, fascists, and other assorted crypto-Nazis operating within the United States. The role of the consequent House investigative body, known as the "Dickstein Committee," was expanded at its namesake's request. As Texas Democrat Martin Dies gained control over the committee, he focused an increasing amount of attention on Communists. It was only then that the Communists objected to the House Committee on Un-American Activities, the very outfit their own fellow traveler was responsible for devising.

The Communist Party actively supported the Smith Act when it was enacted in the early 1940s. The legislation criminalized political parties that sought the violent overthrow of the U.S. government. When the leadership of the Trotskyist Socialist Workers Party was put on trial for violating the Smith Act in the law's very first case in 1941, the Communist Party prepared 14 documents for federal prosecutors, including an item called "The Fifth Column Role of the Trotskyites in the

United States."[30] Communists began to cry foul only when the Smith Act was later used against them.

Long before the major studios announced a boycott of Communists working in the film industry, Hollywood's Left introduced its own blacklist. Writer Martin Berkeley's work, for instance, was held back for more than a year and a half by his agent, a Communist who sought to blackball his own client's career.[31] Studio giant Jack Warner testified that Hollywood Communists blocked anti-Communists from getting jobs.[32] "Hollywood Ten" defendant Dalton Trumbo dutifully cooperated as an informant for the FBI on "antiwar" writers during World War II.[33] A few years later, when the government was interested in his activities in the Communist Party, Trumbo indignantly labeled the inquest an affront to the Constitution. Trumbo and his ilk, however, were not interested in the Constitution. They wanted to save their own hides. Director John Huston later outlined the real reason the Hollywood Ten balked at answering queries about their party membership: "It seems that some of them had already testified in California, and that their testimony had been false. They had said they were not Communists and now, to have admitted it to the press would have been to lay themselves open to charges of perjury."[34]

Representative of too many in her profession, historian Ellen Schrecker denies that Communists were somehow unpatriotic. She euphemistically maintains that American Communists simply "did not subscribe to traditional forms of patriotism."[35] This is a bit like saying that tigers merely practice a different kind of vegetarianism.

It is delusional to suggest that the Communist Party was just another political group, different from the Democrats and the Republicans only in the policies that it advocated. American

Communists existed to serve a foreign power that openly sought the destruction of the United States of America. Party members deferred to Moscow for their thoughts. As party leader V. J. Jerome candidly told a potential recruit, "When the Party makes a decision, it becomes your opinion."[36] Communist leaders often forced "party marriages" on their members, with the largest state party affiliate forcing any members married to a "Lovestoneite" or a "Trotskyite" to leave their spouse or the party.[37] American Communists could not travel abroad without the permission of the party hierarchy and were directed to purchase their tickets through a party travel agency known as World Tourists.[38] When the Soviet Union instructed its admirers in the United States to spy, we know that hundreds of them happily obeyed. Of the scores of instances when a member of the Communist Party of the USA (CPUSA) was asked to engage in espionage, authors Herbert Romerstein and Eric Breindel observe, "We know of no case in which a Party member reported such an offer to the FBI."[39] The charge that American Communists remained mute while their Russian overlords murdered millions—including scores of American citizens—only begins to tell the nefarious story of Communism in America. We now know that U.S. Communists played key roles in murdering numerous people, including Trotsky.[40] Strong evidence suggests that Americans actually murdered other American volunteers for suspected ideological deviationism during the Spanish civil war.[41] In the midst of the Great Terror, when any accusation equaled guilt, the CPUSA was feeding Stalin paranoid accusations against inhabitants of the Soviet Union. One written exchange reported the theft of the files of the much-disparaged former CPUSA leader Jay Lovestone, bragging, "Some of these documents refer to certain persons in the USSR who are mentioned in letters which discuss the trials of the Trotskyite-

Bukharin spies."[42] In another missive a few years earlier, the Americans reported to their ideological brethren, "a food worker here in New York reports that he has overheard Solomon Rechter's brother boasting to somebody else that Solomon Rechter, in Moscow, was carrying on underground work for Zionist 'black shirts'—the Zhabotinsky group."[43] One need not be Sherlock Holmes to deduce that the result of the tattling was not beneficial for the subjects of the gossip.

If there were any doubts that America's Communist Party was controlled by a hostile power, the revelation that the group's budget was heavily subsidized by the Soviet Union put those doubts to rest. During the 1920s, the CPUSA received between one-third and one-half of its budget from the Soviet Union. From 1958 to 1980, two double agents alone delivered $28 million. The illegal subsidies reached the $3 million per annum mark by the late 1980s. Ironically, CPUSA chairman Gus Hall's failure to parrot the Moscow line by criticizing Gorbachev's glasnost and other liberating reforms—the first public rebellion against the Kremlin by a prominent Communist leader since John Reed lambasted Lenin's counsel for American communists to work with industrial labor unions in 1919—resulted in the cessation of the CPUSA's Moscow Gold.[44]

For all but a few holdouts, the party ended for American Communists when the Soviet Union collapsed. One might trace the party's real demise to when Nikita Khrushchev fessed up to the atrocities committed in the Soviet Union under Stalin. The leader of the Motherland confirmed what anti-Communists had been saying for years. This was a bitter pill to swallow for many who had chalked up such charges to capitalist propaganda. From that point forward, the Communist Party played no discernible role in any institution of significance in America. Yet its legacy endures.

If in the wake of the Iron Curtain's collapse American leftists worried that they could no longer rely on Moscow to supply their opinions, they could find solace in the realization that they no longer needed direction. For the circus elephant psychologically conditioned to the futility of breaking away from his chains, a frayed rope is all that is needed to keep him tied down. Similarly, America's far Left had imbibed Moscow's anti-American party line for so long that it had become conditioned what to think. Moscow, like the elephant's chain, was no longer necessary. Communists had alternatively denounced unions as tools of industrial capitalism and embraced them as weapons against industrial capitalism; they ran candidates in elections and urged boycotts of the "sham" electoral process; they were anti-Nazi, then pro-Nazi, and then anti-Nazi again. Amidst all this inconsistency, the one thing you could count on was anti-Americanism. With the exceptions of Earl Browder's "Communism Is Twentieth Century Americanism" campaign of the 1930s and Stalin's alliance with Roosevelt during World War II, Communists maintained a persistent drumbeat of anti-Americanism unmatched by any other organization. While Communists at their apex constituted only a fraction of the American Left, their privileged position within the radical community awarded them great influence among men of the Left. Communism's hatred for America became contagious. Much of the non-Communist Left became infected. For many leftists, it became easier to defer to a preordained anti-American dogma handed down by the Marxists than to think for themselves. To this day, this is a mental straitjacket that many find difficult to divest.

"THE REPRESSIVE IDEOLOGY OF FREEDOM"

EVEN AS TRADITIONAL Communism expanded its dominion and gained starry-eyed converts outside its borders, a competing brand of Marxism emerged. Shifting Marx's focus on economics to the culture, it replaced the worker as Marx's victim of choice with homosexuals, women, and ethnic minorities. Its method mixed Marx with Freud. The result was something alternatively called Critical Theory, Cultural Marxism, or the Frankfurt School. Communists fumed over Critical Theory's loose reading of Marx. With the establishment of the Soviet Union in 1917 and the subsequent spread of so-called workers' states around the world, doctrinaire Marxists questioned the need for this heretical strain of Marxism. Within a generation of the October Revolution, however, the allure of socialism was on the wane. No one, save true believers, claimed that the economic condition—even for workers—was preferable in Communist nations than in free-market ones. By substituting racism, sexism, xenophobia, anti-Semitism, homophobia, and a host of other "isms" and alleged pathologies for the traditional Marxist bogey of capitalism, Critical Theory ensured that Marxism would thrive long after the fall of the Iron Curtain.

As its name implies, Critical Theory criticizes. It eschews a positive program in favor of dissecting a society to point out its perceived flaws. Whereas traditional Marxism focuses on economic inequality, Critical Theory highlights inequalities with regard to race, sex, and sexual behavior.

The group using Marx to assail Western civilization, rather than just Western free-market economics, was known collectively as the Frankfurt School. Max Horkheimer, Walter Benjamin, Erich Fromm, Theodor Adorno, Leo Lowenthal, Herbert Marcuse, and Georg Lukacs were among the more noteworthy intellectuals in the group. Founded in 1923 as the Institut für Sozialforschung, its association with the recently founded University of Frankfurt gave the school of thought its name. Initially, the institute was to be called the Institute for Marxism, but its founders artfully deduced that they would find greater mainstream acceptance for their ideas if they settled on an innocuous name. Thus, the Institute of Social Research was born.

"Who will free us from the yoke of Western Civilization?" Frankfurt School theorist Georg Lukacs asked.[45] Yet it is clear that Cultural Marxists themselves did not want to be free of Western civilization. When Hitler came to power, the Institute of Social Research emigrated to New York rather than Moscow. After the Thousand-Year Reich came to a premature end in 1945, the Institute of Social Research returned to Germany. Never did these academicians employing Western ideas to criticize Western civilization ever seriously consider leaving the society that they claimed was so oppressive. Their hypocrisy was indicative of the hollowness of their theories.

The Frankfurt School's greatest success in influencing the mainstream came via its postwar Studies in Prejudice series, of which the lengthy *Authoritarian Personality* was the most important volume. Written by a team of psychologists led by Theodor Adorno, the 1950 study characterizes America as a Nazi Germany waiting to happen. Its introduction declares, "The present writers believe that it is up to the people to decide whether or not this country goes fascist."[46] Later the reader is ominously warned, "we are living in potentially fascist times."[47]

What was it about America that in the minds of the authors placed the nation precariously close to fascism? The family structure was "authoritarian" (i.e., ruled by parents) rather than "equalitarian," people were obedient to religion and God, patriotism ran high, and the free-enterprise system exalted the strong. Rather than characteristics of actual fascists, these traits seemed instead to be aspects of America that the Left had long bemoaned. To deflect America from its fascist course, the authors suggested a number of left-wing solutions—abandon capitalism, give children a say in democratic families, discourage patriotism, and push God and religion out of its central role in the lives of many.

The authors' assertion that fascism and conservatism are in some way connected is a secondary theme of the book. Sold as a rigorous study in empirical social science, *The Authoritarian Personality* was based on interviews that gauged not whether an individual was an actual fascist but whether he or she was a "potential fascist," whatever that meant. Based on a series of questions, the authors rated interview subjects on scales that purported to measure such things as fascism, anti-Semitism, ethnocentrism, and political conservatism. Many of the survey's standard questions that sought to highlight hidden prejudices, however, did nothing to illustrate the interviewee's affinity for antidemocratic attitudes, as the authors claimed. On a scale measuring prejudice, subjects were asked to agree or disagree on such statements as "Now that a new world organization is set up, America must be sure that she loses none of her independence and complete power as a separate nation," "America may not be perfect, but the American Way has brought us about as close as human beings can get to a perfect society," and "The best guarantee of our national security is for America to have the biggest army and navy in the world and the secret of the atom bomb."[48]

Affirming these statements might indicate a tendency toward conservatism, yet the authors characterized agreement with any of these statements as the mark of an antidemocratic individual. The only possible reason for including questions that might indicate whether one was a conservative—but told us next to nothing about one's tendencies toward ethnocentrism—on a questionnaire designed to gauge ethnocentrism would be to establish a phony connection between political conservatism and racial prejudice. This is precisely what *The*

Authoritarian Personality attempted to do. In fact, so rigged was the "scientific" survey that at least one question used to indicate political conservatism was also used to indicate fascism.[49] By these methods, one could find a direct link between any two things. The authors did not discover a link between conservatism and fascism; they concocted one.

Throughout the Studies in Prejudice series, ideology trumped scholarship. Despite anti-Semitism being a key focus of the series, the program's overseers made it clear that criticism of the anti-Semitism of key political allies would be off-limits. A book in the series that claimed disturbing levels of anti-Semitism within organized labor was spiked because its discoveries were contrary to what the left-wing ideologues running the program had hoped to find.[50] The initial overseer of the project went further than merely covering up politically inconvenient prejudice, choosing to serve as an apologist for one of the world's worst offenders of anti-Semitism. At the height of Stalin's power, Institute of Social Research director Max Horkheimer amazingly claimed, "at present the only country where there does not seem to be any kind of anti-Semitism is Russia. This has a very obvious reason. Not only has Russia passed laws against anti-Semitism, but it really enforces them; and the penalties are very severe."[51] Conspicuous throughout *The Authoritarian Personality* is the association of totalitarianism and authoritarianism with fascism but not with Communism. Indeed, the book actually suggests a connection between anti-Communism and totalitarianism, equates Communists with members of persecuted "out groups," and states that hostility toward the Communists may be a displaced form of anti-Semitism.[52] Released at a time when fascists controlled virtually no countries but Communists controlled nations representing more than a third of humanity, the decision to airbrush out the relationship between Communism and totalitarianism seems quite peculiar.

The legacy of *The Authoritarian Personality* was to give an air of scientific respectability to smearing right-leaning arguments with terms denoting mental sickness—for example, xenophobe, racist, and homophobe. Conservatism was not a political outlook to be debated but a psychiatric condition to be treated. A second legacy was to implant the seed in the brains of the intellectual class that America, the country most responsible for the defeat of Nazism, was not far from being a Nazi state itself. The calumny has stubbornly remained an article of faith for many on the Left.

The Frankfurt School's most influential member curiously had no involvement in its most influential project. Herbert Marcuse came to the United States with his cohorts when Hitler came to power in Germany. Unlike most of his associates, he remained in America after the war. Teaching at such campuses as Columbia, Brandeis, and the University of California–San Diego gave Marcuse an ideal perch from which to oversee the burgeoning counterculture.

Heretofore overlooked amidst his famous colleagues, Marcuse began to make a name for himself in 1955 with *Eros and Civilization*. Like his later offerings, the book would become scripture to the leading figures of the New Left of the 1960s. *Eros and Civilization* gave Marx a fitting makeover for the era of sex, drugs, and rock and roll. Whereas Marx opposed the exploitation of labor, Marcuse opposed the very idea of labor. Similarly, Marcuse expanded Marx's "To each according to his needs" to include the libido's "needs" as well. *Eros and Civilization* argues that man's "labor time, which is the largest part of the individual's life time, is painful time, for alienated labor is absence of gratification, negation of the pleasure principle."[53] Work was to be replaced with a big party. Not surprisingly, Marcuse's message was endorsed as super-groovy by the Flower Power generation.

It was not just a sexual revolution that Marcuse sought. America was so intrinsically evil that its government and guiding principles needed to be overthrown as well. Marcuse called for violent revolution in the era of peace and love, convincing his followers that the three principles were harmonious. Making hypocrisy seem principled would be a running theme throughout his work.

How did the New Left mesh its support for violent radicals with its professed stand of pacifism? Practicing nonviolence for the Left really meant committing violence against the establishment. Defending such violent groups as the Black Panthers and the Weathermen, Marcuse remarked, "If they use violence, they do not start a new chain of violence but try to break an established one."[54]

How can one at once claim to be a part of a "free speech movement" and censor opposing views? Marcuse gave the 1960s generation the answer in 1965. "Liberating tolerance," he famously wrote in his essay "Repressive Tolerance," is "intolerance against movements from the Right, and toleration of movements from the Left."[55] His words became so influential on the Left that even those who have never even heard of Marcuse follow his counsel, particularly denizens of the campuses. Marcuse's screed went even further, calling for the "[w]ithdrawal of tolerance from regressive movements before they can become active; intolerance even toward thought, opinion, and word, and finally, intolerance ... toward the self-styled conservatives, to the political Right."[56]

How could Marcuse reconcile the New Left's professed support for freedom and democracy with its veneration of totalitarian dictators? It is because the "ideology of freedom" is actually "repressive." Marcuse affirmed Rousseau's notion that people "must be 'forced to be free.'"[57] Thus, Marcuse named Vietnam, Cuba, and Mao's China as living examples of the freedom he was referring to.[58] "[F]or a whole generation, 'freedom,' 'socialism,' and 'liberation' are inseparable from Fidel and Che and the guerrillas," he later wrote; "they have recaptured . . . the day-to-day fight of men and women for a life as human beings."[59] America, on the other hand, he likened to Hitler's Germany and its policemen to the SS.[60] "[I]s there today, in the orbit of advanced industrial civilizations," he asked in *One-Dimensional Man*, "a society which is not under an authoritarian regime?"[61] Marcuse's inference was that Great Britain, the United States, Australia, the Netherlands, Switzerland, and Japan were among the many despotic regimes that populated the First World.

After indulging in a steady diet of Marcuse, the New Left was inspired to unleash a wave of violence against the "establishment." In what was to become a recurring cycle of events on campuses, Columbia University students rioted in April 1968, tearing up the campus that had housed the Institute of Social Research during its sojourn in America. Paris erupted in violent chaos shortly thereafter, with agitators seen holding up placards reading, "Marx/Mao/Marcuse."[62] The Weather Underground, a group that adopted a spread-fingered greeting to symbolize the fork that the Manson family had stuck into one of its victims, bombed the Pentagon, Manhattan banks, the New York City police headquarters, and numerous other sites.[63] For Black Panthers, the revolution sometimes meant murdering law enforcement officers. Marcuse's own student, Panther camp follower Angela Davis, went on the run after purchasing the guns used for a failed raid on a Marin County, California, courthouse that resulted in several deaths, including the decapitation of a judge.[64] Davis's efforts were rewarded with tenure at the University of California–Santa Cruz. Typically, Panthers received lifetime appointments of a different sort. Romain "Chip" Fitzgerald, Anthony Jones, Eddie Conway, Mumia Abu-Jamal, H. Rap Brown, David Rice, and Ed Poindexter are among the Black Panther alumni serving life sentences for murdering law enforcement officials. The tumult of the 1960s was too much for some members of the Frankfurt School to handle. One thinks of Dr. Frankenstein and his monster when encountering Theodor Adorno's incredulous utterance, "when I made my theoretical model, I could not have guessed that people would try to realize it with Molotov cocktails."[65]

"WHO'S TO SAY?"

CATCHING SIGHT OF a native toting a Bible, an American serviceman stationed on a Pacific island during World War II is said to have remarked, "We educated people no longer put much faith in that book." "Well," the native responded, "it's good that we do, or you would be eaten by my people today."[66]

The conversation reveals a great paradox of our age. At the same time that educated westerners are turning away from their own civilization, the elites in primitive cultures (but perhaps not in non-Western advanced cultures) rush to embrace our way of life. This latter phenomenon is deeply troubling to cultural relativists.

"The dogma of cultural relativism is challenged by the very people for whose moral benefit the anthropologists established it in the first place," concedes anthropologist Claude Lévi-Strauss. "The complaint the underdeveloped countries advance is not that they are being Westernized, but that there is too much delay in giving them the means to Westernize themselves. It is of no use to defend the individuality of human cultures against those cultures themselves."[67]

Relativism declares all ways of life to be of equal value. "Who's to say," the relativist's familiar refrain goes, that our culture is better than another? This same doctrine is also applied to individuals. Under relativism, the only sin is imposing morality on another person. There is no truth, only perceptions. Relativism exhorts humanity to be nonjudgmental. At the same time, it ironically condemns anyone who passes judgment on morals, cultures, or people.

The primary field used to spread the message that all cultures are equal is anthropology. Its influence extends well beyond a lone academic concentration. Writers, museum curators, and diplomats can usually be counted on to excuse practices in other cultures that they would virulently condemn in their own culture. On anthropological field trips, cultural relativists always seem to find exactly what they are looking for: societies that mirror their own vision of an ideal culture. Theory comes before facts. "Facts" are obtained to support the theory. Facts that undermined the theory are whitewashed or ignored.

Franz Boas, the father of modern anthropology, employed this method during his career. His report on the Kwakiutal Indians of Vancouver Island, for instance, deliberately omitted any mention of the group's practice of slavery.[68] When one thinks of anthropologists fibbing about cultures to bolster the case for relativism, no example comes to mind more readily than Margaret Mead's reports on Samoa.

In August 1925, Margaret Mead, an unknown 23-year-old graduate of Columbia University, landed in Samoa. By reporting what she found on her trip to the South Seas—and some things that she did not find—the twentysomething Mead was transformed overnight into the world's most famous anthropologist. Her book *Coming of Age in Samoa* became the most commercially successful and influential anthropological tome in history.

"The results of her painstaking investigation confirm the suspicion long held by anthropologists," Franz Boas announced in the book's introduction, "that much of what we ascribe to human nature is no more than a reaction to the restraints put upon us by civilisation."[69] Boas, Mead's mentor at Columbia, put the cart before the horse. Mead's "suspicion" was not confirmed by what she found. Rather, it fueled what she found.

Mead's project had two realized goals. The first was to convince others that human behavior is not affected by genetics but is formed almost entirely by environment. By presenting a society that shunned behavior that westerners assumed to be universal, Mead convinced elite opinion that human behavior was extremely malleable. The second goal was to provide a scientific rationalization against such ingrained institutions as the family, capitalism, religion, and marriage. To show a society that rejected these institutions and that was the better for it was to make a compelling case that the West should follow a similar course.

"Were there no conflicts, no temperaments which deviated so markedly from the normal that clash was inevitable?" Mead asked. "Was the diffused affection and the diffused authority of the large families, the ease of moving from one family to another, the knowledge of sex and the freedom to experiment a sufficient guarantee to all Samoan girls of a perfect adjustment? In almost all cases, yes."[70] Mead would have her readers believe that it was the perfect society.

An added bonus of her work for many sociologists, anthropologists, and other academicians was that the societal practices reportedly embraced by Samoans happened to be very similar to those advocated by such intellectuals themselves. Free love, an absence of the competitiveness that plagued capitalist societies, community parenting, and a rejection of religion among Samoans seemingly proved not only that nurture and not nature determined human behavior but also that "Western" practices such as monogamy, parental child rearing, and religion were outdated hang-ups. Mead's book put scientific weight behind the arguments for discarding these assumedly unappealing aspects of the Western world.

Coming of Age in Samoa laments "the evils inherent in the too intimate family organisation."[71] In its place, Mead offered a family system similar to the one purportedly embraced in Samoa. She asked,

> What are the rewards of the tiny, ingrown, biological family opposing its closed circle of affection to a forbidding world, of the strong ties between parents and children, ties which imply an active personal relationship from birth until death? Specialisation of affection, it is true, but at the price of many individuals' preserving through life the attitudes of dependent children, of ties between parents and children which defeat the children's attempts to make other adjustments, of necessary choices made unnecessarily poignant because they become issues in an intense emotional relationship. Perhaps these are too heavy prices to pay for a specialisation of emoti on

which might be brought about in other ways, notably through coeducation.[72]

In addition to the family structure, sex was a second main area in which Mead purportedly discovered radical departures from Western norms. Western readers learned that, among Samoans, "the capacity for intercourse only once in a night is counted as senility."[73] Mead reported, "Samoans laugh at stories of romantic love, scoff at fidelity to a long absent wife or mistress, believe explicitly that one love will quickly cure another. . . . Having many mistresses is never out of harmony with a declaration of affection for each other."[74] "If," Mead posited, "a wife really tires of her husband, or a husband of his wife, divorce is a simple and informal matter, the non-resident simply going home to his or her family, and the relationship is said to have 'passed away.'"[75] The South Seas bacchanalia allegedly included children, too, with preadolescents openly partaking in masturbation, light homosexuality, and expeditions into heterosexuality.[76]

For more than a half century, Mead's work stood as conventional wisdom within intellectual circles. All this changed in 1983, when Harvard University Press published Derek Freeman's *Margaret Mead and Samoa*. Freeman spent more than six years living in Samoa. What his study discovered—not only in Samoa but in Mead's own notes as well—directly contradicts the findings of *Coming of Age in Samoa*.

Freeman tested Mead's assertions about the diffusion of responsibilities of raising children and discovered much that disaffirmed her work. He tracked all 108 children between the ages of 3 and 18 in one village and found that all but three lived with their parents.[77] An "it takes a village" mentality to parenting was not to be found in Samoa. Freeman conducted another experiment that measured the response of infants to their mothers walking away from them and the babies' reaction to other relatives walking away from them. When the mother departed from her own child, that child displayed great anguish. When others moved away from babies who were not their own, the children showed no signs of distress. "The primary bond between mother and child is very much a part of the biology of Samoans, as it is of all humans," Freeman observed.[78]

At the core of the Samoan belief system is a cult of female virginity. Among its features are a public marriage ritual that tests whether the bride's hymen is intact. Each tribe also featured its own *taupou*, or ceremonial virgin. One or several girls fill this role for their community. So prized is sexual purity that Freeman relays one account of a 22-year-old girl who slit her own throat after it became public knowledge that she had lost her virginity.[79] Such a shameful reaction could hardly have occurred in a society that had no moral constraints on eros.

Mead's assertions are even betrayed by the evidence she presents to bolster her argument. Of the 25 adolescent girls from whom she collected sexual information, only 11 claimed to have had sex.[80] More than half, by her own account, were virgins. How these facts mesh with her depiction of a society that venerates free love is not explained. Nor does she explain how the eight girls who were ovulating managed to avoid getting pregnant despite their promiscuity and obvious lack of birth control. She did admit in *Social Organization of Manua* that "the infrequency of pregnancy in the unmarried woman is puzzling."[81] Mead's tortured logic later maintained that "in Samoa" promiscuity seemed to serve as a safeguard "against pregnancy."[82] Freeman's own surveys 20 years later of girls between the ages of 14 and 19 found that 30 out of 41, or 73% of his sample group, were virgins. Among 25 women born in the Samoan village of Upolu between 1924 and 1947, Freeman found that the mean age at the birth of their first child was 20.[83]

Adultery, hardly a sin in Mead's imaginary Samoa, remains a criminal offense and is the reason for the breakup of marriages in a majority of the cases in Samoan divorce court. Others claimed that on discovery of marital infidelity, the most common Samoan reaction is violence.[84] This reality hardly meshes with the idea that adultery is accepted.

Such a sexually libidinous society would erase sexual dysfunction, the theory posits. Thus, *Coming of Age in Samoa* necessarily downplayed the level of rape on the Pacific islands. The young author claimed, "the idea of forcible rape or of any sexual act to which both participants do not give themselves freely is completely foreign to the Samoan mind."[85] This belies Mead's own experiences. Her own notes report two cases of forcible rape.[86] While Mead was in Samoa, Freeman notes, rape was the third most common crime, and incidences of the offense were reported in the *Samoa Times*.[87] It is inconceivable that anyone living in such a small society for more than half a year could be oblivious to the occurrence of such serious crimes. In the 1960s, the rape rate in Samoa was double that of the United States and 20 times that of England.[88] Freeman concludes, "The Samoan rape rate is certainly one of the highest to be found anywhere in the world."[89]

Freeman's thesis that Mead was tricked by Samoan girls telling tall tales was confirmed in 1989, when Fa'apua'a Fa'amu, a Samoan islander who had developed a friendship with Mead in 1925–1926, revealed that the neophyte anthropologist had been the victim of a hoax. The elderly woman professed that in response to Mead's imprudent and incessant questions regarding sex 63 years earlier, she and a friend told their American visitor "that we were out at night with boys; she failed to realize that we were just joking and must have been taken in by our pretences." She imparted to her American friend that it was not uncommon for Samoan men and women to make love 15 times in one night and that girls her age engaged in sexual acts with random boys on a regular basis. She added, "we just fibbed and fibbed to her."[90]

Fa'apua'a Fa'amu'a's fibs massaged Mead's worldview, so she chose to believe them. Mead's mind was not open to all the complexities of Samoan society. It only entertained those aspects of Samoan culture that conformed to her preordained thesis. Mead, like other cultural relativists, was not interested in other cultures as much as she was interested in how presentations of other cultures could be used to advance relativism's assault on the West. A feigned interest in other cultures would also come to mark the ideological designs of relativism's stepchild, multiculturalism.

"DIVERSITY WOULD SUPERSEDE FACTUAL CORRECTNESS"

NO IMAGE CAPTURED the resilient spirit of America following the 9-11 attacks better than the famous photograph of three New York City firemen hoisting the Stars and Stripes amidst the rubble and ashes of Ground Zero. The photo was to the September 11 attacks what the picture of the Iwo Jima flag raising atop Mt. Suribachi was to World War II. Both snapshots conveyed to the public that no matter how dire the situation, America has a habit of rising like a phoenix. So when the city of New York decided to memorialize the firefighters killed in the collapse of the Twin Towers, it naturally sought to immortalize the arresting image of the three firefighters in a statue. What seemed to be the perfect symbol to everyone else was deemed deeply flawed by city officials. The three firemen, to the dismay of city officials, were white. History would need to be rewritten to appease racial bean counters. A 19-foot-tall, $180,000 bronze statue was unveiled depicting the familiar scene of the three rescue workers raising the flag, only instead of three white men, the firefighters had become a multiethnic trio. Confronted with the choice of truth or diversity, city officials chose the latter. "I think the artistic expression of diversity would supersede any concern over factual correctness," stated Kevin James, a spokesman for a minority firefighters' group defending the racially diverse statue.[91]

New York City's controversy was a microcosm of the troubling issues evoked by multiculturalism elsewhere. The fictionalized rewrite of history, the politicization of events, racial quotas, and an allegiance to race and not nation all fueled the controversy over the firefighers' memorial and, not coincidentally, are all key components of what has become known as multiculturalism.

Multiculturalism is a relatively new phenomenon. It crept into the national consciousness at the same time that the Baby Boom generation came of age professionally in the worlds of higher education, the media, and other society shaping institutions during the late 1980s. Richard Bernstein points out in *The Dictatorship of Virtue* that a Nexis search for "multicultural" and "multiculturalism" yielded just 40 articles for the year 1981. Bernstein's same search for 1992 generated a 50-fold increase in articles.[92] Alvin Schmidt, another author on the subject of multiculturalism, observes that the *Reader's Guide to Periodical Literature* had no entry for multiculturalism before the 1990s. By 1993, the guide listed 41 entries.[93] If one were to have fallen into a coma in the mid-1980s and awakened a decade later, multiculturalism would be among the societal phenomena that would appear quite unfamiliar.

"Multiculturalism" is an ambiguous term. To a university apparatchik, it is a code word for anti-Americanism. To a political leader, it may simply mean an appreciation for our diverse ethnic backgrounds. To a job applicant passed over because of his fair skin color, it is a euphemism for reverse racism. To a scholar, it may mean a pursuit of the best that foreign cultures have to offer. To speak against "multiculturalism" in its discriminatory incarnation is also to appear to speak against the "multiculturalism" that broadens our understanding of other societies. Because there are so many differing and at times contradictory perceptions of multiculturalism, one runs the risk of being greatly misunderstood by simply claiming to be against multiculturalism. The word's definition is much too complex to yield a fixed meaning. This nebulous definition has granted multiculturalism widespread immunity from criticism.

If multiculturalism merely meant what its name suggests it means, few would debate it. Who, really, finds learning about other cultures objectionable? In practice, multiculturalism is rarely about promoting other cultures. It is more often about debasing our own. This is why one is likely to find a liberal splattering of, say, Cornel West and Paula Rothenberg on multicultural reading lists but search in vain for Averroes or Confucius. A multiculturalism that read the Bhagavad Gita, studied the life of Muhammad, or discussed the current political situation in sub-Saharan Africa would be embraced by all but the most xenophobic among us. Multiculturalism, however, rarely does this. Instead, it sets its sights on all of Western civilization.

True multiculturalism might see a rise in student exchange programs or foreign language courses. The multiculturalism that we get in its place is preoccupied with removing the dreaded dead white males from the literary canon, museum exhibits, and even national holidays. Multiculturalism is therefore a misnomer. A more apt term is "monoculturalism," whose adherents are more obsessed with America and the West than were the supposedly jingoistic educators of the past that these modern "multiculturalists" claim to be rallying against.

At the core of multiculturalism, then, is not an appreciation or understanding of other cultures but a deep animus toward America and the West. When a donor gave $20 million to Yale University to implement a program in Western civilization, for instance, English professor Sara Suleri asked, "Western Civilization? Why not a chair in colonialism, slavery, empire, and poverty?"[94] A professor at the University of Massachusetts–Amherst introduced his course by informing his students, "This class will be consistently anti-American."[95] Ali Mazrui, a distinguished professor of political science at the State University of New York at Binghamton, calls America "a breeding ground of racism, exploitation and genocide."[96] Barbara Johnson defines multiculturalism as "the deconstruction of the foundational ideals of Western civilization."[97]

Multiculturalism is a political program masked as a project of cultural appreciation. Those who accept its tenets see the world through a lens that divides us into oppressor and oppressed. Whites, males, the rich, Christians, and heterosexuals are all considered members of privileged groups. Racial minorities, females, homosexuals, immigrants, and the disabled are classified as victim groups. One's status on the hierarchy of victimhood is determined by the number of "oppressed" categories one falls under. A handicapped black lesbian, therefore, would be exalted by multiculturalism, while a straight white male would be detested. This belief in categories of oppression results in multiculturalists seeking to "level the playing field" by favoring "victim" groups while punishing those perceived as privileged. Because one's sexual preference or skin color tells us next to nothing about one's privileged status in Western society, multiculturalism's method of analysis is deeply flawed.

As is the case with all ideologies, multiculturalism's most fervent adherents seek to silence those who question it. This often manifests itself in outright censorship. Examples of this might include a racially frank book such as *Huckleberry Finn* being pulled from school reading lists or a black conservative speaker being shouted down on campus. More often, however, it is intimidation and name-calling and not censorship that is used to silence critics. Rather than debate the merits of his adversary's argument, the multiculturalist promiscuously hurls accusations of "racism," "sexism," or "homophobia" at him—and why not? The fear alone of being branded a bigot is enough to shut someone up. Once the accusation is leveled, its recipient is almost always cowed and crying uncle. If he's not, he's damaged goods anyhow—forever smeared with the broad accusatory brush of racism, sexism, anti-Semitism, homophobia, and so on. The multiculturalist's gains in name-calling are twofold. Not only does his adversary back off or lose his effectiveness, but the multiculturalist is saved from having to defend an intellectually bankrupt position. Words such as "racist" and "sexist" still retain a degree of currency, and those who throw them around without regard for their accuracy still do so with impunity. Until this changes, opponents of multiculturalism will be at a disadvantage.

The corruption of the language that categorizes the attack terms (e.g., racist, sexist, and homophobe) relied on by multiculturalists also taints the language employed in defense of their ideology. "Diversity" is transformed into a word that endorses a rainbow of skin shades but only one coloring of political opinion. The term thus becomes a euphemism for its antonym. "Tolerance" takes on a new meaning in the multiculturalist lexicon as well. A word that implies a recognition of the right of others to follow a different course now is incorrectly defined as an active support of that different course. Tolerance is confused for endorsement. Thus, someone who adheres to a "live and let live" philosophy with regard to homosexuals is characterized as "intolerant." To be considered "tolerant," one must go further to support special laws that punish the attackers of homosexuals more heavily, call to outlaw any private group that does not admit gays as members, or demand that lawmakers use tax funds to indoctrinate schoolchildren into believing that homosexuality is morally desirable. Despite demanding endorsement and not mere respect for their own program, multiculturalists do not extend even mere toleration to their adversaries. Tolerance is for multiculturalists alone. The familiar buzzwords of "sensitivity" and "civility" are meant to apply only to the conduct of their adversaries. The multiculturalist is absolved from any obligation to conform to such niceties.

Ostensibly, multiculturalism demands equal respect for all cultures. In reality, there is one culture that multiculturalists exhibit a blatant disrespect for. That culture, of course, is our own. On the other hand, multiculturalists call for sensitivity toward other cultures. To this end, one schoolteacher's manual advises educators, "Avoid dwelling on the negatives which may be associated with a cultural or ethnic group. Every culture has positive characteristics which should be accentuated."[98] Some fanatical multiculturalists go beyond this suggested bias and simply concoct histories that enhance the aura of their favored group.

In *They Came Before Columbus*, Rutgers University professor Ivan Van Sertima asserts that Africans and not Columbus discovered the Americas.[99] Other Afrocentrists claim that Aristotle stole his ideas and knowledge from Africa, specifically the Library at Alexandria. A simple date check reveals that the famous library was not erected until after the Greek philosopher had died.[100] More obvious, the Greeks themselves founded the famous library to advance their civilization. Had the Greeks rifled the library for their theories and wisdom, they would be stealing merely from themselves. *African-American Baseline Essays*, a teacher's manual developed in Portland, Oregon, imparts that black Africans invented energy-generating batteries and flew around in primitive airplanes in ancient Egypt. This very silly book has been used as a guide for teachers in Detroit, Washington, D.C., and Atlanta.[101]

University of Massachusetts–Boston professor Charley Shively claims that Abraham Lincoln had numerous gay affairs. "For his taste in men," Shively writes, "Lincoln was clearly an ass rather than a crotch man." What is Shively's evidence? Well, Lincoln, it seems, shared a bed for a while with his friend Joshua Speed—a practice that was common and not thought much about in the 19th century. Shively claims that George Washington was gay as well. Normally, Shively's "scholarship" might be considered laughable. Just how unfunny it is becomes clear when confronted with the reality that the Los Angeles Unified School District—based on Shively's work—instructed teachers to inform homosexual youth that Lincoln was "gay" to boost student self-esteem.[102]

The state of New York has directed that its public schools teach children that one of the two primary influences for the U.S. Constitution was the government of the Iroquois Indians.[103] Professors Donald Grinde and Bruce Johansen echo this claim by asserting that America's Founding Fathers relied heavily on the philosophical tradition of Native Americans to form our government. "Someday," the confused scholars write, "when the dominant society becomes more concerned about reciprocity and less concerned about superiority and domination, we may all be able to join hands and celebrate the diverse roots of the American democratic tradition without the blinders of indifference and cultural arrogance."[104]

Perhaps the most unforgettable example of multiculturalism subverting the truth in favor of political expedience is the case of Rigoberta Menchu. Exploding on the intellectual scene in the early 1980s with her book *I, Rigoberta Menchu*, the diminutive Guatemalan reported that the typical poor Central American bought into every faddish ideology exalted on campus—Marxism, environmentalism, feminism, liberation theology, and so on. Because its conclusions meshed with their ideological predispositions, leftist intellectuals made her book one of the most popular assigned readings on college campuses throughout the 1980s and 1990s. Her success within the academic community soon permeated mainstream society.

The fashionable Menchu held court with a plethora of figures of great import, including the pope, the Dalai Lama, Nelson Mandela, and UN Secretary-General Boutros-Boutros Ghali. This woman who gloried in her past illiteracy was ironically awarded more than a dozen honorary doctorates and appointed a goodwill ambassador by the United Nations Educational, Scientific, and Cultural Organization. In 1992, 500 years after Columbus landed in the New World and in the midst of peace talks aimed at ending her nation's protracted civil war, Menchu won the Nobel Peace Prize.

In 1999, Middlebury College professor David Stoll released *Rigoberta Menchu and the Story of All Poor Guatemalans.* The author spent years inspecting court records and interviewing hundreds of Menchu's fellow villagers, friends, and family. To his consternation, Stoll discovered that *I, Rigoberta Menchu* was largely a fraud.

It is undeniable that Menchu suffered greatly during Guatemala's brutal civil war. Equally undeniable is the fact that her book is filled with lies designed to cast a positive light on the causes she holds dear.

One brother who dies of malnourishment in *I, Rigoberta Menchu* is actually alive and well. He was located still living in Guatemala, quite puzzled about the news of his death.[105] Another brother who was graphically tortured and burned to death in her book was indeed killed, but not in such an attention-grabbing manner.[106]

Menchu's claim that she was illiterate was a fraud designed to endear her more to Western intellectuals. She reports in her autobiography that her father feared that schooling would be treason against their class and ethnicity.[107] During the period that she purports to have labored as a migrant worker active in the revolutionary movement, Menchu was actually attending a prestigious Catholic boarding school. The Menchu of *I, Rigoberta Menchu* forgoes an education in favor of a life as a revolutionary. The truth is quite different. "I interviewed six women who studied with Rigoberta," reports Stoll, "plus three others who had heard stories about her." All agreed that Menchu attended a Catholic school.[108] The *New York Times* interviewed four nuns who were teachers at a school in which Menchu was a student.[109] Additional testimony came from members of her family. "Her way of talking was no longer that of ours," remembers a brother of her visits home from school. "She admonished us to speak correctly."[110]

The central theme of *I, Rigoberta Menchu* is that of prolonged strife between the protagonist's family and the merciless white landowners. "My father fought for twenty-two years," Menchu maintains, "waging a heroic struggle against the landowners who wanted to take our land and our neighbours' land. After many years of hard work, when our small bit of land began yielding harvests and our people had a large area under cultivation, the big landowners appeared."[111] Her book claims that her parents were "forced to leave town because some ladino families came to settle there. They weren't exactly evicted but the ladinos just gradually took over. . . . The rich are always like that."[112] Later she describes her father's jailing at the hands of these rich descendants of Europeans who bribed the courts to keep him imprisoned.[113] Court documents and the unanimous recollection of Menchu's fellow villagers prove that her family's problems were with other indigenous peasants, with the consensus being that it was Rigoberta's family who exploited other peasants. The fight was apparently an interfamily dispute.[114] Her father was not a political prisoner, as she suggests, but was jailed at the instigation of other Indian peasants.[115]

Rigoberta Menchu may have provided multiculturalists with made-to-order propaganda, but they have paid her back generously by continuing to exalt her fraudulent book.

Wellesley professor Margorie Agosin told the *Chronicle of Higher Education*, "Whether her book is true or not, I don't care."[116] Professor John Peeler of Bucknell excuses the discrepancies in the book by claiming, "the Latin American tradition of testimonial has never been bound by strict rules of veracity."[117] Stanford professor Timothy Brook told the *Stanford Re-*

view, "Authenticity and reliability are problems in all texts, this controversy does not inauthenticate Menchu's book." Brook added that rather than dropping the book, he is thinking about bumping it from secondary to required reading in his course.[118]

As was the case with the historically incorrect (but politically correct) New York City memorial to firefighters killed while evacuating the World Trade Center, partisans of *I, Rigoberta Menchu* cared little if what they were pushing happened to be true. What mattered to them was that it conformed to the ideological precepts of multiculturalism. Truth is not the concern of multiculturalism; ideology is.

CONCLUSION

CULTURAL MARXISM, COMMUNISM, relativism, and multiculturalism are the religions for the people who mock religion. While these sects differ in their finer points, they are denominations within the same overriding faith. At their core exists a hatred of America and the West. Their creed of anti-Americanism has become dogma for much of the Left.

The ideologies examined in this chapter come complete with taboos, rituals, zeal, and saints but with little of the social good that religions provide. The jihadists within these ideologies believe that theirs is a divine mission, even if they do not believe in a divinity. Anyone who gets in their way is treated as an impeder to salvation. This is why, for instance, Communists did not hesitate to kill those who stood in their way. If one believes an ideology can manufacture heaven on Earth, which is what many ideologues do in fact believe, then why is it surprising to find ideologues who lie and kill for what they believe? The sacred texts of these various faiths, books such as *The Communist Manifesto* and *I, Rigoberta Menchu,* are immune from criticism. One who questions these holy books is excommunicated out of any society that the ideologues control, be it something as small as a faculty social club or as large as an entire nation. Similarly, it is considered blasphemy to criticize the canonized figures within these ideologies. The religious fervor that grips the ideologies' adherents often blinds them to reality. Most important, like all religions, these ideologies have a devil. That devil is the United States of America.

These anti-American faiths are all cons. The central tenets of these quasi-religions claim that our country's main contributions to humanity are racial discrimination, the oppression of women, environmental rape, the exploitation of workers, and various other wicked crimes. Reality, as we will see, begs to differ.

CHAPTER 3

ANTI-AMERICAN CHIC

THEY MADE THE trek to New York City from as far away as Toronto, Paris, and Miami. They held signs espousing a diverse array of causes: "Queers Against Israeli Occupation," "Say No to Racial Profiling," "Let Iraq Live." They chanted. A popular mantra was "It's bullshit! Get off it! The enemy is profit!" Others shouted "1, 2, 3, 4 . . . I am not a corporate whore! 5, 6, 7, 8 . . . Third World countries liberate!" Some wore masks, while others donned street-theater costumes. An American flag could be seen flying with the field of 50 stars replaced by the logos of Nike, Microsoft, and other corporations.[1]

The impetus for the winter 2002 pilgrimage to the Big Apple was the meeting of the World Economic Forum, held at the Waldorf Astoria Hotel from January 31 through February 2. Unlike at earlier meetings of the global elite in Seattle and Genoa, there were no riots, looting, mass acts of vandalism, or rock throwing at police. Erroneously dubbed "antiglobalization protestors" by much of the media, those gathered came to demonstrate against capitalism, not globalism. As the largest free-market economy in the world, America served as a figurative punching bag—just as actual Starbucks shops and McDonald's restaurants had served as literal punching bags at earlier violent demonstrations—for many of the anticapitalist activists.

So what were the protestors so angry about?

"We are against American imperialism," explained Walter Daum. "The United States dominates the world militarily, economically, and politically." Regarding the terrorist attacks on his city, the mathematics instructor at the City University of New York remarked, "It's the misery that American economic policies and military policies impose on the entire world that makes it possible for terrorists like this to have an audience—to recruit people." Not only does Daum believe that American policy is indirectly responsible for the attacks, but he argues that the United States itself is a greater terrorist threat than the al-Qaeda network. "The country is dominated by capitalism and imperialism, and, in fact, our policies make the United States the greatest terrorist power on the globe these days."[2]

The protesting math teacher was not alone in his beliefs.

Eric Josephson, the head of a local track workers' union, conceded that the 9-11 terrorists were "criminals." But, he maintains, "They are small criminals as against the big bloody criminals who run United States imperialism." We live in a dysfunctional world where, Josephson contends, "[a] few wealthy advanced powerful countries dominate the rest of the world, particularly the United States, and they suck the rest of the world dry." Most major problems facing America today, the transit worker believes, are caused by capitalism, which serves as the source of his enmity toward the United States. These problems include racism, sexism, environmental degradation, and political repression. "Capitalism is by its nature racist and sexist. I don't believe that you can fight racism off in a corner without taking on the capitalist system." Then why is there more racism and sexism in countries that do not have free-market systems? Josephson explains this anomaly away by maintaining that minority groups attained increasing levels of justice in spite of capitalism, not because of it. Leftists view the relationship between democracy and the free market not as symbiotic but as antagonistic. "It's not immediately evident, and it's not around the corner, but capitalism less and less can afford democracy. You see that now in this country."[3]

Phil Houser traveled all the way to the Big Apple from Ft. Lauderdale, Florida. His grievance was American policy as well, which he blames for much of the misery in the world. For Houser, it is U.S. foreign policy, rather than just its economic policies, that infuriates. He charges the United States with the extermination of entire peoples. "I learned about a year ago that the United States had deliberately blocked the Iraqis from having water treatment facilities, knowing full well in 1991 that they would end up dying with typhoid, hoof and mouth disease, and dysentery—looks to me like deliberate genocide." Houser continued, "But do you know what really kills me? When I found out that the United States had dropped depleted uranium bombs on civilians—and I'm talking hundreds and hundreds of pounds of depleted uranium on civilian populations—and seeing the birth defects and genetic abnormalities caused by United States uranium bombs, I can't keep quiet." The cause of this confabulated genocide? You guessed it: capitalism.[4]

If you hate capitalism, it is hard to love America. The Left despises capitalism. Being the foremost adherent of the free market in the world, America is naturally hated by many of the same people who hate capitalism. America is to the Left what the old Soviet Union was to the Right. Both countries symbolize economic systems viewed as inherently evil by their detractors. It is therefore not difficult to understand why a socialist might hate America.

The anti-Americanism of the activists gathered outside the Waldorf Astoria in New York City is motivated by a hatred of the economic policies embraced by the United States. But just as not everyone who hates capitalism hates America, not everyone who hates America does so out of revulsion toward capitalism. So what are the other issues that drive Americans to hate America?

DIVERSITY OR DIVISION?

STARTING AT THE origins of the republic, people of color have marked themselves among our greatest patriots. One of the Revolution's earliest casualties, Crispus Attucks, was a mix of African and Indian. Giving your life for your country, like Attucks did, is the most radical expression of patriotism one can make. People of color, constituting a disproportionately high percentage of the military, show themselves more willing to make this supreme sacrifice than the white population. The second most extreme manifestation of love for America is the act of abandoning one's own life elsewhere to come here. A great many people of color are American by choice and not by chance. There was obviously something that appealed to them about America that motivated them to uproot their lives and come here. Our country, past and present, is replete with examples of heroic acts of patriotism by Americans of every hue. Even when their country did not return their love, Americans of color have loved their country.

Despite this rich history of patriotism, there are some that would have us believe that you cannot be a real black person or a genuine Hispanic if you love America. These peddlers of racial animosity form groups to exploit historical grievances for current political gain. It is in their interests not to make things better but to sow division along ethnic and racial lines. The advocates of these "antiracist" causes are often mirror images of the white racists that they purport to oppose.

The Hispanic student group MEChA (Movimiento Estudi-antil Chicano de Aztlán) boasts campus affiliates at more than 400 colleges and universities. MEChA's literature emits the putrid stench of Nazism. The group's motto is "For our race, everything. For those outside our race, nothing."[5] MEChA calls for Mexicans to take over the American Southwest, regularly employs racially derogatory language against whites in its literature, and calls for Mexican Americans to show loyalty to Mexico and not the United States. "In the spirit of a new people that is conscious not only of its proud historical heritage but also of the brutal 'gringo' invasion of our territories," reads the group's mission statement, "we, the Chicano inhabitants and civilizers of the northern land of Aztlan from whence came our forefathers, reclaiming the land of their birth and consecrating the determination of our people of the sun, declare that the call of our blood is our power, our responsibility, and our inevitable destiny."[6]

American Indian Movement (AIM) leader Russell Means labels Native Americans who have assimilated into American culture "apples"—red on the outside, white on the inside.[7] AIM accuses contemporary U.S. governments of "cultural genocide," directs Indians to separate from the society surrounding them, and generally blames whites for any problem facing American Indians. Currently, the group expends much of its energy opposing holidays such as Thanksgiving and Columbus Day. In 2000, Means and his cohorts tried to block Italian Americans from marching in a Columbus Day parade in Denver. AIM's tactics included dumping red liquid in the path of the marchers and taunting the Italians gathered for the celebration. Nearly 150 anti-Columbus activists were arrested. "I'm sorry, but the day of Gandhiism and Martin Luther King tactics are over," Means candidly admitted to his supporters after his release from jail.[8]

The now defunct Black Panthers are glorified in movies like *Panther* and in popular histories of the 1960s and 1970s. The fictionalized Panthers are preoccupied with community education and breakfast programs for the poor. The real Panthers were a racist gang that included drug dealers, robbers, rapists, and murderers within its ranks.[9] Their 10-point party platform called for "education for our people that exposes the true nature of this decadent American society" as well as for jails to release all blacks, black secession from the United States, and full employment for blacks.[10] Several decades after their heyday, the Panthers reunited—at least the ones not dead or in jail. At a 2002 conference, speakers referred to the killing of policemen as "military actions" and the men convicted of these murders as "prisoners of war." Thunderous applause followed a description of the murder of two prison officials.[11] The Panthers are long gone as an organization (although a self-proclaimed New Black Panther Party has sprung up), but their jaundiced view of America lives on. Today, it is not Martin Luther King's desire for blacks to share in America's promise but the Panthers' view that blacks need special protection from our thoroughly corrupt society that pervades the thinking of Louis Farrakhan, Jesse Jackson, Al Sharpton, and other self-proclaimed civil rights leaders.

Despite the extremist message of these groups, they enjoy a great deal of success in attracting admirers. By focusing exclusively on wrongs committed against members of their respective ethnic groups, such organizations demagogically gain support. Tributes to their success can be seen all around us.

Tennessee state representative Henri Brooks recently balked at standing when the legislature recited the Pledge of Allegiance. Brooks complained, "This flag represents the former colonies that enslaved our ancestors."[12] True enough, but does it not also represent the government that freed her ancestors? The cause célèbre among Native American activists is freeing fellow activist Leonard Peltier, who murdered two FBI agents in 1975. Peltier's guilt is widely established—his rifle left 114 shell casings at the scene, he admits to shooting at the agents, eyewitnesses state that he was the murderer, and so on.[13] Rather than the facts of the case, Peltier's hate-filled political diatribes against America attract followers such as director Oliver Stone, actor Ed Asner, and musician Robbie Robertson. Pat Buchanan points out, "When the U.S. soccer team played Mexico in the Los Angeles Coliseum a few years back, the 'Star-Spangled Banner' was hooted and jeered, an American flag was torn down, and the American team and its few fans were showered with water bombs, beer bottles, and garbage."[14] Minority demagogues have joined white racists in using race as a wedge to separate Americans from their fellow countrymen.

Race, then, like economics, is used to engender toxic feelings toward America. That is the bad news. The good news is that unlike the socialists, whose hatred of capitalism quite logically leads to a hatred of the United States, those who portray patriotism as incongruous with membership in certain ethnic groups base their view on false premises—a phenomenon we will explore in greater detail in the next chapter.

A POP CULTURE AGAINST ITSELF

WHEN ACTOR DANNY GLOVER and director Robert Altman spoke out against their country in the aftermath of September 11, their perspective represented the long-standing opinion of many in their field. "The United States is a land that has raped every area of the world," claimed Susan Sarandon shortly after making *Thelma and Louise*. At around the same time, Sean Penn could be heard professing, "I was brought up in a country that relished fear-based religion, corrupt government, and an entire white population living on stolen property that they murdered for and that is passed on from generation to generation."[15]

What is shown on the silver screen reflects the out-of-touch views of people like Sarandon and Penn. The fictional hero of Academy Award–winning *Dances with Wolves* is a traitor. Ten years later, the Best Picture award was given to *American Beauty*, a venomous indictment of our society that skewers the life-draining corporate conformity faced by the husband, the Tony Robbins–style self-improvement of salesmanship adopted by his wife, and the high school inhabited by their daughter that serves to manufacture such people. Rarely does Hollywood produce films of this caliber; frequently does it serve up a product that matches the two films' malevolence against our society.

Tinseltown's most poisonous venom is reserved for the military. Other than Mel Gibson's *We Were Soldiers* or movies starring Chuck Norris, how many Vietnam-themed films do not portray veterans of that conflict as bloodthirsty lunatics, doped-out losers, or sufferers from some other severe form of mental illness? While the Vietnam War certainly inspired many excellent movies, it spawned few accurate ones. Hollywood's propaganda on the conflict's veterans has been so successful that its take has become conventional wisdom.

The revulsion felt for the military—interrupted by a recent wave of patriotic war movies—goes beyond Vietnam-themed flicks. Recent cinematic offerings depict crackpot Marines attempting to nuke San Francisco (*The Rock*) or approving the killing of an out-of-step private (*A Few Good Men*). From watching *The General's Daughter*, one gets the idea that the typical rapist is not an inhabitant of the urban jungle or of a correctional institution but an officer candidate at West Point. Classics such as *The Sands of Iwo Jima*, *The Longest Day*, and *Sergeant York* are lambasted for being pro-military propaganda. Yet the events depicted in these movies really happened. Films like *The Rock* are only the product of a writer's warped perception of the armed forces, making it more of a propaganda film than any midcentury war movie. Despite all the negativity, there is reason for optimism. The success of films such as *Saving Private Ryan*, *We Were Soldiers*, and *Black Hawk Down*, coupled with the public's growing intolerance of glib cynicism in the wake of September 11, make it increasingly unlikely that there will be a pot of gold at the end of the rainbow for propagandistic scripts railing against America. Money talks nowhere as loudly as it does in Hollywood.

A negative depiction of our country is reinforced through popular music. Many of rap's most vaunted acts—NWA, Public Enemy, Ice-T—profited from peddling the idea that America is a giant concentration camp for blacks. In this tradition, a rap duo known as The Coup began promoting their new compact disc, inappropriately titled "Party Music," shortly before 9-11. The album's ill-timed cover, which was later changed amid public outrage, featured the witless twosome blowing up the World Trade Center.

Some rock acts idolize John Lennon or Jimi Hendrix. Others emulate Pete Townshend. Pearl Jam and REM, among others, cite a more peculiar figure as a leading artistic influence: Noam Chomsky. No intellectual has been as persistently anti-American over the past three decades as the Massachusetts Institute of Technology professor, which is precisely what endears him so much to rockers half his age. From labeling the Cambodian genocide anti-Communist propaganda to claiming that the United States conspired with Nazis after World War II for the purpose of world domination, Chomsky has never been one to let facts stand in the way of his imaginative broadsides.[16] Chomsky's rhetoric is music to the ears of leading rockers. REM tried in vain to coax Chomsky to open their concerts with a speech. Bad Religion used a Chomsky lecture as the B-side on one of their singles. When Pearl Jam set up temporary "pirate" radio stations on stops during a mid-1990s tour, songs like "Rearview Mirror" and "Jeremy" were interspersed with clips of the MIT linguist's angry rhetoric. "Rock and Roll is a fruitful area to spread [Chomsky's message] because rock musicians are natural anarchists in terms of their personality, even if they don't know it," expounds Charles Young, a Chomsky admirer and music critic for *Playboy* and *Musician*. "It makes complete sense to me that Chomsky has been picked up in these circles rather than among Hollywood moviemakers." Chomsky's philosophical appeal to rock stars, Young assures, is genuine. "It's not just fuck-youism."[17]

Another group of Chomsky disciples, Rage Against the Machine, has sold millions of albums "raging" against the country that made them rich. Like the corporate schlock they purport to despise, the rap/metal group maintains a cookie-cutter approach to producing hits: predictable, politically charged lyrics set to tunes that evoke feelings of déjà vu for listeners wondering whether what they are hearing is the band's last single. By shrewdly clothing their off-putting message in beats and rhythms congenial to the ears of youth, the political activists masquerading as musicians assure that their idiosyncratic views receive a hearing amongst an audience that normally wouldn't pay them any attention. With an upside-down flag gracing an amplifier, Rage Against the Machine fans mosh to such numbers as "Bullet to the Head," "CIA (Criminals In Action)," and "Take the Power Back," which waxes poetic, "Bam! Here's the plan/Motherfuck Uncle Sam."[18] MTV favorite Marilyn Manson offers fans a nihilistic mélange of suicide, drugs, and Satanism in his lyrics. The bane of his existence is the only society tolerant enough to give him a stage.

Silencing these "artists" would be the most un-American reaction citizens could have. The second most un-American response would be silence itself. The makers of anti-American propaganda films and the millionaire musicians who rail against our capitalist system deserve our scorn, not our dollars.

In fiction, where any theory or characterization, no matter how absurd, can be made to work, readers, listeners, and viewers are conditioned to believe what they see or hear. With enough repetition, the creator's imagination is often processed as reality. This is why so many ideologues flock to the arts. In their utopia, even the most outlandish ideas can appear to make sense.

A NEW HISTORY

THE ENTERTAINER'S OBLIGATION to accuracy is less stringent than the historian's. Some leeway is afforded to films that fudge the facts. Artistic license, however, is not the prerogative of chroniclers. So when we see historians play fast and loose with truth, it is more irksome.

To view America through the eyes of the Left is to witness a dark place. One sees a nation built on slavery, genocide, the oppression of women, racial discrimination, severe class stratification, and ecological degradation. It is the Frankfurt School's Critical Theory unleashed on American history. Indeed, the federal government's *National Standards for United States History* put forth a history with one mention of George Washington and no references to Thomas Edison, the Wright Brothers, or Robert E. Lee. In their place were scores of appearances of the word "slavery," 19 mentions of the Ku Klux Klan, and 17 references to Joe McCarthy and so-called McCarthyism.[19] Schoolchildren are taught that theirs is a country to be hated, not loved.

There are two major problems with the New History. The first is that it frequently sacrifices factual accuracy for ideological purity. The second is that it lacks context. Both phenomena serve to darken rather than enhance our understanding of the past.

When one reads the federal government's *National Standards'* section on the Revolutionary War and glimpses its lone picture on the conflict—a painting of a woman immersed in battle—one quickly understands that conveying an accurate portrait of what happened is secondary for the authors.[20] Starting with the idea that Europeans rather than the diseases they brought with them wiped out the Native American population, contemporary historians present a tissue of lies designed to serve their ideological interests rather than truth. We are incorrectly taught that World War II internment policies affected only Japanese Americans, that domestic anti-Communists conducted a witch-hunt against imaginary foes, and that a replay of the Great Depression took place during Ronald Reagan's presidency. In our history books, politics overrides accuracy.

The baleful effect of political correctness trumping factual correctness is compounded by presentations of the past without reference to historical context. Judging past events, ideas, and people by our current standards—presentism—divorces them from their context. An example of presentism can be found in the New Historians' condemnation of the American founding. "Though the Declaration of Independence stated that 'all men are created equal,' race, religion, ethnicity, class, and gender limited the rights of many Americans to participate in the Constitution's promise of democratic government," maintains a 2002 Smithsonian exhibit.[21] "African Americans and women struggled throughout the 19th century for rights that only white male property holders had been granted in the 18th century." The college text *Approaching Democracy* echoes the characterization of the republic's infant government as quite regressive. "Only a minority of people—white, landowning males over the age of 21—could exercise full citizenship rights in 1787."[22] Aside from being untrue (some states had no suffrage property requirements, women voted in New Jersey, and free blacks voted in several states), the statements miss the point of the American founding.[23] What is remarkable is not that certain people were denied the right to vote—that was the case everywhere in 1787—but that anyone voted at all.

The negative depiction of our heritage starts with the discovery of the Americas and continues through the modern age. It is hardly confined to textbooks. Movies, theater, museums, political leaders, pop culture, art, and monuments increasingly portray American history as a continuum of shame.

Christopher Columbus alchemized from heroic explorer to genocidal maniac in the 1990s. By virtue of his extending Europe's dominion, the Left holds Columbus responsible for any harm caused by those who followed his footsteps to the

New World. The sins of the sons, both real and imagined, are ascribed to the father. In 1990, the National Council of Churches condemned honoring Christopher Columbus with a holiday, calling the day a celebration of an "occasion of oppression, degradation, and genocide."[24] For these same reasons, the University of Massachusetts–Amherst and the University of California–Berkeley replaced Columbus Day with something called Indigenous Peoples' Day.[25] New York's Lincoln Center greeted the quincentennial of the Italian explorer's discovery of the Americas by hosting *New World: An Opera About What Columbus Did to the Indians.*[26]

Fast-forward to the arrival of the Pilgrims at Plymouth Rock, and America's early settlers are viewed as sex-obsessed prudes, 17th-century versions of Ken Starr. Worse still, they are cast as culpable in the decimation of the native population. American Indian groups have declared Thanksgiving a "National Day of Mourning," annually descending on Plymouth, Massachusetts, during the holiday to express outrage—at times violently. A leader of the protestors maintains that the Plymouth celebration of Thanksgiving is a "glorification of genocide. It's like the Ku Klux Klan re-creating a cross burning because 'that's the way history was.'"[27]

The founding of our nation is degraded. Several years ago, a group at the University of Massachusetts–Amherst—aided by administrators and faculty—attempted to strip the school's "Minuteman" nickname from the university's sports teams and merchandising. Their rationale? The Minutemen, they claimed, were racist white men who carried guns![28] The city of New Orleans went so far as to remove the name of George Washington from one of its schools.[29] Historian Connor Cruise O'Brien writes that Thomas Jefferson should be ejected from our pantheon of national heroes.[30] A bill requiring schoolchildren to re-cite brief passages from Jefferson's greatest accomplishment, the Declaration of Independence, was defeated in New Jersey, with every Democrat voting in the negative. The Declaration, ac-cording to one of the bill's opponents, is "anti-women, anti-black and too pro-God." "You have the nerve to ask my grandchildren to recite the Declaration," remarked state senator Wayne Bryant. "How dare you? You are now on notice that this is of-fensive to my community."[31]

As the republic grew in population, it moved west. The New History uniformly condemns westward expansion as the culmination of a genocidal campaign against the Indians. Yet the only party guilty of genocide against Native Americans was Mother Nature, not the U.S. government. The continent's in-digenous population was depleted almost entirely through the introduction of foreign diseases, such as smallpox, after the arrival of Europeans and Africans. To allege white culpability in genocide of the Indians is tantamount to blaming Africans for AIDS, Asians for the Black Plague, or Indians for syphilis. Even far-left historian James Loewen concedes that between 1840 and 1860—prime years in the western migration—pioneers killed 426 Indians, while Indians inflicted 362 deaths upon whites.[32] This hardly resembles genocide. As evidenced by mas-sacres at Deerfield, Fort Mims, and Little Bighorn, U.S.–Indian relations are more nuanced than the New History lets on. The role-reversing reenactments of the old "good guy versus bad guy" cowboys and Indians films that today's history books adopt in telling the story of U.S.–Indian conflicts is simply bad history.

Like the displacement of Native Americans, slavery is a part of our heritage that is so shameful that one might think activists need not exaggerate it to attaint our nation. Yet reparations activists and much of the media create an impression that the institution of slavery was somehow unique to America. On the occasion when these ideologues do concede that human bondage did occur elsewhere, they downplay the harm that non-U.S. slavery wrought. Dorothy Benton-Lewis, co-chair of the National Coalition of Blacks for Reparations in America, maintains that slavery in other parts of the world was relatively benign compared to slavery in the United States. "It is American slavery that put a color on slavery," she contends. "And American slavery is not like the slavery of Africa and ancient times." How so? She opines that American slavery differed in that it was "dehumanizing, brutal, and barbaric slavery that subjugated people and turned them into profit."[33] John Henrik Clarke, emeritus professor at Hunter College, alleges that slavery in Africa "had few similarities" to the slave system adopted by whites. Unlike the supposedly benign black slave masters, whites "totally dehumanized the slave and denied his basic personality." "In the United States," he writes, "an attempt was made to destroy every element of culture of the slaves." In contrast, he claims, South American and West Indian slave masters "did not outlaw the African drum, African ornamentations, African religion, or other things dear to the African, remembered from his former way of life."[34] An activist at the University of Wisconsin dismissed the reality of slavery in Africa by maintaining, "That's a totally different type of slavery."[35] It is clear that what is discomforting to these activists is the United States and not slavery.

The New History even condemns the Civil War, which led to the abolition of slavery.

The conflict is depicted as a war fought because the rich sought to blind the lower classes to the stratified economic conditions of the country. Howard Zinn, for one, writes that "on the eve of the Civil War it is money and profit, not the movement against slavery, that was uppermost in the priorities of the men who ran the country."[36] One would think that historians, heretofore dwelling on slavery during the infancy of America, would welcome the emancipation of slaves. This would be to mistake their real interests. The New Historians are not concerned with slavery per se—which is why they take a jaundiced view of America's abolition of it—but are instead concerned with twisting any event to make America look bad. Slavery easily serves this purpose, but other events need to be more carefully molded to depict America in the worst possible light. The theme of Zinn's chapter on the Civil War in his *People's History of the United States* is that the conflict was a ruse to give the ruling class all it coveted and to stem the impending workers' revolution. "Class consciousness was overwhelmed during the Civil War, both North and South, by military and political unity in the crisis of the war," the book claims. "That unity was weaned by rhetoric and enforced by arms. It was a war proclaimed as a war for liberty, but working people would be attacked by soldiers if they dared to strike."[37] In Zinn's Marxist take on America, which loudly boasts more than 500,000 copies sold on its cover, the slave system is kept in place by the conspiratorial forces of wealth and privilege and then is strangely abolished by those very forces. Zinn never explains the cause of the about-face. In fact, the book conveys the notion that every major occurrence in U.S. history is caused by the desire of the wealthy for more and more profits. Zinn's many readers learn, "The psychology of patriotism, the lure of adventure, the aura of moral crusade created by political leaders, worked effectively to dim class resentments against the rich and powerful, and turn much of the anger against 'the enemy.'"[38] No matter what course America follows, it cannot win—even in abolishing slavery—in the eyes of the New Historians.

America's transition from economic backwater to industrial powerhouse is characterized as an age of robber barons and greed. The *National Standards for United States History* instructs students and teachers to "Conduct a trial of John D. Rockefeller on the following charge: *'The plaintiff had knowingly and willfully participated in unethical and amoral business practices designed to undermine traditions of fair and open competition for personal and private aggrandizement in direct violation of the common welfare.'*"[39] Was Rockefeller engaging in "private aggrandizement" when his generosity helped develop the vaccine for yellow fever, eradicated the boll weevils that had long bedeviled Southern crops, helped save Belgium from famine during World War I, or launched the University of Chicago and Spelman?[40] Rockefeller's business practices pioneered win-win employee shareholder programs, which made his workers part owners of the company. He gave the United States the lion's share of the world's oil market. The impact of his "amoral business practices" was a drop in kerosene prices from 23.5 cents per gallon when Standard Oil was launched in 1870 to 7.5 cents per gallon two decades later. He once instructed a colleague, "We must remember that we are refining oil for the poor man and he must have it cheap and good."[41]

The "common welfare" of consumers, employees, charities, and the nation all benefited from John D. Rockefeller. The textbooks' treatment of Rockefeller is emblematic of their treatment of other leading creators of wealth. If one seeks to discredit capitalism, what better way is there than to demonize capitalists? In the jaded lens of the partisan historian, the era of capitalism's great triumphs becomes a "gilded age" or the time of the "robber barons." Left-wing historians view rapid wealth creation as a bad thing. Corrupt schemes of the age that married the state to business are blamed on free-market economics—despite that philosophy's aversion to government involvement in the economy—rather than on the government. Profit-hungry businessmen are similarly blamed for pushing America into World War I as well as causing the Great Depression.

The discussion of World War II in the *National Standards* exemplifies the misplaced priorities of the New History. D-Day merits a fleeting reference, while Iwo Jima, Guadalcanal, and other important battles are completely ignored. What is deemed significant about the war is the internment of Japanese Americans and questioning the "appropriateness" of President Truman's decision to drop the atomic bomb.[42]

President Truman is labeled a mass murderer and a racist for using atomic weapons on Hiroshima and Nagasaki. A proposed exhibit at the Smithsonian's Air and Space Museum was canned in 1995 after critics labeled it anti-American propaganda. A Massachusetts congressman pointed out that the prospective exhibit displayed 97 graphic photographs detailing Japanese suffering, compared to a mere 8 photos relaying the hurt caused by Japan's aggression.[43] Veterans complained that the museum display gave scant attention to the *Enola Gay* and its crew. Others wondered why the Smithsonian would base its exhibit almost entirely on memorabilia from the Hiroshima Peace Memorial Museum, an institution funded by the same government that makes it illegal for public schools to teach World War II from any perspective save its own. In the end, the politicized display gave way to a more neutral account, which infuriated critics of Truman's use of atomic weapons. Twenty protestors attempted to block the gates of the museum on the exhibit's opening day. Another man threw red paint meant to symbolize blood on the featured display.[44] American University staged its own exhibit utilizing much of the unused material from the Smithsonian. ABC News aired a documentary, "Hiroshima: Why the Bomb Was Dropped," which suggested that the United States employed atomic weapons to flex its muscles to scare off the Soviet Union. Penn State University professor Robert James Maddox called the Peter Jennings–hosted broadcast "the worst piece of garbage I've seen."[45] What Truman's critics fail to admit is that the bomb undoubtedly saved lives (both Japanese and American) by ending the war and preventing a tortured land invasion. Their argument that the Japanese would have surrendered anyhow is more obviously flawed. Even after the *Enola Gay* released its payload over Hiroshima, Japan still refused to surrender. The Empire of the Sun stubbornly sacrificed another of its cities before it would concede defeat.

Like slavery and the displacement of the Indians, ethnically based internment policies besmirch the reputation of the United States on their own without the aid of overstatement. Still, some find the idea of discrediting America so inviting that they resort to exaggeration and outright deception.

The Smithsonian Museum of American History's 2002 exhibit "A More Perfect Union: Japanese Americans and the United States Constitution" exceeded the Air and Space Museum's *Enola Gay* piece in its dishonesty. "On February 19, 1942, President Franklin D. Roosevelt issued Executive Order 9066," one learns upon setting foot in the exhibit. "It authorized military authorities to exclude 'any and all persons' from designated areas of the United States to protect the national defense. The language of the order implied that any citizen might be removed. In reality, the order applied only to Japanese Americans." Further on, "A More Perfect Union" asserts, "Little serious thought was given to the incarceration of German or Italian resident aliens."[46] The facts belie these proclamations.

The treatment of internment in textbooks is similar in tone. Typical is the account in the widely assigned college history text *The Enduring Vision*. The book explains that, during World War II, "[t]he worst abuses of civil liberties" involved "the internment of 112,000 Japanese Americans." Those interned were placed in what the authors label "concentration camps." This injustice, states the book that is read by hundreds of thousands of students, occurred despite the fact that "military intelligence had [not] uncovered any evidence of disloyal behavior by Japanese Americans."[47]

Both the Smithsonian and our textbooks get the story of World War II internment wrong.

It is claimed that more than 100,000 Americans were interned during World War II. The true figure barely exceeds 30,000. More shocking than this is that of all those who were internally detained, roughly half were Europeans living in America.[48] Historians don't dare question the loyalty of some Japanese Americans. To do so would be to undermine their thesis that there was no rational (rather than racial) motivation for internment. Yet more than 5,000 Japanese Americans renounced their citizenship following Pearl Harbor, and additional thousands joined the Japanese war effort.[49] While the Smithsonian did quietly note that many Japanese Americans renounced their citizenship and refused to fight, the museum excuses their shameful conduct by claiming that they did so "under confusing and stressful circumstances."[50] Historians ignore the internment of Europeans. This inconvenient occurrence delegitimizes the idea that internment unfairly targeted the yellow Japanese but not the white Germans.

To the shame of the United States, tens of thousands of Japanese Americans, in addition to the 15,000 or so ethnic Japanese internally detained, were forced to relocate from the West Coast. Historians use the concepts of "forced relocation" and "internment" interchangeably, even though each was quite different than the other. This is why, presumably, historians have cooked up the figure of 112,000 for the total number of Japanese interned. Confusion might explain this error, but what are we to make of the total omission of non-Japanese internment and relocation? In contradiction to what the Smithsonian says, the government forced thousands of Italians and Germans to relocate and detained others in internment centers. Just a few months after his son incredibly hit in 56 consecutive games for the New York Yankees, San Francisco fisherman Giuseppe DiMaggio was barred from practicing his trade and even from traveling to his son's local waterfront restaurant. As it did with scores of Italians, Germans, Bulgarians, and others, the government placed a five-mile limit on DiMaggio's travel from his home. The federal government forced thousands of others, such as world-famous opera singer Ezio Pinza, into detention centers.[51] Still others living near areas of strategic importance were compelled to move. Unlike the Japanese, the Germans and Italians forced from their homes were not given the option of relocating to federally funded centers that offered free food, clothing, housing, medical care, and education.[52] The Smithsonian hyperbolically describes these relocation centers in a section called "Concentration Camps, U.S.A." The museum display states, "Although we may not be comfortable with the term, the fact remains that these facilities were, by definition, American concentration camps."[53] Yet the camps had the highest life expectancy rates and the lowest infant mortality rates during the war. While those in the camps had been made to leave California, Arizona, Oregon, and Washington, living in the government centers was optional (35,000 Japanese chose to live on their own elsewhere). When the war ended, the Japanese American Citizens League sued to keep them open.[54] The author is willing to go out on a limb and say that none of the inhabitants of Kolyma or Auschwitz objected to closing down those real concentration camps.

Pop culture and the intelligentsia depict the Cold War as a time when our public officials suffered from paranoid delusions, seeing Communists around every corner and under every bed. We now know better. Even the more ridiculed warnings against Communists in government underestimated the problem of domestic subversion. The opening of the Soviet archives and our own government's declassification of the Venona program prove that hundreds of Americans were indeed acting as Stalin's agents.[55] Historians choose to ignore all this and instead paint anti-Communism as an irrational movement caught up in an unfounded hysteria.

What Communists did in this country only partly inspired anti-Communists. What Communists did in other countries primarily motivated the anti-Communist movement. If all you knew about the role of the United States in the 20th-century world came from the leading college textbooks on American history, you would know nothing of Communism's murder of 100 million people. You would not know what a gulag is, nor would you have any familiarity with the term *laogai*. Widely used college history texts *A People and a Nation, The National Experience,* and *The Enduring Vision* mention Mao Zedong's name dozens of times. Yet nowhere do they even reference his slaughter of 60 million of his fellow countrymen. With the exception of one vague reference to Stalin's "brutality" against his own people, you would have no idea from reading these texts of the tens of millions of deaths he was responsible for.[56] A great deal of the context for America's opposition to Communism in these books is erased like Trotsky airbrushed out of an official Soviet photograph. Our history texts' presentation of Lenin, Stalin, Mao, and their minor league impersonators is a bit like learning about the character of Adolf Hitler with that part about the Holocaust unmentioned. The sins of omission are often more misleading than outright lies.

Hollywood reinforces the Alice-in-Wonderland view of anti-Communists as the bad guys and Communists as harmless idealists. *The Front, Guilty by Suspicion, The House on Carroll Street,* and *Daniel* are among the scores of films depicting the evils of "McCarthyism." Contrast the plethora of movies portraying anti-Communists as villains with the paucity of films about life under Communism. Individuals risking their lives over the Berlin Wall or in the seas south of Florida, real-life Oceanas such as North Korea, and tales of survival during Stalin's liquidation campaigns would all make potentially interesting backdrops for silver-screen offerings. Hollywood has thus far balked at presenting any of these real-life dramas to the masses. Certainly the wrenching stories of once-Communist agents such as Whittaker Chambers and Elizabeth Bentley are exponentially more spectacular than many of the fictional stories that we see. They too have been ignored by the entertainment industry.

In Oxford University Press's *The Unfinished Journey: America Since World War II,* President Reagan is described as a "reactionary," derided for holding a "monolithic worldview," and blamed for "95 percent of the problem" with regard to the debt. The end of the Cold War, the textbook informs students, "was above all a gift of Gorbachev." Reagan's was an America "so weak from economic stagnation and out-of-control deficits at home as to seem in free-fall decline."[57] This hardly meshes with the unprecedented levels of uninterrupted peacetime economic growth that America experienced from November 1982 until July 1990.[58] A chart in the text *A People and a Nation* informs students, "While the Rich Got Richer in the 1980s, the Poor Got Poorer." Only when you read the fine print do you learn that the chart begins the 1980s in 1977.[59] This lumps Carter's years of doom and gloom with Reagan's unprecedented prosperity. In reality, all groups—rich, poor, and middle class— saw their incomes grow during the 1980s.[60] The textbook *The National Experience* even includes the discredited allegation that Reagan's 1980 campaign team worked with the Iranian government to keep the hostages in captivity until Reagan won the election.[61] Even the most liberal members of the press judge the notion of an "October Surprise" as utterly baseless, yet supposedly objective textbooks continue to promote it.

If all this is what you learned about our country, how could you love America? Weaned on these tales, one could not help but hate America.

And it is these tales that Americans are inundated with. The Left's vision of U.S. history is now the prevailing account. College professors, who teach the next generation of social studies teachers and write high school and college history texts, belong to a one-party profession. Stanford University's history department, a mid-1990s survey revealed, housed 22 Democrats and just 2 Republicans.[62] Among history professors registered to vote locally at Dartmouth University, Democrats outnumbered Republicans 13 to 0.[63] The daily student newspaper at the University of North Carolina–Chapel Hill found that their history faculty contained 46 Democrats but just 1 lonely Republican.[64] The University of Colorado, a hotbed of diversity according to its administration, employs 27 Democrats in history but not a single Republican.[65] Cornell University's history department, which fields 29 Democrats, completely excludes the GOP as well.[66] In total, the five schools employ 137 Democrats in history but a mere 3 Republicans. Academia's rigid conformity is matched in Hollywood, which, in stark contrast to its halcyon days, turns out film after film reinforcing a negative view of America. Our most esteemed national museum, the Smithsonian, suffers from national self-loathing as well. Even the federal government's guidelines for teaching U.S. history were so rabidly anti-American that they were condemned 99 to 1 by the U.S. Senate.[67]

For the self-hating American, our heritage is not the winter at Valley Forge, the 13th Amendment, the promise of Ellis Island, Edison turning on the lights, the *Spirit of St. Louis* touching down at La Bourget, hitting the beach at Normandy, or the discovery in Jonas Salk's lab. It is the slave master's whip, Wounded Knee, melted corpses at Nagasaki, My Lai, the homeless, and the murder of Matthew Shepard. Patriotic America's collective haze of confusion that greets the burning of an American flag or the ugly statements justifying the 9-11 attacks suddenly dissipates when we come to grips with what our past evokes in the minds of some. The Left's alienation from our community starts to make perfect sense when we think about just what they were taught.

NEW HEROES

WE ONCE MEMORIALIZED those who built our country. Because intellectual elites view our nation as something to be ashamed of, the men who sacrificed to improve America are now depicted as villainous figures. Columbus Day morphs into Indigenous Peoples' Day, the Minutemen become armed racist white men, and Washington's name is sandblasted off the schoolhouse.

On campus, those currently making great sacrifices for their country join the heroes of the past on the persona non grata list. Faculty at Washington University voted in March 2002 to exclude military men and women from a school program that partially repays the loans of students who go into public service after they graduate. The military's "don't ask, don't tell" policy barring out-of-the-closet homosexuals from serving acted as the impetus for the punitive rule against law students opting for careers in the armed forces. Under a spell of twisted logic, Professor Karen Tokarz claimed that by discriminating against members of the armed forces, she hoped "that sometime in the future, one or two of them [the excluded graduates] will say, 'My teachers showed me a commitment to nondiscrimination.'"[68] When Marine Captain Felix Rodriguez attempted to make a recruiting pitch to interested students at the University of Nevada–Las Vegas in the fall of 2001, faculty and administrators shouted him down. The university employees objected to the armed forces' policy on homosexuals, so they blared the sound of a pro-gay video and shouted whenever the Marine officer attempted to speak to students in the room he had reserved. "We have a group of people over there who really hate the military," regent Tom Fitzpatrick frankly conceded.[69] At the very time that several Ivy League schools accept lucrative grants from the Department of Defense, they forbid their students who participate in the Reserve Officers Training Corps to meet on their campuses. Harvard University, which accepted millions of dollars from the bin Laden family fortune, refuses to allow students who accept scholarship money from the American military to train on campus.[70] Some money, it seems, is too dirty for the 365-year-old school.

Patriots are out of fashion on the Left. Today, America's cultural institutions honor those who sought to destroy our country. They are America's new "heroes."

Rutgers and Penn State Universities honored Paul Robeson, winner of the 1952 Stalin Peace Prize, by naming campus cultural centers for him.[71] The visage of his intellectual mentor, W. E. B. Du Bois, graced a stamp. Two Pulitzer Prize–winning hagiographies by David Levering Lewis focused on Du Bois, as did laudatory documentaries airing on PBS. In 1996, the University of Massachusetts–Amherst named the tallest public building in the Bay State, the campus's 26-story tower library, in honor of Du Bois, a Stalinist proponent of racial separatism who renounced his American citizenship.[72] New York's Bard College boasts an Alger Hiss Chair of Social Studies, named for the Soviet spy and convicted perjurer.[73] For a time, a branch of the City University of New York even awarded $500 scholarships honoring Ho Chi Minh and Assata Shakur—the former the leader of the Vietcong, the latter a Marxist cop killer now living in Cuba.[74]

These are the saints for those whose religion is anti-Americanism. Columbus, Washington, and Jefferson are among their devils. Just as deceased haters of America are venerated, living homegrown enemies of the United States are rewarded with plush jobs, hefty speaking fees, tenure, and positions of prestige.

Angela Davis, fugitive from justice after supplying the guns in a failed courthouse raid that resulted in numerous deaths, was awarded the University of California's highest academic honor, the Presidential Chair. Along with the $90,000 she was given with the honor, Davis commands lucrative speaking fees from the country's most prestigious colleges.[75] Alex Rackley, accused of being a police informant by the Black Panthers, was subsequently tortured with ice picks, cigarettes, and boiling water. The end came for Rackley when he was shot in the head by Warren Kimbro, who subsequently confessed to the nefarious deed. Rackley is dead. Kimbro was appointed an assistant dean at Eastern Connecticut State College.[76] Bill Ayers gleefully admits to being a terrorist during the 1970s. He has since traded in his bombs for a lectern and chalkboard. Now the former Weatherman serves as the Distinguished Professor of Education at the University of Illinois–Chicago.[77] Kirkpatrick Sale gushed that the "Unabomber Manifesto" was the product of "a rational and serious man, deeply committed to his cause, who has given a great deal of time to this expression of it," while a publishing house announced that it had secured the rights to a book by Theodore Kaczynski.[78] Mumia Abu-Jamal murdered Philadelphia police officer Daniel Faulkner in cold blood, shooting him in the back and then in the face at point-blank range. Yet his books are sold at Barnes and Noble and Borders. He has delivered commencement day addresses at Antioch College, Evergreen State College, the University of California–Santa Cruz, and Occidental College. The *Yale Law Journal* and *The Nation* have published his writings. Pacifica Radio broadcasts his radio commentaries. Oliver Stone, Michael Stipe, Susan Sarandon, and Whoopi Goldberg are among the stars that fawn over him.[79] For leftists such as Abu-Jamal, Kimbro, Ayers, and Davis, crime pays.

The Left has neither cornered the market on anti-Americanism nor acquired a monopoly on adherents who perform acts of terrorism in its name. Where the Left is truly unique is that while believers of other domestic political programs aggressively shun their ideological relatives who commit violence for their cause, leftists enthusiastically embrace murderers and terrorists who partake in crimes under the guise of "social justice." In fact, the commission of a crime need not even be done with political motives in mind to secure its architect a place of honor. To merely be a leftist and be guilty of some nonideological crime is sufficient to earn the designation of "political prisoner" and become a cause célèbre among radicals.

No libertarian book publisher salivated over the prospect of publishing a manifesto of Timothy McVeigh's beliefs. No educational institution run by the religious right would ever seek to host the murderer of an abortionist as its commencement speaker or hire the bomber of an abortion clinic for its faculty. On the contrary, such figures are vehemently denounced within such circles. Yet several institutions of higher learning currently employ unrepentant left-wing terrorists. The Left portrays convicted murderers such as H. Rap Brown, Leonard Peltier, and Mumia Abu-Jamal as heroes. It is not as though the promoters of the Left's criminal celebrities are spaced-out dropouts or inhabitants of communes. They are university presidents, magazine editors, A-list Hollywood actors, major book publishers, platinum recording artists, and even political leaders. While their views may occupy the fringe, their station within society is center stage. This is precisely what is so alarming.

The Left's veneration of killers and terrorists bespeaks a malevolence toward America so great that those under its spell are willing to overlook any crime as long as its composer subscribes to the "correct" ideals. Similarly, figures who betrayed their country, such as Alger Hiss, are the subject of memorials. Hating America, not helping to build it, is now the prerequisite for receiving honors from our cultural commissars.

Orwell wrote, "Who controls the past controls the future: who controls the present controls the past."[80] Today's reality is that the Left is in complete control of the institutions charged with chronicling the past.

A Freedom Forum poll reported that in the 1992 election, 89% of journalists polled cast their ballots for Bill Clinton, while an anemic 7% voted for George Bush.[81] Earlier surveys found that in the seven previous presidential races, never had less than 80% of national journalists voted for the Democratic candidate—even though these elections witnessed several historic Republican landslides.[82] A Luntz poll revealed that among Ivy League professors who voted in the 2000 election, 84% voted for Gore and 9% for Bush.[83] Other surveys of a variety of departments at individual schools reveal an even greater imbalance in the political leanings of college professors. Surveys revealed a Democrat-to-Republican faculty ratio of greater than 9 to 1 at Stanford, 25 to 1 at Cornell, and 31 to 1 at the University of Colorado.[84] In controlling the present, the Left seeks to rewrite the past. True patriots are targeted for removal from the pantheon of heroes. America's most venomous critics are slotted to take their place.

Just as Orwell suggested, the objective in controlling our past is to control our future. America's past is based largely on capitalism and Christianity. It was shaped—for better or worse—by white men. This offends the multiculturalist mindset. Thus, a new history must replace the old. In doing so, the Left hopes to chart a new course for the future.

THE TRUE BELIEVERS

"ALL ACTIVE MASS movements strive," Eric Hoffer avows in *The True Believer*, "to interpose a fact-proof screen between the faithful and the realities of the world. They do this by claiming that the ultimate and absolute truth is already embodied in their doctrine and that there is no truth nor certitude outside it."[85]

We see shades of Hoffer's "true believer" in the campus activists who viewed the September 11 attacks as our just deserts. We see it in the intellectuals who craft history to fit their theories rather than the facts. We see it in racialist groups that blame their individual problems on white people they have never met.

The common denominator of "true believers" of every stripe is that they tightly hold on to ideas that appear quite irrational to the rest of us but to them are the keys to understanding every possible question. Consider the case of the protestors outside the World Economic Forum gathering that we met at the outset of this chapter.

The activists invoked theory, no matter how inapplicable to the situation, to explain the attacks on America. The Marxists submit the bizarre idea that multimillionaire Osama bin Laden targeted us because of global inequality. Because their ideology reduces all questions to economics, the Left's brainwashed minds refuse to consider, say, the religious or cultural motives of bin Laden. Instead, they defer to Karl Marx's writings 125 years ago to explain an event far removed from anything addressed by the German scribbler. The blinding hatred for America reduces the killing of thousands of its citizens to a "small crime." The true believers view America as omnipotent. The United States is as equally to blame for problems halfway around the world as it is for not fixing them. Wild conspiracy theories, usually involving the Central Intelligence Agency, serve to link America to tragedies outside our borders that our government seemingly had nothing to do with. Evidence against the conspiracy theory merely reinforces the true believer's faith in it. The conspirators are so cunning, true believers argue, that they erase any trace of their involvement. The true believer's bitterness is so consuming that when U.S. interests coincide with his professed aims—such as the case of Afghanistan when the United States liberated a people from an oppressive band of patriarchal clerics—he redefines his long-held positions to put himself again at odds with U.S. policy.

Attempting to reason with the true believer demonstrates the limits of reason. It is impossible to reason with people who embrace unreason. Trying to find a rational motivation for all his ideas and actions is similarly fruitless. Irrational people do not act or think rationally.

The fuel that powers the true believers' hatred toward America is varied. For the socialists protesting the World Economic Forum, it is chiefly our economic policies. Demagogic appeals to racial solidarity serve as a wedge between some minorities and their nation. Still others have bought into a history based on ideology and not truth.

What our society's discontents purport to demand can usually be found in the very land that they denounce. Human rights, a just economy, and equal opportunity for people of all ethnic backgrounds are rarities in our world but not in our country.

A generation ago, Yale Law School professor Alexander Bickel wrote, "to be a revolutionary in a society like ours, is to be a totalitarian, or not to know what one is doing."[86] The "revolutionaries" who gathered to protest the World Economic Forum, as well as those who welcomed the attacks of September 11, detest America. Yet America is the world's greatest force for democracy, human rights, free speech, religious liberty, the rule of law, peace, prosperity, and individual autonomy. What is it, really, that they are denouncing? Either, as Professor Bickel wisely observed, self-hating Americans are totalitarians or they are simply ignorant. Let's hope it is the latter.

PART 2

A CITY UPON A HILL

CHAPTER 4

THE FIVE BIG LIES

JOSEPH GOEBBELS, HITLER'S chief propagandist, perfected the practice of the Big Lie. Shout a lie loud enough, repeat it frequently, and rhetorical alchemy transforms falsehood into truth. While Goebbels may have been the most astute and diabolical practitioner of the Big Lie, he was neither the first nor unfortunately the last to employ the technique. Ideologues of all stripes promote falsehood when it advances their vision of what is correct for the rest of us. Ideology, for the fervently committed, is truth. As Lenin remarked to the Young Communist League in 1920, "The class struggle is continuing and it is our task to subordinate all interests to that struggle. . . . We say: morality is what serves to destroy the old exploiting society and to unite all the working people around the proletariat, which is building up a new, a communist society."[1] In other words, murder, repression, and especially lies all are truly moral acts when committed in the service of the cause. For the ideologue, ideology is the big "truth" to which all "smaller" truths are subservient.

For much of the Left, anti-Americanism is an article of faith. Whatever denigrates the society they hold in contempt, even lies, is encouraged. Whatever places the country they dread in a positive light, even truth, is denied. The overall "truth" that the United States is the national equivalent of a moral leper is deemed more important than "minor" truths that contradict this thesis. Above all else, the goal is to debase the country that embraces the policies that their theories vehemently oppose. To these ends, the Left forwards a number of general assertions, backed by dubious premises, about the United States. On examination, these assertions do not hold up under scrutiny. We will examine the more oft repeated claims regarding race, sex, class, the environment, and foreign policy.

For Hoffer's "true believer," reason, logic, and facts fail to persuade. Not everyone who is influenced by anti-American myths, however, has leased his or her mind to an ideology. For the open-minded merely hoodwinked by this Big Lie—that is, that American society is a racist, sexist, classist, environmentally abusing, bloodthirsty empire—truth can win out.

Lies learned can be unlearned.

MYTH #1: AMERICAN WOMEN LIVE UNDER A PATRIARCHY

ALEXIS DE TOCQUEVILLE wrote of the United States, "I have nowhere seen woman occupying a loftier position."[2] More than 170 years later, his observations remain applicable. Opportunities open to all women in America are unknown to most women outside Western civilization.

A more jaundiced view of the status of women emanates from domestic feminists. Angry Andrea Dworkin labels Western women "the ultimate house-niggers, ass-licking, bowing, scraping, shuffling fools." Women's "minds are aborted in their development by sexist education," the feminist academic writes. "[O]ur bodies are violated by oppressive grooming imperatives," the disheveled Dworkin complains, and "the police function against us in cases of rape and assault." Her rant continues, "the media, schools, and churches conspire to deny us dignity and freedom . . . the nuclear family and ritualized sexual behavior imprison us in roles . . . which are degrading to us."[3]

One would be hard-pressed to find many feminists willing to defend Tocqueville's perspective. It would not be very difficult to find large numbers of feminists, both inside and outside the academy, who agree with the substance of Dworkin's tirade. This speaks volumes about contemporary feminists. Feminist theory posits that an ambiguous force known as "patriarchy" keeps women down. With key components (e.g., religion, family, and capitalism) of the patriarchy warmly encouraged by American culture, feminists vent special ire toward the United States. Ironically, the country that feminists denounce in the harshest of terms stands as the greatest ally in equality of opportunity for women.

It is telling that the feminists most vociferously decrying America as the dreaded "patriarchy" are notoriously prone to overstatement and issuing baseless claims. In her book *Who Stole Feminism?*, Christina Hoff Sommers documents such dishonesty among women's issues activists. For example, several years ago the presidents of the National Organization for Women and the National Women's Studies Association declared domestic violence the leading cause of birth defects. Media outlets such as *Time*, the *Chicago Tribune*, and the *Arizona Republic* repeated the claim, citing a nonexistent March of Dimes report as evidence. Like the March of Dimes study, the idea that domestic violence causes a large proportion of birth defects is a feminist-generated hoax.[4] Another widely believed fraud posits that a national anorexia epidemic kills tens of thousands of young women annually. If these figures on anorexia put forward by the likes of Gloria Steinem and Naomi Wolf were true, one might quite logically conclude that our culture inflicts tremendous harm on young women. But the figures promiscuously bandied about have little relation to the truth. In reality, the approximate number of deaths per year from anorexia in the United States is a more modest but still tragic 100.[5] Accuracy, one concludes, is not a strong suit of feminists.

Some feminists are actually quite honest about their dishonesty. Feminist scholar Kelly Oliver writes, "in order to be revolutionary, feminist theory cannot claim to describe what exists, or, 'natural facts.' Rather, feminist theories should be political tools, strategies for overcoming oppression in specific concrete situations. The goal, then, of feminist theory, should be to develop *strategic* theories—not true theories, not false theories, but strategic theories."[6] Other feminists avouch that all truth is socially constructed. Feminists deride the conventional tools used to arrive at truth, such as logic, reasoning, and science. *Thinking About Women*, a leading women's studies textbook, imparts, "despite the strong claims of neutrality and objectivity by scientists, the fact is that science is closely tied to the centers of power in this society and interwoven with capitalist and patriarchal institutions."[7] When we come to grips with the fact that for feminists "strategic" interests trump ridiculed concepts such as science and truth, we are better equipped to understand the rationale for feminism's wild claims, particularly its closely guarded tenet that the patriarchy governs our affairs in the West.

If women in the United States live under "patriarchy," what term could accurately describe the situation faced by women in other parts of the world?

Are the problems that preoccupy American feminists—the lack of taxpayer-funded abortions, low self-esteem for schoolgirls, an unequal number of sports teams for women—in any way comparable to something like clitorectomy, a culturally ingrained practice that has mutilated the genitals of more than 100 million living African women? Is the patriarchy that forces women to abort their unborn children in China the same "patriarchy" that "oppresses" women in America? What is there to compare between the status of women in the West and the status of women in the Arab world? Is it honest to use the term "patriarchy" to describe both the Western form of marriage, where women are free to choose their husbands, and arranged marriages in India, which sometimes lead to the bride's death because her family provided an "insufficient" dowry?

"Patriarchy," a term that adequately describes societies in many parts of the world, loses its currency when applied to the West. The effect of mislabeling America a "patriarchy" is as likely to endear people to the patriarchy as it is to repel them from America. The feminists abuse language by freely hurling about terms without regard for their meanings.

Think of any major problem affecting our society. Chances are, that problem disproportionately affects males. Males are both the victims of most crimes and their perpetrators. The population behind bars is an overwhelmingly male population. Almost 19 out of every 20 prisoners are men.[8] Homelessness is predominantly a male problem. Men constitute 70% of the adult homeless population.[9] Men abuse alcohol and other drugs in far greater numbers than women.[10] The suicide rate for men is more than four times greater than the rate for women.[11] More males lack health insurance than females.[12]

Girls get better grades, are more likely to be enrolled in advanced placement courses, and are involved to a greater extent in all major extracurricular activities save sports. Boys, on the other hand, are suspended from school more, are three times more likely to be enrolled in special education, and constitute the vast majority of high school dropouts.[13] Knowing this, should we be taken aback when we learn that the majority of students who have enrolled in college for each of the past 24 years have been women?[14]

Women in the United States tend to live nearly seven years longer than their male counterparts.[15] Cancer, heart disease, and the remaining 15 leading causes of death all victimize men in greater numbers than women.[16] In the United States, AIDS is an overwhelmingly male disease.[17] Men make up 54% of the workforce yet fall victim to 92% of all deaths in the workplace.[18]

Of course, there are many areas where women generally find themselves on less than equal ground with men. To name just two: The average woman earns less money than the average man, and women occupy fewer political offices than men. Just as no institutional force compels men to commit crimes or abuse drugs, no governmental or societal force keeps women from seeking greater wealth or political power. Unlike in other nations, economic and political opportunities are completely open to women here.

Women in the West lead better lives than women in the Third World. More important, according to numerous statistical indicators, American women are healthier, better educated, and less susceptible to various cultural pathologies than are American men.

If American men conspire to oppress women, as theories of "patriarchy" assert, they are not doing a particularly effective job of carrying out their plot.

MYTH #2: AMERICA IS THE WORLD'S LEADING THREAT TO THE ENVIRONMENT

INVENTING "FACTS" TO promote one's political objectives is certainly not a phenomenon confined to feminists. Radical environmentalists also willingly twist the facts when attempting to promote a political agenda. The more politicized the agenda, the deeper their belief seems to become.

- Environmentalists claim that humans have depleted the forests for their own selfish motives. Some of the more extreme green activists implant steel spikes in trees to injure loggers or place themselves in trees to prevent timber harvesting. Reforestation and advances in fire-fighting technology, however, have ensured that America has more trees now than at any point in over 100 years. As John Tierney points out in a *New York Times Magazine* article, "Yes, a lot of trees have been cut down to make today's newspaper. But even more trees will probably be planted in their place. America's supply of timber has been increasing for decades, and the nation's forests have three times the amount of wood today than in 1920."[19]

- In his best-selling book *Earth in the Balance*, then senator Al Gore commented, "We now know that [automobiles'] cumulative impact on the global environment is posing a mortal threat to the security of every nation that is more deadly than that of any military enemy we are ever again likely to confront."[20] Do we really "know" this? Cars averaged around 14 miles to the gallon in the mid-1970s. Today, they average more than 30 miles to the gallon. Automobiles rolling off the assembly line today emit 99% fewer hydrocarbons, 96% less carbon monoxide, and 90% less nitrogen oxide than cars hitting the street 30 years ago.[21] Things are getting better, not worse.

- "The battle to feed humanity is over," Paul Ehrlich's *Population Bomb* famously proclaimed in 1968. "In the

1970s, the world will undergo famines—hundreds of millions of people are going to starve to death." *The Population Bomb* prophesied that "a minimum of ten million people, most of them children, will starve to death during each year of the 1970s. But this is a mere handful compared to the number that will be starving before the end of the century. And it is now too late to take action to save many of those people."[22] Needless to say, this modern-day Malthus erred. Since intellectuals and journalists deemed Ehrlich's ideology correct and cared less about his incorrect facts, the Stanford professor has become a media darling, and his book has gone on to sell millions of copies.

Perhaps the greatest myth advanced by environmentalists posits that the primary villain responsible for the planet's ecological problems is the United States. An anticapitalist protestor curiously described the September 11 terrorists as "lashing out against the American foreign policy, which is basically to protect the American lifestyle, which is an unsustainable lifestyle. . . . We will never have peace until everybody basically lives the same way."[23] Apart from the disingenuousness of projecting one's personal ideology on the terrorists, does the rest of the world demand that we adopt their standard of living, or do they instead envy our prosperous position? "Economically, we can only hope that other nations will never achieve our standard of living, for if they did, the earth would become a desert," author James Loewen opines, proposing that nations regress to "zero economic growth" even if it takes an international body to enforce the goal.[24]

Yet it is not technology or the United States that threatens the environment. Americans breathe cleaner air and drink cleaner water than almost anyone. The World Resources Institute's rankings of the world's most polluted cities list no U.S. metropolises in its top tier. In fact, China boasts 9 out of the 10 most polluted cities.[25] An Asian magazine's study listed Beijing, Mexico City, Kuala Lumpur, Bangkok, and Hong Kong as the globe's most environmentally inhospitable cities.[26] Pollution in many other countries is far worse than it is in the United States. An inconvenient fact confronts environmentalists who are quick to blame America for ecological ills: It is not the United States that pollutes Lanzhou, New Delhi, or Mexico City.

The United States is a more environmentally considerate nation than it was just a few decades ago. The air is cleaner. Of the six air pollutants that the Environmental Protection Agency began tracking in 1975, all six are down significantly today. Some of the pollutants measure a mere fraction of their former presence. Lead stands at less than a tenth of its 1975 level, while carbon monoxide has slipped to less than half its 1975 level.[27] The amount of forest acreage has risen dramatically. The U.S. Forest Service reports that the number of new trees has exceeded the number of trees cut down in every year since 1952.[28] The water is cleaner. Scenes such as the Cuyahoga River aflame are a distant memory. Now people actually fish in the Cuyahoga. The United States compares favorably to other industrialized nations in the cleanliness of its waterways. The Mississippi, for instance, is cleaner than the Seine, the Rhine, and the Thames.[29] Would anyone prefer drinking from the Ganges or the Volga than from the Colorado?

New Republic writer Gregg Easterbrook points out that we have much to cheer about regarding the environment. Industrial toxic emissions declined by nearly half from 1988 to 1996, several formerly endangered species now thrive, the government and the private sector cleaned up a third of all Superfund toxic waste sites, and forest area continues to expand. He further states,

> Twenty-five years ago, only one-third of America's lakes and rivers were safe for fishing and swimming; today two-thirds are, and the proportion continues to rise. Annual wetlands loss has fallen by 80 percent in the same period, while soil losses to agricultural runoff have been almost cut in half. Total American water consumption has declined nine percent in the past 15 years, even as population expands, especially in the arid Southwest. Since 1970, smog has declined by about a third, even as the number of cars has increased by half; acid rain has fallen by 40 percent; airborne soot particles are down 69 percent, which is why big cities have blue skies again; carbon monoxide or "winter smog" is down 31 percent; airborne lead, a poison, is down 98 percent. Emissions of CFCs, which deplete stratospheric ozone, have all but ended.[30]

Technological innovation has at times harmed the environment. Today, technology serves the environment. Pesticides and genetic engineering have increased crop yields, feeding the millions of people the environmentalists warned would surely starve by now. Sewage treatment is so advanced that the same water some Californians flush down their toilets eventually recycles back clean through their faucets.[31] Energy now burns cleaner, with technological advances allowing some alternative energy sources to cause no pollution at all. Yet the naysayers persist. Doomsday prophet Paul Ehrlich and his wife, Anne, maintain, *"Most people do not recognize that, at least in rich nations, economic growth is the disease, not the cure."*[32] The facts vindicate the very opposite view. The growth in the U.S. economy over the past quarter century coincided with and resulted in a healthier environment.

As implied by the "ism" affixed to it, environmentalism sometimes acts as a surrogate religion for its followers. The zeal of the committed environmentalist is based on faith—and faith in something false, at that. Logic and reason play next to no role in swaying the radical environmentalist's devotion to his creed's sacred tenets, such as the belief that economically advanced nations threaten Mother Nature. Since many environmentalists believe that they've received an enlightenment that passed the rest of us by, they rationalize their use of deception to achieve their desired ends. When you're saving the world, what's the harm in telling a few lies to achieve your objective?

The problem is that, although environmentalists may cavalierly think that they are saving the world, they are not doing anything of the sort. Their more misguided crusades have inflicted pain on a great number of people. Victims include loggers harmed by "tree sitters" and other activists, apple growers put out of business by the phony Alar scare, and Africans placed at greater risk for malaria because of the ban on DDT. While a need for a movement that safeguards the health of the environment clearly exists, we could do without the kind of environmentalism that relies on deception, dogmatically forgoes cost-benefit analyses of its policy prescriptions, and seeks laws whose results frequently betray their intentions.

In the wake of 1992's Earth Summit in Rio de Janeiro, a group of scientists released a document decrying "the emergence of an irrational ideology that is opposed to scientific and industrial progress and impedes economic and social development." The Heidelberg Appeal, as the statement became known, eventually bore the signatures of 3,000 scientists, including more than

70 Nobel Prize winners. "The greatest evils which stalk our earth are ignorance and oppression, not science, technology, and industry," concluded the document.[33] Environmentalists blaming American technology and energy use for the world's ecological maladies would be wise to heed the message of these men of science.

MYTH #3: AMERICA IS A RACIST NATION

MANY AMERICANS BELIEVE that their country invented racism. That is the bad news. The good news is that this notion is built on a series of myths. The Left charges bigotry not from a longing to stem racism but out of a desire to use it as an issue to discredit the country they hate. The Left's cynical and deceptive depiction of historical events validates this hypothesis.

The Left points to the fact that the Constitution counted each slave as three-fifths of a free person as proof of the malignant nature of America's founding. This bespeaks a complete ignorance of what was at stake in counting slaves equally alongside free men. The proponents of slavery sought to classify each slave as a full person to enhance their representation in the House of Representatives and the electoral college, thereby ensuring the survival of their inhumane institution. It was the opponents of slavery who sought not to count slaves at all. The three-fifths rule was the result of a compromise between the two sides. The irony of all this is that certainly the slaves themselves would have preferred that they not be counted at all or that they be counted as three-fifths of a free man rather than be counted whole to enhance the political power of their masters. All this is ignored because the "three-fifths" myth makes for good propaganda. These critics similarly point to the Declaration of Independence's lofty words that "all men are created equal" to indict the American system for hypocrisy. Yet the Declaration's ideal served as the basis for most antislavery rhetoric for the four score and seven years that followed. By appealing to the American tradition and invoking the nation's most-quoted document, abolitionists gained converts and ultimately found success. The Declaration of Independence's ideal of equality, which contradicted the actual legal condition of slaves in 1776, actually paved the way for emancipation. Had the slaveholder Jefferson made his words consistent with his practices, African Americans certainly would have been enslaved for an even longer period of time.

Just as the Left deliberately mischaracterizes the American founding, sins of commission and omission mark their presentation of the history of slavery as well. With slaves singularly portrayed as black, many have the mistaken impression that the global institution targeted one race. We forget that the term "slave" derives from the name for the widely enslaved "Slavic" people. A parochial view of slavery likewise portrays the United States as the world's greatest purveyor of slavery. David Horowitz writes,

> In the years between 650 and 1600, before any Western involvement, somewhere between 3 million and 10 million Africans were bought by Muslim slavers for use in Saharan societies and in the trade in the Indian Ocean and the Red Sea. By contrast, the enslavement of blacks in the United States lasted 89 years, from 1776 until 1865. The combined slave trade to the British colonies in North America and later to the United States accounted for less than 3 percent of the global trade in African slaves. The total number of slaves imported to

North America was 800,000, less than the slave trade to the island of Cuba alone. If the internal African slave trade—which began in the seventh century and persists to this day in the Sudan, Mauritania and other sub-Saharan states—is taken into account, the responsibility of American traders shrinks to a fraction of 1 percent of the slavery problem.[34]

What is truly peculiar about America's "peculiar institution" is that a great number of people found it peculiar. Outside Western civilization, slavery was considered part of the natural order of things. Only westerners (besides the slaves themselves) questioned this order. "Never in the history of the world, outside of the West, has a group of people eligible to be slave-owners mobilized against the institution of slavery," Dinesh D'Souza points out; later, he adds, "In numerous civilizations both Western and non-Western, slavery needed no defenders because it had no critics."[35]

Anti-American hatred motivates lies on more recent occurrences as well. A typical myth forwarded by racial demagogues is the story of Charles Drew's death. Drew, who pioneered the effective use of blood banks, was critically injured in a 1950 car wreck. "Yet tragically," a too widely used Afrocentric teacher's guide maintains, "he encountered white racism at its ugliest—not one of several nearby white hospitals would provide the blood transfusions he so desperately needed, and on the way to the hospital that treated black people, he died. It is so ironic that the very process he developed, which had been saving thousands of human lives—was made unavailable to save his life."[36] Arthur Schlesinger observes, "It's a hell of a story—the inventor of blood-plasma storage dead because racist whites denied him his own invention. Only it is not true."[37] No hospital turned Drew away; several white surgeons tried in vain to save his life. The graphic tale is a complete concoction. What else but base hatred for America motivated the architect of this canard?

The Left slanders America by claiming that the country sent members of minority groups to fight the Vietnam War while whites avoided the fray. This myth is so widely accepted that it even finds its way into mainstream pop culture references. One thinks of the hilarious scene in *South Park: The Movie*, for instance, when the cartoon soldiers directed to do the actual fighting are conspicuously all black. The commanding officer directs the other troops, who just happen to be all white, to stay in the rear. The humor works because it relies on a grievance that many believe to be justified. Yet there is no truth to support the claim that minorities disproportionately died in the Vietnam War. No significant statistical deviation exists between the percentage of blacks in the general population during the Vietnam War era and the number of blacks who died in Vietnam. During the Vietnam War, blacks made up more than 13% of the draft-age population but constituted 12.5% of the servicemen who perished in the war.[38] Blacks served admirably in the Vietnam War, just as they have in other wars. The assertion that generals sent them to their deaths to save whites, however, is pure calumny.

If racism in America is so bad, why are self-described antiracist activists compelled to lie to make their point?

Such rhetoric and inventive stories serve neither truth nor the common good. Racial propaganda inevitably results in engendering animosity. Susan Sontag, no doubt having imbibed a steady stream of the fiery racial rhetoric of the times, wrote in the 1960s, "The white race *is* the cancer of human history."[39] The University of Massachusetts–Amherst's Radical Student

Union held an event in the spring of 2002 titled "Abolish the White Race."[40] Amongst self-styled intellectuals, a new field called "whiteness studies," dedicated to denigrating Caucasians, has emerged. A recently launched journal in the field, *Race Traitor*, boasts the motto "Treason to whiteness is loyalty to humanity."[41] It does not require a great deal of imagination to ask the inevitable question: What might the reaction be if one substituted "black" or some other racial or ethnic category for the word "white" in any of these examples?

As racial discrimination has abated, more than one observer has noted, public discussion of racism has paradoxically reached unprecedented levels. "Conditions are worse—much worse— for the masses of black people," maintained activist Frank Kellum at a reunion of the Black Panthers, "than they were 35 years ago. And from the way it looks, they're going to get worse."[42] In some key areas (e.g., crime, illegitimacy, and drug use), Kellum's statement is valid.[43] For the most part, however, blacks are much better off than they were a generation ago. This is especially true in areas where racism had traditionally affected opportunities in a major way. With discrimination marginalized culturally and, in some instances, outlawed legally, previously locked doors are now open. An objective look at economics, political rights, law, and education shows the remarkable progress that blacks and all Americans have made in just a few short decades.

President Timothy Jenkins of the University of the District of Columbia, a predominantly black college, recently pointed out that not a single African American was registered to vote in Alabama's overwhelmingly black Lowndes County in 1965.[44] Jenkins's story, unfortunately, stopped in 1965. Today a black man, Congressman Earl Hilliard, represents the people of

Lowndes County in Washington, D.C. According to cynics, nothing has changed. Yet would even a handful of blacks living in Lowndes County prefer residing there in 1952 instead of 2002? Times have changed. No person in Lowndes County, Alabama, or anywhere else in America is any longer denied the right to vote on account of skin color. With unrestricted access to the ballot comes political power. Today, African Americans serve as the secretary of state and the national security adviser. A black sits on the U.S. Supreme Court. And African Americans, including Earl Hilliard, occupy 37 seats in Congress as well.

Educational opportunities have increased. Apart from the obvious departure from separate but unequal schools in various parts of the country as a result of 1954's *Brown v. Board of Education* decision, educational opportunities abound. In 1967, a mere 13% of college-age African Americans attended college. Today, more than 30% do. No other ethnic group has experienced as dramatic a rise in college enrollment over the same period.[45]

Black economic gains have been dramatic as well. African Americans have the fastest economic growth for any major group in the United States over the course of the past three decades. In inflation-adjusted terms, black per capita income has more than doubled since 1970. Blacks still lag behind whites and Asians (though not Hispanics), but the income gap is getting smaller, not larger.[46]

Black people in the United States are wealthier than black people anywhere else. Per capita income for blacks in America is 30 to 40 times higher than per capita income for blacks in Africa. The income gap between the inhabitants of the poorest countries on the African continent and black Americans differs by a factor of 100.[47] There is no country in which blacks find more success than in the United States.

Nonblack minorities, such as Vietnamese, Cubans, and South Asian Indians, continue to achieve success in America as well. The incessant waves of non-European immigrants that have reached our shores for almost four decades find greater tolerance and acceptance than some European immigrants, such as the Irish, experienced 100 years ago. America, always a melting pot of various ethnicities and hues, has never been so welcoming.

Like every diverse nation, America has its share of racial problems. Considering ethnic wars in Sudan, Yugoslavia, and Rwanda; race-based expropriation in Zimbabwe; government-enforced discrimination against minority groups in China, Iran, and Ethiopia; and vestiges of the caste system in India, things could be a lot worse.

MYTH #4: THE UNITED STATES IS AN IMPERIAL POWER

ON APRIL 20, 2002, nearly 50,000 people converged on the Mall in Washington, D.C., to protest. The diverse targets of the activists included Israeli occupation of the West Bank, the School of the Americas, the World Bank, and the War on Terrorism. The inhabitants of the government buildings surrounding the protestors received the blame for many of the international ills that the activists sought to cure.

The protestors' chants, signs, and rhetoric targeted the United States. Kenneth Stewart, a Vietnam veteran from Maine, bluntly opined, "We are a terrorist nation."[48] A North Carolina college student remarked, "I think the United States of America is a culturally and emotionally diseased country."[49] "Who's the real Axis of Evil?" State University of New

York–Brockport student Chris Powers rhetorically asked. "If any country's really an Axis of Evil, it's us."[50]

Their nation, the activists uniformly contended, seeks to conquer the world through empire. Imperialism is the most threatening manifestation of the evil that they see inherent in America. As sign-carrying New Yorker Charles Freed expressed, "The United States, being the one lone superpower, thinks its manifest destiny is to rule the world."[51]

If the United States is an imperial power, where is our empire? What are the names of the colonies we possess? What wars of conquest did we fight to gain this territory?

The British Empire ruled Ireland, India, Arabia, Rhodesia, and numerous other locales. The French Empire cast its dominion over Vietnam, Algeria, and Lebanon, among other places. The Roman Empire claimed Britain, Judea, Gaul, Macedonia, and points beyond. The American "empire" rules no one.

American imperialism, the Left maintains, is not necessarily characterized by stealth fighters, M-16s, or navy destroyers. It is more nuanced than that. The corporate logos of Starbucks, Coca-Cola, and The Gap are the images evoked by American empire. These seemingly benign symbols suggest just how threatening American "imperialism" really is to the rest of humanity. Something is obviously amiss when the same word used to describe a McDonald's opening up in a Third World country is also used to describe the horrors that occurred in the Belgian Congo.

In the lexicon of the Left, the term "empire" possesses an amazing elasticity. "An empire does not only necessarily consist of actual colonial countries that one owns," Charles Freed insisted. "The real empire is owning all these countries in terms of dollars."[52] Beverley Anderson, who traveled to the Washington rally from California, maintained that America's foreign policy is "imperialism disguised as human rights, and building economies, and wiping out poverty."[53] Student Rachel Garskof-Leiberman sees American imperialism as "much more dangerous because if you see someone taking over with a gun . . . and you see traditional imperialism it has negative connotations that are obvious. But an economic imperialization is so much worse because you look at Starbucks and Starbucks isn't threatening. [Third World people] don't think of imperialism. They think of comfort."[54]

Where did these activists get their ideas? "No country is exempt from [the brutal force of the U.S. military], no matter how unimportant," famed Massachusetts Institute of Technology linguist Noam Chomsky writes in the popular pamphlet *What Uncle Sam Really Wants*. A possible socialist success story, Chomsky alleges, threatens the economic order and sparks the capitalist states to crush even tiny rebellions against free enterprise. "If you want a global system that's subordinated to the needs of U.S. investors, you can't let little pieces of it wander off."[55] Howard Zinn labels the recent relationship between U.S. corporations and the Third World "a classical imperial situation, where the places with natural wealth became victims of more powerful nations whose power came from that seized wealth."[56] Gore Vidal tags his homeland "a seedy imperial state."[57] The aging literary crank advances the theory that the military retaliation against Afghanistan for the 9-11 attacks had nothing to do with stopping terrorism but was in fact "a great coup on the part of the United States to grab all of the oil and natural gas of central Asia."[58]

By now, the reader is perhaps familiar with the Left's response to military action around the globe. Radicals inevitably hypothesize that the United States is pulling the strings behind the scenes, usually through the Central Intelligence Agency, even in the cases where no evidence links the United States to the conflict. The non-Americans engaged in the actual fighting, they suggest, serve as our proxies. Far from casting doubt on their analysis, the absence of proof linking the United States to, say, a coup in the Third World merely confirms the Left's view of the CIA's cunning and conspiratorial acumen. Similarly predictable is the Marxian analysis attributing financial motives to all military actions by free-market democracies. The financial motivation usually takes the form of oil, even when the enemy in question—such as the Taliban's Afghanistan—boasts no great oil reserves. If one gets feelings of déjà vu after speaking with leftists about America's role in global affairs, it is because activists lower on the information food chain devour the party line of Zinn, Chomsky, and others.

A problem for the "American Empire" school of thought is that the masses in developing countries enthusiastically welcome what the Left describes as imperialism. When a clothing line sets up a factory in Central America, no one forces anyone at gunpoint to work the jobs. In fact, the opposite scenario occurs. The people flock to work there. Coca-Cola's omnipresence around the world similarly stems from voluntary choice, not force. For better or worse, Third World people embrace both the production and the consumption components of corporatism. How do leftists explain the enthusiasm of the masses for what they describe as imperialism? "The masses," explained one young man, "are uneducated."[59]

The Left's contention that the United States holds a disproportionate share of military power certainly is valid. It does not follow, however, that great military power necessarily translates into imperial designs. If the United States sought to impose its will on other nations, it certainly could have a great deal of success. It chooses, however, not to do so. This is a conspicuous deviation from the historical pattern. Nations holding power vis-à-vis other nations have traditionally used that power to claim dominion over others. America refrains from this course of action. In fact, the major wars involving the United States since it became the world's preeminent military power have been fought to prevent empires—Nazi imperialism, Japanese imperialism, Communist imperialism, and Iraq's attempt at an oil empire. After all these wars, America's territory remained essentially the same.

The rise of American hegemony notably coincided with the decline of colonialism. The American Century witnessed the fall of, among others, the British, French, and Soviet Empires. Normally, the ascendant power fills the vacuum left by the falling powers. We defeated the Soviet Union, but we do not rule over it. We helped liberate Eastern Europe from its Soviet overlords, but, unlike with the Soviets' rule replacing the vanquished Nazis' rule, we declined to exert our will in governing the affairs of these nations. America's example is a historical anomaly.

The fallacy that one nation's fortune causes another's misfortune inspires much of the hatred of U.S. foreign policy. America's wealth did not come at the expense of other nations. On the contrary, the economies of other nations benefit from Western wealth. The theory behind the false notion of American imperialism posits that U.S. policy aims to transfer the wealth of the rest of the world to the elites of this country. This has not happened. The United States has certainly grown wealthier during the past century. The rest of the world has, too, and at a more dramatic pace. In relative terms, the wealth shift has been away from the West and toward the rest of humanity. Samuel Huntington guesses in *The Clash of Civilizations* that the West's portion of the economic pie reached a high of around 70% after World War I and will decline to the 30% mark by 2020.[60] More important, this time period witnessed remarkable economic progress for non-Western countries in absolute terms as well.

The idea that the United States obtained its wealth by bleeding the rest of humanity dry is a gross inversion of reality for another reason. From the close of World War II until today, the United States has given more than $500 billion in aid to the rest of the world. This figure is roughly $500 billion more than the aid the rest of the world has given the United States. If adjusted for inflation, the $500 billion figure would be quite larger. A survey by the Congressional Research Service estimates that the actual cost to the taxpayer for foreign aid (as a result of interest payments on the borrowing that finances it) stands at over $2 trillion during this period. Again, this massive amount of money is in non-inflation-adjusted dollars.[61] The foreign appropriations budget for fiscal year 2002 lays out more than $15 billion for foreign countries and international programs. The $15 billion, which represents about two-thirds of government spending on foreign governments and international programs, includes money for more than 130 countries.[62] One might logically argue that the federal government milks its own citizens for the benefit of foreigners. Holding that the federal government milks foreigners for its own citizens' benefit belies the objective numbers.

The Left's ideology presumes that the drive for profits from capitalist countries results in attempts at political, economic, and military domination. The facts resist this theory. Preferring ideology to reality, the Left persists in claiming that the dictates of their theories are reality—even when everything around them says otherwise.

MYTH #5: THE RICH GET RICHER, THE POOR GET POORER

WRITER JAMES LOEWEN laments the fact that publishers refrain from printing "a textbook that would enable readers to understand why children of working-class families do not become president or vice-president, the mythical Abraham Lincoln to the contrary."[63] Without a hint of irony, the author penned these words when the occupant of the Oval Office was a man abandoned by his father and raised in poverty by his struggling mother in Hope, Arkansas. The writer's ideological myopia regarding class and success in America is a central tenet of leftist philosophy. The Left's propaganda campaign has been so effective that a majority of Americans now believe that the American system benefits the rich at the expense of the poor. A December 2001 Harris poll, for instance, revealed just how the belief in class rigidity remains entrenched in the collective consciousness. Sixty-nine percent of Americans agreed with the assertion that, in their country, "the rich get richer and the poor get poorer."[64] The facts do not support this popular belief. Nor do they buttress the idea that the system is set up to benefit the rich.

The burden of taxation overwhelmingly falls on the rich. The federal government relieves the poor of paying even a nominal amount of income taxes. The Internal Revenue Service reports that in 1999, the richest 1% paid more than a third of all income taxes it received. The richest 5% paid well over half of all federal income taxes. Only $1 out of every $25 collected by the IRS came from taxpayers on the bottom half of the economic ladder.[65] To state that such a system unfairly benefits the rich, as many politicians perennially do, requires an abandonment of the facts as well as common sense.

The poor's share of the economic pie has undeniably shrunk, however slightly, in recent decades.[66] But the size of the entire pie has grown larger. Every economic class now receives a larger piece because they feast on a larger pie. From 1967 through 2000, the household income of the poorest tenth of the population increased by more than 33% in inflation-adjusted dollars.[67] Surely it is better to have a smaller piece of a massive pie than it is to have a larger piece of a small pie. Countries exist, of course, where income equality is more pronounced among the masses. Economic equality for the populace (but not the leadership) is far more evident in China, Cuba, and Libya than it is in the United States. But what good is equality if it results in making everyone equally poor? Only one consumed by envy prefers equality of condition to increased prosperity for all.

A $9 trillion economy hardly leaves much room for what the rest of humanity considers true poverty. In more than 100 countries, America's poor would be considered the moneyed elite.[68] To its critics, the obscenity of our free-enterprise system is that some still go poor in a nation that houses Bill Gates and Leona Helmsley. Strangely, the system where everyone equally shares financial degradation equally earns higher marks from such critics. Such utopians fail to realize that only the system that keeps in place the natural rewards for hard work and ingenuity realizes the desired widespread prosperity. Government schemes that remove incentives seal the degraded fate of their own citizenry.

The United States is a free country. Any country that values liberty necessarily shuns the socialist's conception of equality.

The two ideals are incongruous. Nobel laureate Friedrich Hayek astutely observed in *The Constitution of Liberty*,

> From the fact that people are very different it follows that, if we treat them equally, the result must be inequality in their actual position, and the only way to place them in an equal position would be to treat them differently. Equality before the law and material equality are therefore not only different but are in conflict with each other; and we can achieve either the one or the other, but not both at the same time.[69]

A variety of income levels usually reflects the health of freedom in a nation. What truly would frighten would be no differences in income.

Ignoring the absolute gains of the lowest economic class while stressing their relative losses serves as one example of the mathematical legerdemain the Left plays in the service of class warfare. A second trick involves the portrayal of "the poor" as a static group of individuals rather than as an economic class whose membership constantly rotates. The people we refer to as "the poor" today are not at all likely to be the people we refer to as "the poor" a few years from now. This reality alone rebuts the notion that the rich get richer while the poor get poorer. Today's rich are often yesterday's poor.

Hard statistics demonstrate that economic mobility is widespread. A Treasury Department study tracking class movement from 1979 to 1988 discovered that 86% of 1979's poor no longer remained in the lowest income quintile in 1988. More of 1979's poorest quintile actually found themselves in the richest 20% of Americans in 1988 than were still mired in the poorest 20%.[70] Considering that the bulk of the survey focused on the

Reagan years, the very time the Left describes as an era of unprecedented misery for the poor, the numbers are quite devastating to any claim of a static class structure.

An Urban Institute study at around the same time yielded similar results. The group found that the greatest proportional income gainers from 1977 to 1986 were 1977's poorest quintile. This bottom fifth of the economic ladder saw their incomes climb 77% during the time period. By way of comparison, the average income gain during the 10-year period was 18%. Conspicuously, 1977's richest quintile experienced an anemic 5% increase in their earnings.[71] In many ways, the Urban Institute's findings merely confirm common sense. Poor people, having nowhere to go but up, experience more rapid proportional gains in income than the rich. To advance an ideology that ignores this reality flies in the face of common sense.

Over the past two decades, the U.S. Census Bureau has tracked individual income fluctuation from one year to the next on seven occasions. Even over a period as short as two years, the studies reveal a startling fluidity in the economy. In each of the Census Bureau's seven two-year studies, at least three-fourths of all individual incomes fluctuated up or down by 5% or more.[72] The studies affirm that the average American sees his earnings change significantly from year to year. A similar Census Bureau study of poor people in the mid-1990s found that nearly one-quarter of impoverished citizens in the first year of the study escaped poverty by the end of the next.[73] Again, the poor are not a fixed group of people. Poverty is a condition that different people find themselves in at different times. Students, the young, and newly arrived immigrants may constitute "the poor" during one still frame but live quite comfortably once we fast-forward their lives.

Just as the extremely poor are not typically chronically impoverished, the extremely rich usually were not born into affluence. Historians generally regard John Jacob Astor as the first man to be worth $10 million, Cornelius Vanderbilt, $100 million, and John D. Rockefeller, $1 billion. Significantly, each of these men earned his own wealth and rose from a fairly modest background. When we look at the rich today, the tradition of self-made wealth still holds true.

The self-made rich constitute the majority of wealthy people. Someone born into wealth stands a far greater chance of dying wealthy, of course, than someone born into poverty. But this hardly supports the claim that "the rich get richer and the poor get poorer." Nor does it indict the American system. The advantages of inherited wealth occur not just in the United States but everywhere else in the world as well. In viewing the *Forbes* 400, the annual ranking of America's superrich, one finds quite a few spots on the list that, like the publisher's chair of the magazine compiling the report, are occupied by the inheritors of great wealth. Sam Walton's wife and children constitute half of the *Forbes* top 10. A brood of Rockefellers populate the list. Five generations after the launch of Johnson & Johnson, numerous members of *Forbes*'s exclusive club bear the genes of the company's founders. Old money has its advantages.

Yet these people are the exception. A perusal of the most recent list of the 400 richest Americans yields a count of 252 men and women, 63% of the total, described by *Forbes* as "self-made."[74] Their stories are truly amazing.

Texan Red McCombs (ranked at 158), the son of an auto mechanic, made billions selling the cars his dad was paid a few dollars to fix. Equaling McCombs in wealth is Kenny Troutt (158), a man who grew up in a housing project, only to establish one of the most successful communications companies in the United States. Andrew McKelvey (172), founder of Monster .com, got his start selling eggs. He later graduated to peddling ad space in the Yellow Pages, which undoubtedly planted the seeds in his mind for his successful Internet classified-ad company. Both Marcus Bernard (60) and Arthur Blank (136) grew up in dilapidated tenement housing in and around New York City. After Bernard and Blank were fired by the Handy Dan home improvement store, they decided to launch their own venture. Handy Dan is out of business. Home Depot is one of the most successful stores in history. West Coast financier Leslie Gonda (136) escaped the Holocaust.[75] The odds do not get much worse than that. Yet he made it. The lives of Mississippi sharecropper's daughter Oprah Winfrey (280), college dropout Steve Jobs (158), and paperboy, horse breaker, and greeting card salesman H. Ross Perot (47) all serve as testimony to the reality of the American Dream.

These aren't Horatio Alger stories. The rags-to-riches tales found in the *Forbes* 400 really happened. If the American Dream can become real for a Jew fleeing from under the jackboot of Nazism, whom can't it become real for?

CONCLUSION

MACHIAVELLI SAID, "One who deceives will always find those who allow themselves to be deceived."[76] The Big Lies told about America find a ready-made audience willing to embrace their deception without inspection. Lies that massage our beliefs often find acceptance without analysis. The nature of the Big Lie, however, is that through volume and repetition it influences the perspectives of those who may not be ideologically predisposed to accept its findings. This is why the previously mentioned anti-American myths present severe danger. The majority of the people who have fallen for them typically are not deluded fanatics. They are regular people.

The uniformly negative portrayals of the American Dream, domestic race relations, women's rights, the state of the environment, and U.S. foreign policy are not the only lies told to discredit America; they are merely the most effective. Wholesale condemnations of the nation's criminal justice system and democratic institutions, for instance, have become staples of leftist rhetoric as well. In these cases, there fortunately do not seem to be as many buyers for what self-described progressives are selling.

America's success contradicts various left-of-center theories touting the failings of religion, cultural assimilation, free enterprise, and the nuclear family. Thus, committed leftists feel compelled to denigrate America so as not to bring discredit to their sacred ideology. To borrow the phrase of a self-hating American of an earlier generation, leftists feel called to besmirch the name of America by any means necessary—even if it means advancing myths. As the following chapter will demonstrate, a second impulse of the anti-American Left involves stifling honest discussion about what really goes on in foreign cultures. To favorably contrast the miserable cultural practices of many parts of the world with those of the United States requires a great deal of dishonesty as well. Because placing America in its worst possible light involves slandering the United States and sugarcoating the practices of foreign lands, the Left does both.

Determining the truth can be an arduous process. Sports fans may argue the play at the plate or whether the point guard released the last-second shot in time. Religious people may debate the one true faith. Eyewitnesses to a crime may give honest but conflicting accounts of what happened.

Determining a lie poses no similar difficulty. Once deceit has been exposed, we all know what it is—whether we care to admit it or not.

CHAPTER 5

SOME CULTURES ARE MORE EQUAL THAN OTHERS

IN THE LATE 1980s, Jesse Jackson led hundreds of Stanford University students in a protest of the school's required "Western Culture" course. That such an exclusionary class was required, demonstrators claimed, constituted institutional racism within Stanford. In the place of a course on Western civilization, the activists demanded a "multicultural" course, teaching students about cultures outside our own. The protestors famously chanted, "Hey hey, ho ho / Western culture's got to go." University administrators agreed. Stanford, as many other schools would soon do, abandoned the course on the West and replaced it with a mandated class on multiculturalism.[1] The mob's angry chant not only questioned the value of Western civilization but also seemed to suggest that westerners have neglected the study of external cultures for too long. On the charge of ignorance of foreign cultures, most Americans are certainly guilty. This is especially true of the vast majority issuing such charges.

Only a simpleton would deny the contributions of other cultures. The Chinese were the first to develop vaccinations, gunpowder, the compass, block printing, the seismograph, and paper money.[2] Of the religions that most westerners practice, none began in Europe or the Americas. From India we received our system of numerals, which we can truly appreciate when we try calculating roman numerals or are reminded that the Egyptian sign for 1,000,000 was an amazed man with his hands placed above his head in wonderment that there was a number that great.[3] It is perhaps at the dinner table that other cultures receive their most enthusiastic endorsements.

Just as we find much to admire in cultures outside our own, we naturally find much to detest. This is particularly true of less advanced societies. Well into the 19th century, the Skidi Pawnee tribe of Nebraska sacrificed human beings to the Morning Star, a deity these Plains Indians worshiped.[4] Children born to tribes in Madagascar were killed if they were born in March or April, on certain days of the week, or during the last week of the month.[5] The males of the Fore tribe of Papua New Guinea so deprived women and children of food that their wives and kids were compelled to dine on human corpses and developed kuru, a disease caused by cannibalism.[6] It is these ugly aspects of primitive societies that multiculturalists choose to ignore and relativists ask us to reserve judgment on.

What upsets us most about foreign cultural practices are the things that most often anger us about our own culture: We see the weak subjugated by the strong. We see maladaptive customs that serve only to harm our fellow man. In short, we see evil and stupidity, and our impulses tell us to right these wrongs. As the West grew in power after the 15th century, its sphere of dominion expanded, and it found itself in the position of being able to alter native practices in its growing number of colonies. When wrongs could be corrected, westerners often tried to do so, eliciting quite accurate charges of cultural imperialism. What seems peculiar is not that we imposed our will on native populations—after all, Russian, Egyptian, Aztec, Arab, Chinese, and Mongolian conquerors have all complied with this pattern—but that many of the cultural changes the West introduced actually helped the colonials.

The English put an end to the killing of newborn twins by Nigerian Ijaws by administering the death penalty to its practitioners.[7] Forgotten are the human sacrifice, cannibalism, and constant conquest that marked Aztec culture. Incessantly invoked is the cruelty of the Spanish conquerors. The French removal of the veil from the faces of Algerian women was deemed an offense akin to rape by Frantz Fanon, the self-proclaimed partisan of the oppressed.[8] The Indian tradition of suttee, the suicide of widows on their husbands' funeral pyres, ran afoul of English gentlemanly sensibilities. Despite being ingrained in Indian culture, suttee was for the most part eradicated through decades of colonial rule. When Sir Charles Napier, conqueror of the Sindh, instituted his plan to end the dehumanizing practice, Brahmins complained to him that his edict violated national custom. "My nation also has a custom," Napier curtly replied. "When men burn women alive, we hang them. Let us all act according to custom."[9]

Napier's absolutist vision of right and wrong would be frowned on today. Our prevailing ethos can be summed up by a proclamation by anthropologist Theodosious Dobzhansky: "No culture's way of life is better than another; people live differently and that is all."[10] But is that all?

Relativists axiomatically state that all cultures are equal. Common sense tells us that they are not. Cultures are not equal because the worth of their contributions to the happiness and betterment of mankind vary. An M-1 tank is not merely different from a slingshot. It is a more effective weapon. The telephone and smoke signals are not just alternative ways of sending messages. They are unequal methods of communication. "Arabic" numerals, born in India, are superior to the West's "roman" numerals, born in Greece.

Multiculturalists demand that westerners look at other cultures with tolerance; however, they discourage that same trait for those inspecting our own society. In the multicultural vernacular, tolerance has a double meaning. For Third World cultures, it means uncritical appreciation and praise. For the First World, it means highlighting faults. Thus, slavery becomes a Western invention while its popularity among primitive societies is ignored.

Cultural equality is achieved the same way most equality is achieved: through leveling. The principles of Marxism are applied to cultures. "Rich" ones are knocked down a few rungs, and "poor" ones are given a boost upward. The need to do this, of course, is an admission that some cultures really are better than others and that cultural equality can come only by artificial means.

Intellectually curious people don't defer to slogans (e.g., all cultures are equal) when assessing cultures. As sentient beings, we have the ability to inspect, evaluate, and judge. When one looks at America vis-à-vis other cultures, it quickly becomes apparent why anti-American academics are so hesitant to do just that—inspect, evaluate, and judge.

A real multiculturalism would give us the good, the bad, and the ugly about the world outside our door. Because the picture that we are often presented with of other cultures serves to delude rather than to enlighten, we are truly shocked when confronted with the harsh reality of life outside America. Forced abortions, ethnic concentration camps, tongue amputations for vocal contrarians, slavery, and genocide are among what await the rising generation in various spots around the world. When we open our eyes to what really exists rather than what some ideologues want us to believe exists, the anti-Americanism promoted by Marxism, multiculturalism, Critical Theory, relativism, and other like-minded ideologies becomes absurd.

PATRIARCHY IN THE THIRD WORLD

"IT'S THE CHRISTIAN patriarchal system of the last 1,000 years," claims one New Age feminist, "that has really screwed the world."[11] Raise the question of the West's treatment of women at a meeting of the National Organization for Women (NOW) or in a women's studies seminar, and you likely will get a similar response. A more humane, feminist-friendly world, they insist, awaits us outside our cultural borders. The question naturally arises: where?

By any statistical measure, women in non-Western countries are treated as inferiors to their male counterparts. The condition of these women is far below that of their sisters in the West as well. While men vastly outnumber women in China, 70% of all illiterates are of the gentler sex. Kenya's illiteracy gender gap is the same. In India, the male/female literacy disparity is 66% to 38%, in Chad 62% to 35%, and in Egypt 63% to 34%.[12] The exclusive right of males to marry additional spouses is legal in the entire Islamic world and most of Africa, where polygamy is an accepted practice in more than 25 countries.[13] India, poised to become the world's most populous nation later this century, boasts a mortality rate for females higher than that for men.[14]

Today, female genital mutilation affects women in the vast majority of countries on the African continent. The practice, which dates back thousands of years, usually involves excising a young girl's clitoris and slicing off her labia minora. An even more gruesome procedure involves a total excision of a girl's external genitalia and stitching of the vaginal opening, leaving a hole only large enough for menstrual blood or urine to seep out but little else. Both procedures create obvious complications for childbirth and sex and occasionally result in immediate death. "For me, sexual intercourse is painful and I find it difficult to find pleasure," notes one woman from Burkina Faso. Elsewhere on the continent, in Egypt, Somalia, Sudan, Mali, Eritrea, Sierra Leone, Djibouti, and Ethiopia, the practice is nearly universal, affecting 85% or more of the female population in each of these nations. The World Health Organization estimates that between 100 million and 140 million African women have undergone female genital mutilation.[15] Listen to Western feminists, and it is eating disorders, the self-esteem of schoolgirls, and a lack of subsidized abortions that are the major problems confronting women. Outside America, there are more serious issues at hand.

Foot binding, the long-standing Chinese custom of compressing girl's feet begun in the 10th century, was one of the more thankful casualties of the 20th century. Chinese women, unfortunately, are still treated as subhuman.

Chinese women living in cities are permitted to have only one child, with some rural mothers of girls allowed to get pregnant a second time in hopes of having a boy. China's satellite state, Vietnam, also puts a ceiling on the number of children women can have. The Chinese Communist Party dictates that all "unplanned pregnancies must be aborted immediately." Unwed mothers are almost nonexistent because they are forced to abort their babies. Women who might be at risk for passing on defective genes are forcibly sterilized, a procedure performed on more than 10 million people in the country. It should come as no surprise that in a society so patriarchal as to dictate when and how many children women can have, most of the children that are allowed to be born are males. Men outnumber women by 100 million or more in China. For every 100 girls who are born, there are 117 male births. A study of second children born in one county revealed a ratio of 306 males to 100 females. Sex-selection abortions are normal. Female infanticide is far from unheard of. Because women are at a premium, forced prostitution and abductions for the purpose of marriage are serious problems.[16]

Calling women in Islamic nations second-class citizens would be to elevate their actual status. Islamic courts weigh a woman's testimony as worth half that of a man's.[17] Koranic rules dictate that female heirs are to get half the inheritance that men get.[18] Men control the travel of their wives and daughters in almost every nation in the Middle East. Even in so-called moderate nations such as Kuwait, Jordan, and Egypt, husbands must grant permission to wives, and fathers to daughters under 21, to travel outside their nation's borders.[19] In more extreme countries such as Yemen and Saudi Arabia, women need permission to travel outside their own homes.[20] While the severity of dress codes varies from country to country, cultural norms dictate that women cover their heads in much of the Islamic world. Police beat women for removing the veil, for instance, in Iran and Saudi Arabia.[21] In March 2002, religious police in Mecca prevented rescue workers from saving the lives of schoolgirls trapped in a fire. "They forced the girls to remain inside the school and didn't allow them to leave, saying that their hair wasn't covered and they weren't wearing the abaya [long robe]," reported a local newspaper. Fourteen girls died in the conflagration.[22]

Traditionally, and in some Muslim nations by law, females must gain permission from their closest male relative to marry. Women often have little choice in whom they wed. In Yemen and Iran, for instance, families can legally marry off girls as young as nine years old.[23] It is quite common for Islamic states to outlaw marriages between a Muslim woman and a non-Muslim man; the same prohibitions do not apply to men.[24] Muslim men alone are allowed to take many spouses, including, in some traditions, partaking in an infinite number of temporary marriages that can last for as little as 30 minutes. Husbands' ability to divorce is easy, while the process for their mates is arduous, and the male's ability to gain custody of children—with the exception of small children—is usually automatic. Women in many Middle Eastern countries are unable to even confer citizenship on their own children.[25]

"Honor killings," in which male relatives murder women for shaming their family, are common throughout the Middle East. Egypt, Qatar, Jordan, Yemen, Pakistan, and Lebanon are among the countries that grant leniency to men who commit "honor killings."[26] Iraq grants immunity to murderers who can prove that "honor" was their motive.[27]

The men who rule much of the Islamic world treat rape frivolously. Shaheen Akhtar, a 15-year-old Pakistani rape victim, was charged with adultery and placed in prison after telling her story to the authorities. Her alleged attackers, however, were not charged. Akhtar was kept in chains under detention. She contracted tuberculosis in prison and died.[28] In neighboring Bangladesh, a 13-year-old Christian girl was raped by a Muslim man and became pregnant. No one was able to produce the requisite four male Muslim eyewitnesses to generate a rape indictment, so the teenager's rapist was not arrested. The pregnant 13-year-old, however, was put on trial for her "crime."[29] Of the 2,130 rapes that were prosecuted in Bangladesh in 2000, there were a mere 63 convictions. In both of these South Asian countries, it is common for rape victims to be placed in prison for their "protective custody." It is uncommon for rapists to be punished for their crimes.[30] In Iraq, rape is used as a political tool to terrorize opponents of the state. Having defected in the mid-1990s, General Al-Salahi received a videotape in June 2000 showing Iraqi security forces gang-raping a female relative.[31] It was not until 1999 that the Egyptian government revoked a law that gave immunity to rapists who agreed to marry their victims.[32]

In Bangladesh and Pakistan, rejected suitors often resort to throwing acid in the faces of the women who denied them. In 2000, a human rights organization documented 181 such cases in Bangladesh.[33] Devadasi, the practice of poor families sacrificing a daughter to become a sexual slave for Hindu priests, persists in southern India. Female infanticide claims the lives of more than 10,000 Indian children annually. As in China, the proportion of male births vastly outnumbers female births. Female illiteracy is nearly double that of men, and the harsh lives that women are forced to lead in Hindu culture remarkably leads to lower life expectancy rates for females. Tradition in Near Eastern countries requires a bride to provide a dowry to her new family. Women who fail to meet their new family's dowry expectations are often killed. Crime statistics in India, for instance, list 6,917 dowry killings for 1998.[34]

At the opposite end of the spectrum from the dowry is the paying of a "bride-price," which endures in such African countries as South Africa, Lesotho, Cameroon, and the Republic of the Congo.[35] As its name suggests, the bride-price reduces one-half of humanity to property and forces women to spend their lives married to men they may find repulsive. Consistent with the idea that women are "property" to be purchased is the practice of "inherited wives" that occurs in Tanzania, Uganda, and Zimbabwe.[36] The tradition dictates that on the death of the husband, his wife is to be inherited by the deceased man's eldest brother. Other maladaptive and misogynist traditions include the rape of women by suitors to ensure marriage in Benin and abduction marriages in Ethiopia.[37] In keeping with these anti-women practices, polygamy is available to men throughout much of the continent.

Outside Western patriarchy, one finds more patriarchy. More significant, one finds real patriarchy. The non-Western world of sexual equality exists only in the imaginations of feminists, who have projected their own ideals on cultures we know little about. Their hope is that we will buy into the existence of a world that stands in positive contrast to our own. The place they outline is imaginary. What is real is the West. Although far from perfect, the West is the only major civilization on earth where women have tasted equality.

RACIAL AND ETHNIC HATRED

LIKE SEXISM, RACISM is depicted as a problem almost unique to the West, particularly America. When we look at the world, our existing racial problems actually appear comparatively benign. Ethnically motivated killings that are commonplace, say, in Nigeria or Indonesia are so infrequent in America that when they do occur they make national headlines for weeks. When we look at our own history, we see that our current status is preferable to what existed just a few generations ago. While civil rights activists are wont to deny our improved situation, the issues that now consume their energies belie this fact. The Confederate battle flag waving atop a building, standardized tests, and slow service at Denny's are hardly as menacing as Bull

Connor's German shepherds, segregated schools, or Alabama church bombings. A familiar refrain from those obsessed with race is that while racism no longer operates overtly, it continues covertly. Overseas, racism and ethnocentrism are not covert. They're brutally overt.

For the past 20 years, Sudan has been embroiled in a civil war pitting Arab northerners against black southerners. Africa's most populous nation has seen more than two million of its inhabitants slain and more than four million displaced in the conflict. Perhaps more shocking to westerners are the race-based raids conducted by Arabs on blacks that have resulted in the enslavement of nearly 100,000 human beings.[38] Further south on the continent was the setting for the multination ethnic war between Hutus and Tutsis that claimed more than a million lives in the mid-1990s. As the carnage transpired in Rwanda, Burundi, and elsewhere, a more publicized, if less bloody, ethnic conflict engulfed the former Yugoslavia. Bosnians, Serbians, Croatians, and Albanians took turns killing each other. As was the case in Sudan, the ethnic divisions in Yugoslavia were compounded by religious differences. China's enduring occupation of Tibet is a textbook example of genocide. Since 1950, more than a million Tibetans have died as a result of the occupation. Cultural symbols, such as the Tibetan flag and the Dalai Lama's picture, are strictly outlawed. China is slowly replacing the native language with Mandarin in the schools. The nation's borders have been erased, and the Chinese government has conducted a resettlement program to populate the area with ethnic Chinese. Almost all the nation's Buddhist monasteries have been closed, more than 12,000 religious leaders have been forcibly expelled from their dwellings, and three-fourths of the political prisoners are monks or nuns. The Chinese government even kidnapped the six-year-old Panchen Lama, a holy

Buddhist figure who is believed to be able to identify the next Dalai Lama.[39] All traces of Tibet—religious, linguistic, ethnic, cultural, and geographic—are targeted for extinction.

Killing is the most extreme manifestation of racism. State-sponsored discrimination frequently takes less violent forms. Qatar bans the hiring of Egyptians.[40] Liberia reserves citizenship exclusively for blacks.[41] Majority quotas and state-sanctioned discrimination against the Chinese minority persists in Malaysia and Indonesia.[42] Ethnic minorities in Bhutan need permission to enroll in school, receive government employment, or partake in certain professions. All citizens are forced to adopt the dress code and Buddhist religion of the majority.[43] Race-based slavery endures in Mauritania and Sudan.[44]

Ethiopia conducts a campaign of government-sanctioned discrimination against ethnic Eritreans who are citizens of Ethiopia. Ethiopian citizens are deported to Eritrea by the thousands. The east African government's internment camps now house nearly 75,000 Eritreans, most of whom are Ethiopian citizens.[45] Iraq's "Arabization" policy unleashes unique brutality on its Kurdish population. The destruction of Kurdish villages, forced relocations, and chemical weapons attacks are among the methods used by Saddam Hussein to oppress this minority group.[46] Minority groups in Burma face a similar fate. In recent years, the government forcibly relocated tens of thousands of ethnic minorities. The 1982 Burmese Citizenship Law denies citizenship to minority-group members who have not only lived in Burma their whole lives but whose ancestors have as well.[47]

Ethnocentrism is often so strong that it overrides the positive economic benefits that come from a more tolerant society. Foreign investment is restricted—to the host nation's detriment—in scores of countries. Foreigners are barred from owning land, for instance, in Armenia, Azerbaijan, Bahrain, Belarus, Bulgaria, Cuba, Kazakhstan, Kuwait, the Kyrgyz Republic, Laos, Mauritius, Mongolia, Nigeria, Tanzania, and Turkmenistan.[48]

Unfortunately, there is not a society on Earth, including our own, where ethnically inspired hatred does not exist. To contend that the ugly racial crimes that have occurred in America are somehow unique to our culture is to blind us to the truth. In the world today, one's ethnicity can ensure one's death or enslavement. It can prevent one from attaining the rights that one's neighbors possess. It can serve as the rationale for imprisoning someone in a concentration camp. In 21st-century America, race and ethnicity can do none of these things. However imperfect the United States of America is, most nations would gladly trade their racial problems for ours.

FREEDOM OF RELIGION

FREEDOM TO EXERCISE the religion of one's choice is a right taken for granted by many Americans. If this right is not taken for granted elsewhere, it is only because religious freedom rarely exists outside the West. In some countries, religion is banned entirely. Others mandate that citizens practice the religion endorsed by the state. Religious extremists and atheist zealots have different objectives, but the result of their ruling a country is always the same: Individuals are denied the ability to worship their own God and practice their own religion.

The Koran and the tradition of the Prophet Muhammad serve as the constitution of Saudi Arabia. All religions save Islam are illegal. Mosques are constructed at government expense, and taxpayers pay the salaries of imams. Churches and synagogues cannot be built, wearing a cross or a Star of David is a criminal offense, and Bibles and other non-Islamic religious books are subject to government bans. Religious police, or Mutawwa'in, scour the nation looking for people deviating from the mandated dress code, women driving cars, or people committing some other perceived offense against Islam. In November 1998, these Mutawwa'in murdered an elderly religious leader for repeating the call to prayer twice, a Shi'a practice that is forbidden by the Saudi Sunni majority. The Saudi government refused to prosecute (perhaps because the religious police were doing what was asked of them) and claimed that the old man had died of high blood pressure. In early 2000, 16 Filipinos were arrested for practicing Christianity in a private home. In April, Hashim Al-Sayyid Al-Sada, a Shi'a cleric, was arrested and held incommunicado for practicing a form of Islam contrary to the Sunni majority's. Later in the year, the government confiscated Bibles during a crackdown on a Christian religious service. Conversion from Islam to any other religion is a capital crime.[49]

A Shi'a mirror image of the Sunni religious oppression in Saudi Arabia can be found in neighboring Iran, which proclaims itself an Islamic state. The government has murdered numerous evangelical Christians in the past decade, with several dozen additional evangelicals mysteriously disappearing. Among the missing are Christian converts from Islam. With apostasy a capital offense in Iran, there is little doubt regarding their fate. Jews are singled out for discriminatory laws, such as prohibitions against their traveling abroad with their families. Thus, in the two decades since the Islamic revolution, the Jewish population in Iran has evaporated to a third of its former size. As is the case in Saudi Arabia, floggings await those who deviate from the dress code or ignore the call to prayer. Grocery stores owned by non-Muslims are required to post religious identifications on their storefronts. Similarly, non-Islamic inhabitants of Iran must possess special identification. Special persecution is reserved for Islamic coreligionists of differing sects. In 1998, the Sunni imam Bakhsh Narouie was murdered, with most of his followers believing government involvement. Members of the Baha'i faith, an offshoot of Shi'a Islam, are detained, harassed, and beaten. Because Baha'i marriages are not recognized, Baha'i women are occasionally arrested as "prostitutes" and their children deemed illegitimate. In 2000, two followers of Baha'i were executed for "actions against God."[50]

Elsewhere in the region, the situation does not differ greatly. Other states that have established Islam as the official religion and officially discriminate against other faiths include Algeria, Bahrain, Egypt, Jordan, Kuwait, Oman, Tunisia, the United Arab Emirates, Yemen, Sudan, Bangladesh, and Pakistan.[51] Christians, Hindus, Jews, Buddhists, and other non-Muslims are unable to fully practice their faith in any one of these nations. Ironically, what is also true is that in none of these countries are Muslims as free to practice their faith as they are in the United States.

In sharp contrast to the Islamic world, with its requirement that its inhabitants worship a particular God, are China and its several satellite states, which demand that their citizens worship no God. In September 1999, Communist Party general secretary Jiang Zemin made clear Red China's view of religion to anyone who may have forgotten: "Party members of all ethnic groups must have a firm faith in socialism and communism, cannot believe in religion, cannot take part in or organize religious activities, and cannot take part in feudal superstitious religion."

Hundreds of Falun Gong followers have been executed by the government in recent years, with an exponentially higher number committed to mental institutions. Thousands of churches, mosques, and places of worship have been destroyed or closed. Practitioners of Islam, Christianity, and various other religions are routinely thrown in jail and sometimes killed.[52] During the 2001 Christmas season, for instance, Hong Kong businessman Li Guangqiang was sentenced to death for exporting 16,280 Bibles to a Christian group within Communist China. Although Li's sentence was later commuted to jail time, countless others have not been as fortunate.[53] Noting the revolutionary power of religion, one Beijing official candidly stated, "If God had the face of a seventy-year-old man, we wouldn't care if he was back. But he has the face of millions of twenty-year-olds, so we are worried."[54] Laos, North Korea, and Vietnam are apparently worried, too, playing follow the leader to China's policy of religious persecution.

Every predominantly Christian nation in the West protects the freedom of conscience of practitioners of the other major faiths. There is little reciprocation. Christian minorities are often forcibly converted, forbidden to erect churches, persecuted for blasphemy, and denied the ability to celebrate mass. Something as essential to the Christian faith as the Bible is censored in a diverse array of states, making it perhaps the world's most banned text. Islamic states such as Mauritania, Qatar, Comoros, and Oman prohibit the printing, public distribution, and import of Bibles.[55]

Atheism is the encouraged belief system of the remaining Communist nations. As with many faiths, its followers' unwavering belief in its rectitude results in extreme intolerance against those who believe otherwise. Laos bans the import, public distribution, and printing of religious texts. In February

1999, the Cuban government confiscated thousands of King James Bibles, which were burned.[56]

Burma bans the Bible and other non-Buddhist religious texts. The Buddhist nation of Bhutan forbids the import of Bibles into the country.[57]

Naturally, governmental encouragement of intolerance quite often leads to sectarian violence in religiously mixed areas. In February 2002, a horde of Indian Muslims incinerated a train carrying Hindus, killing 58. Within days, more than 400 Hindus and Muslims lay dead as a result of the ensuing violence.[58] Jewish Israelis and predominantly Muslim Palestinians have engaged in sporadic fighting for much of the past several decades, leaving thousands dead. In the aftermath of fighting in East Timor that resulted in 200,000 deaths, hostilities between the Indonesian Muslim majority and the Christian minority have resulted in more than 10,000 lives lost over the past three years. On Christmas Eve 2000, a series of church bombings resulted in 19 deaths. A year later, the leader of an Islamic group wished Christians "a merry and bloody Christmas."[59] Global hot spots that have each witnessed 10,000 or more deaths in religiously related wars in recent years include Nigeria, Tibet, Yugoslavia, Sudan, Chechnya, the Philippines, and Kashmir. While religious zealotry may not be the sole motivation for each of these bloody conflicts, its role is central. More specifically, the followers of one religion conspicuously find themselves as participants in the majority of these grisly conflicts. "Muslims make up about one-fifth of the world's population but in the 1990s they have been far more involved in intergroup violence than the people of any other civilization," Samuel Huntington's best-selling *Clash of Civilizations and the Remaking of World Order* points out. "The evidence is overwhelming."[60]

The American tradition of religious toleration stands athwart the more popular tradition of religious persecution found elsewhere in the world. "The legitimate powers of government," Thomas Jefferson wrote in his lone full-length book, "extend to such acts only as are injurious to others. . . . it does me no injury for my neighbor to say there are twenty gods, or no god. It neither picks my pocket nor breaks my leg."[61] What Jefferson seemed to be saying is that a government's proper role is to protect our freedoms from the encroachments of others, not to encroach on those freedoms itself. A coerced faith benefits neither God nor individual souls. It is only when we are free and not forced that the practice of our faith becomes in any way meaningful. Future generations of Americans affirmed Jefferson's wisdom by viewing religion as the business of the individual and not the state. The world largely disagrees, making religion the business of the state and not the individual.

FREEDOM OF SPEECH

FREEDOM OF SPEECH is such an unchallenged aspect of life in America that Americans sometimes naively assume that it is a right shared by the rest of the world as well. It is not.

Imagine a life in which the only news you heard on the radio or saw on television was what the government wanted you to see. People living in Algeria, Egypt, Bahrain, Iran, Iraq, Jordan, Kuwait, Libya, Morocco, Oman, Saudi Arabia, Syria, Yemen, Maldives, India, China, Cameroon, Djibouti, Mauritania, Rwanda, Seychelles, North Korea, Laos, Vietnam, Turkmenistan, Burma, and Cuba do not have to try very hard to conceptualize such a place. They live there.[62] A majority of the earth's population resides in countries where free and independent broadcasting of the news is illegal. It is the state, not independent journalists, that reports the news.

"The pen is mightier than the sword." One would be hard-pressed to find more committed believers in this old saying than the rulers who preside over their fellow countrymen without their consent. The average nonwesterner lives in a country where journalists and activists are jailed, gatherings and demonstrations occur only when the government approves, and films, art, and literature are censored. Political parties and associations are strictly forbidden in many African, Arab, and eastern Asian states. Government ownership of printing presses, radio, Internet service providers, and television further limit the average person's ability to speak out. Governments view free speech as a threat to their power; thus, they circumvent the power of their subjects to voice their ideas.

Government abridgements of speech, assembly, association, and the press often occur extralegally. That is to say, while no written law actually prohibits the frowned-on activity, the government uses force to outlaw it anyway. As this threat always looms, citizens bite their tongues and practice self-censorship. Some governments, however, are very open about their contempt for free expression. Certain artistic, political, and religious expressions are explicitly forbidden. Kuwait bans speech that "affects the value of the national currency," "spreads dissension among the populace," or "creates hatred."[63] Senegal's press law prohibits views that "discredit" the state.[64] Bhutanese citizenship is revoked for "speech" that is "disloyal in any manner whatsoever to the King, country, and the people of Bhutan."[65] Azerbaijan's Law on Mass Media restricts coverage that "insults the honour and dignity of the state and the Azerbaijani people" or "is contrary to the national interest."[66] Seychelles bars words that are "objectionable" or go against the "national interest."[67] Uruguay's constitution muzzles speech that is "insulting to the nation, the State, or its powers."[68] In Togo, people who "offend the honor, dignity or esteem" of government officials are subject to imprisonment.[69] Yemen prescribes a five-year jail term for "the humiliation of the State, the Cabinet, or parliamentary institutions."[70] Zimbabwe bans subversive statements and views that threaten the "interest of defense, public safety, public order, state economic interests, public morality, and public health."[71]

The consequences for those who violate the written or unwritten rules against speech can be dire in some locales.

China's constitution claims to give its citizens a right to speak freely. In 2000, Li Lusong naively took this proclamation at face value. He complained to Communist Party officials about the dismal state of a local schoolhouse. The officials' idea of correcting the situation involved having Mr. Li beaten up and declining to fix the school. Shortly thereafter, Li stubbornly spoke out again, posting comments against the corruption of party officials in Shanxi Province. Unable to effectively silence him initially, the police incapacitated Li with a stun gun, used pliers to pull out his tongue, and then sliced it off.[72]

Libyan soccer fans found out the hard way that cheering against the team favored by Colonel Gadhafi's sons can cost you your life. In 1996, a referee made a questionable call, enabling the team the dictator's sons were rooting for to score a goal. Outraged fans responded by chanting anti-Gadhafi slogans. The brutal dictator's sons opened fire on the crowd, sparking a riot. The gunfire and the stampede it caused claimed as many as 50 lives by some estimates.[73]

North Koreans are executed for such thought crimes as "ideological divergences" and "opposing socialism." Defacing a picture of the late Kim Il Sung or his son Kim Jong Il is a serious offense. Family members of small children who unknowingly damaged pictures of the leaders of the prison-state's personality cult have been sent to jail for their children's "illegal" actions.[74] Tongue amputation has joined the death penalty as punishment for criticism of Saddam Hussein. In September 2000, a critic of the Iraqi dictator had his tongue removed. The unfortunate man was subsequently carted around in a truck to advertise to the populace the consequences of speaking freely.[75]

Iraq, North Korea, China, and Libya are particularly brutal regimes. Their barbarous punishments are fortunately rejected by all but a few nations. Yet their belief that mere speech can be a crime is embraced almost everywhere.

In guaranteeing freedom of speech, America separates itself not just from the Third World but from the majority of industrialized nations as well. Canada, for instance, prohibits speech that "degrades" or "dehumanizes" women.[76] Vladimir Putin's government shut down Russia's sole remaining private television network, which consistently voiced criticism of the regime in Moscow, in the opening weeks of 2002.[77] A Parisian newspaper columnist was found guilty of "provoking hate" for calling the country's influx of foreigners a "proliferating invasion." The "crime" cost the writer a large fine.[78] Battered by half a century of totalitarian occupation, Hungary bans the swastika and the sickle and hammer.[79] A law prohibiting "hatred against any section of the public in Great Britain distinguished by color, race, ethnic, or national origins" criminalizes "abusive" and "insulting" speech.[80] Just because there is a First Amendment to our Constitution does not mean that every constitution contains such an amendment.

The great irony, of which the reader is by now well aware, is that the complainers who here carp that their nation is an "oppressive" and "intolerant" regime would be thrown in jail in most places. The freedom and ease with which their odious sentiments are expressed in America proves just how wrong they are.

DEMOCRACY

DEMOCRACY IS NOT just rare outside the West; it's almost a novelty. In nearly every country in Europe and the Americas, citizens exercise their legal right to peacefully change their government by vote. Outside the West, only a small fraction of humanity chooses its own leaders.

When democracy prevails in non-Western countries, it usually does so because representative government is forced on those countries. The citizens of Japan, for instance, can choose their own leaders only because the United States imposed a republican government on the vanquished nation after World War II. The concept of democracy was introduced to India after generations of British rule. These governments are anomalies in an antidemocratic world.

No Arab nation is a democracy. Of the more than 30 predominantly Muslim nations in the world, only two—Turkey and Albania—have governments that could be said to be democratic. Both nations are the beneficiaries of geography, standing between the Christian and Islamic worlds. Like India and Japan, these nations have partly inherited the political traditions of the West. The Middle East is the exclusive domain of monarchs, mullahs, and dictators. There are more than a billion Muslims in the world. The few who have a say in electing their leaders live, for the most part, in countries such as the United States, Great Britain, India, and Germany—not Saudi Arabia, Egypt, or Pakistan.

Asia is dominated by autocratic regimes that deny the people any say in how their governments are run. Four of the five remaining Communist dictatorships—China, North Korea, Vietnam, and Laos—can be found in the region. The Far East's longtime repressive regimes of Burma (Myanmar), Cambodia, Indonesia, Mongolia, and Thailand continue to hamper political freedom as well. The sheer number of people in the Far East who are denied a choice in their leaders approaches almost two billion, a third of the earth's population.

Being generous, one could say that slightly less than a quarter of the 54 African governments practice something resembling democracy.[81] Leaders of nondemocratic nations and their supporters in the West deny this. They point to elections held in African nations as proof of democracy. Yet just labeling your country a "people's republic" or feigning to hold an election does not a democracy make.

Cameroon restricts freedom of speech and assembly, jailing demonstrators and journalists. The state has nationalized all television and radio, making it impossible for dissenting voices to reach the people. When the leading opposition candidate announced that he would be running for president, the sitting president had him arrested.[82]

Tanzanian officials arrested journalists, a priest, and 18 members of parliament for criticizing the government in 2000. Antigovernment demonstrations were routinely broken up, with protestors forced to lie in urine. On election day, the state arrested more than 150 opposition party activists. The opposition candidate, who had been pulled off the stage by the government during a campaign speech, was declared ineligible for office by a judge.[83]

The Ivory Coast's government owns all television stations and dominates other media outlets, making it difficult for opposing voices to gain access to the airwaves or newsprint. When journalists expressed criticism of the state, government security forces attacked media offices. Demonstrations require government approval, which is rarely granted. When demonstrations were held in 2000, the government killed more than 100 protestors. Others who escaped with their lives were forced to eat dirt and human waste by the police and had their genitals beaten with bats wrapped in barbed wire. The country's supreme court, which is controlled by the executive branch, disqualified 14 of the 19 men running for president. Despite all this (or perhaps because of it), the ruling party's candidate fared poorly in the presidential election. Soldiers rectified this inconvenience by storming election sites, ejecting observers, and declaring that their candidate, who had been trailing badly, had actually come from behind to win.[84]

Prior to Ethiopia's 2000 elections, 500 supporters of the opposition party were arrested. The state, which owns all printing presses and the only television station, jailed 24 journalists during the election cycle. Opposition demonstrations were banned. The government killed opposition supporters in the days leading up to the vote. On the day of the actual vote, two women were killed for refusing to vote for a state-endorsed candidate.[85]

There is reason for restrained optimism regarding political freedom. Indonesia, Ghana, Mongolia, and other countries that once denied citizens the right to elect their own leaders have shown real signs of abandoning their repressive pasts. Latin America shifts back and forth between strongmen of the left and the right and attempts at democracy. Today, most Latin American countries follow the latter path; tomorrow, who knows? The situation in the former Soviet Union remains precarious as well. While democracy seems firmly entrenched in the Baltics, the former Islamic provinces of the Soviet Union are as firmly in the grip of authoritarian rule. The political direction of other components of the late superstate, including Georgia, Ukraine, and Russia itself, is uncertain. The conventional wisdom of the early 1990s that a rejection of Communist totalitarianism necessarily meant an embrace of representative democracy appears rather naive in retrospect. Despite these unsettled prospects for democracy, the situation is markedly better than it was just a few years ago.

Democracy is not the panacea for the world's problems. The mob, after all, can be as oppressive as any medieval king or banana republic dictator. It is also true that in some locales, notably the Middle East, democracy might prove to worsen rather than better the condition of the people. When we witness the popular support for the Iranian revolution or the Taliban, we are given pause in the belief that the democratic principles that work here work everywhere. Despite all these caveats, democracy still is, as Winston Churchill reminded us, "the 'worst' form of government except all those others that have been tried."[86] The unmistakable reality of the world today is that freedom, civic rights, and equality under the law are given their greatest protections in countries where the political leaders are popularly elected.

CRIMINAL JUSTICE

DOSTOYEVSKY WROTE, "The degree of civilization in a society can be judged by entering its prisons."[87] A liberal interpretation of the Russian novelist's aphorism might also include looking at how a nation treats criminals and suspected lawbreakers not just in its prisons but at every step of its justice system.

Trial by ordeal, the backward practice of determining guilt or innocence by how the accused responds to life-threatening situations (such as submersion in water) is still in use in

Liberia.[88] Amputation is a legal form of punishment in Saudi Arabia, Sudan, and Nigeria's Muslim north.[89] China markets the organs of executed criminals, which, critics claim, drives up the number of capital sentences.[90]

Police in China, Pakistan, Nigeria, Cameroon, the Democratic Republic of Congo, Somalia, and Equatorial Guinea arrest family members of suspected criminals when they have difficulty apprehending the suspects themselves.[91] Libya's "Collective Penalty Law" punishes "any group, whether large or small," including towns, families, or tribes, for the crimes of their individual members. Punishments include shutting off water or electricity to those groups and the withholding of state funds. Families of guilty individuals, the country's leader himself has proclaimed, should be thought of as guilty, too.[92] North Korea's policy of "collective retribution" punishes individuals whose families or ancestors ran afoul of the Communist government.[93]

Rights, which are in short supply for law-abiding citizens, are a rarity for the typical criminal suspect. The right to an attorney, to a jury of one's peers, to a speedy trial, and against self-incrimination are scarce. Defendants in criminal cases in Japan, Saudi Arabia, China, Egypt, Colombia, Indonesia, Chile, and scores of other nations, for instance, face trials without the benefit of a jury of their peers. Corrupt and inefficient judicial systems contribute greatly to the fundamental unfairness that suspected lawbreakers face. Suspects are often jailed for a longer time awaiting trial than the maximum sentence that their alleged crimes call for. In Ghana, for example, a man accused of robbing a taxi driver of $30 appeared in court 17 times in the late 1990s without having his case heard. Finally, after four and a half years in jail, he was released by a judge who affirmed that he did not know when the man would get his day in court.[94] One accused thief in Kenya waited four years in jail before his trial began.[95] In Niger and Rwanda, some prisoners have waited up to six years to be charged with a crime.[96] In Uganda, where three-fourths of the prison population are arrestees waiting for trial, a man was let out of jail 15 years after he was charged with murder without ever having a trial.[97] Justice delayed, the old saying goes, is justice denied. It is justice denied to the aggrieved but also to the accused.

Prison conditions outside the West are abysmal. Food is scarcely provided to prisoners in many African countries. Families are normally compelled to provide food for jailed relatives in Nigeria, Benin, Burkina Faso, Ghana, and Madagascar.[98] Visitation is often the sole prerogative of families with enough money to bribe guards. Juveniles are regularly housed with adults in the prisons of many countries on the continent. Coed jails persist in the Central African Republic, Madagascar, Mali, Nigeria, and Equatorial Guinea.[99] More than 100 people stuffed into a cell in Mozambique died of asphyxiation.[100] In August 1999, 29 helpless inmates in Niger choked to death after their cells were flooded with tear gas.[101] In the Ivory Coast, 27 prisoners were trampled to death after the government unleashed tear gas on them.[102] In the Republic of Congo, 12 of the inmates stuffed into an overcrowded cell died.[103]

The state's contempt for the rule of law often serves as a bad example for the populace. Tanzania, Benin, Indonesia, and Kenya each were home to hundreds of lynchings in 2000.[104] In the span of a few short years, the total victims of mob justice in each of these nations will eclipse the number of lynchings in all of U.S. history. The official response to the pervasive lawlessness in many South American societies is more lawlessness. Brazilian police, who are tried in their own noncivilian courts, take the law into their own hands with impunity. In Rio de Janeiro and São Paulo alone, more than 1,000 killings by the police took place in 2000.[105] Ecuador similarly exempts police from civilian courts.[106] In Venezuela, where politicians recently ran for office on such slogans as "bullets for the underworld" and "the only good criminal is a dead criminal," vigilantism runs amok. In 2000, mobs lynched several dozen criminal suspects, and police killed several thousand more.[107] Prison officials in Argentina were recently caught engaging in a profitable scam allowing overnight releases for inmates who agreed to return to the jails with stolen booty for their overseers. The scheme turned deadly when citizens witnessed an inmate, who was supposed to be languishing behind bars, kill a policeman. Later, the corrupt prison officials suspiciously reported that they found the inmate's body hanging in his cell.[108]

China offers no right to remain silent, no right to an open trial, no right against self-incrimination, no credible appeals system, and no prohibition of double jeopardy. Some defendants do not even rate the formality of a Chinese trial; many verdicts and sentences are handed out administratively. The Communist dictatorship lists 65 capital offenses, including economic and political crimes. Among the thousands of Chinese executed in 2000 were small-time government officials convicted of "corruption" and a man who had allegedly set a forest fire.[109]

Cable television, conjugal visits, intramural basketball leagues, and weight rooms are not what await criminals outside the United States. Follow Dostoyevsky's logic, and one comes to the unmistakable conclusion that civilization is nonexistent in many parts of the world.

ECONOMIC LIBERTY

JUST AS FOREIGN governments are generally more contemptuous of unfettered expression, political liberty, and freedom of conscience, they seek control over the economic sphere as well. Compared to the United States, the average country boasts more government ownership of key industries, higher taxes, greater impediments to investment, more restrictive tariffs, a more freewheeling inflationary policy, state dictation of prices, a higher threat of expropriation, more burdensome and less transparent regulations, and weaker protections for intellectual property, such as inventions, songs, and literature.[110] Freedom is the first casualty of these unwise policies. Prosperity is the second.

At the extremes are the five remaining Communist dictatorships as well as countries like Burma, Rwanda, and Mozambique, which forbid private ownership of land.[111] A milder yet nonetheless still harmful version of Marxism persists elsewhere. State-mandated pricing of major consumer goods, long considered in the United States to be a relic of failed socialist economics, continues in a large number of nations.[112] Another of Marx's tenets—the state controlling the means of production—directs the policies of most non-Western nations, where state ownership of key industries continues unabated more than a decade after the fall of the Berlin Wall. For instance, the dominant banker is the state in Angola, Azerbaijan, Bangladesh, Bosnia-Herzegovina, Burma, China, Costa Rica, Cuba, Egypt, Ethiopia, India, Iran, Iraq, Kazakhstan, Laos, Libya, Nepal, North Korea, Qatar, the Republic of Congo, Russia, Sri Lanka, Syria, Tajikistan, Togo, Tunisia, Turkmenistan, Ukraine, Uruguay, Uzbekistan, Vietnam, and Yugoslavia.[113] Other industries, such as the media and oil, are nationalized in much of the world as well.

Private property continues to be threatened by envious government officials. Embracing the legacy of its fallen overlord, the former Soviet province of Belarus recently passed a law giving its leader broad powers to nationalize private property. Ostensibly, the law targets enemies of the country.[114] In practice, however, such laws have been traditionally used to punish political opponents or legalize theft from the wealthy. Ideology and class are just two motivating factors behind expropriation. Bangladesh's Enemy Property Act of 1976 ordains non-Muslims as enemies of the state, allowing the government to confiscate their land. Hindus, whose portion of the population has dropped from 28% to 12% in recent decades, claim that 60% of their property has been seized by the Muslim government since the passage of the law.[115] The "enemies of the state" in Zimbabwe, according to President Robert Mugabe, are white people. The government and veterans awarded blanket immunity by Mugabe have conducted a race-based campaign of land expropriation against the white minority. Thousands of white-owned farms have been seized and scores of white farmers killed in the racist land grab. After a 48-year-old farmer who had vowed to keep his farm was killed by shotgun blasts to the head and back, the aging president declared that the stubborn murder victim "had it coming."[116] If the wealth one works hard to accumulate will be eventually confiscated by the government on some pretext (race, religion, class, ideology, etc.), what is the point of pursuing wealth? The economies of countries that pursue property nationalization schemes invariably suffer—just as the once thriving Zimbabwean economy is suffering now. Zimbabwe's campaign of state-sponsored theft is particularly frustrating in that expropriation has been tried over and over again in neighboring countries with horrendous results. In the early 1970s, Uganda's target was Indians rather than whites. The assets of Asians—including those who were citizens—were seized, and they were forcibly deported from the country. The Asian population dropped from 96,000 in 1968 to a mere 1,000 five years later. The economic quick fix transferred Asian wealth to the African government but in the long run removed the Asians' productivity from the Ugandan economy. More than a generation later, the Ugandan economy has yet to fully recover.[117] How long will the people of Zimbabwe have to suffer because of their leader's shortsighted greed? Chasing the wealth producers out of a country will always hurt that country.

The *Index of Economic Freedom*, published annually by the Heritage Foundation and the *Wall Street Journal*, gauges economic liberty in more than 150 nations. With few exceptions, the countries judged to be the most economically free were also the countries with the most wealth. Conversely, the countries with the most intrusive governments tended to be the poorest.[118] It is reasonable to conclude that it is not luck that unleashes America's prosperity but rather its free-market policies.

The aversion to market-based solutions by socialist governments, we are told, is sparked by a compassion for workers. How one helps workers by robbing them of the fruits of their labor is left unexplained by partisans of government-based economic solutions. Equally vexing for socialists are the many socialist governments that ban unions, collective bargaining, and strikes. Workers' strikes, for instance, are illegal in Saudi Arabia, Equatorial Guinea, Sudan, Egypt, China, North Korea, Cuba, Iraq, Libya, Oman, the United Arab Emirates, Bhutan, and numerous other nations.[119] Labor activists attempting to organize workers in the People's Republic of China are routinely jailed. Occasionally, they are committed to psychiatric wards. In December 1999, for instance, Xue Jifeng was committed against his will to a mental hospital after he attempted to unionize workers who had been victimized by a financial scheme. A year later, Chinese officials institutionalized and drugged labor activist Cao Maobing. He Chaohui, Yue Tiangxiang, and Zhang

Shangguang were among dozens of labor activists who are serving prison sentences for their work. Others simply disappeared.[120] Clearly, it is not just the freedom of wealthy capitalists that socialism threatens.

While governments monopolize cash-rich industries, lay claim to the produce of labor, and pursue other tired Marxist policies, an even more ancient and pernicious scheme endures: slavery. Slavery haunts the 21st-century world, not just as a dark memory of a crueler age but as a living nightmare for thousands of presently enslaved Africans. One might think that this injustice would provide an outlet for the many activists in Western countries in search of a cause. It has not. The tragic drama of present-day slavery is uninteresting to them. Its villains— slaveholding blacks and Saharan Muslims—are not straight out of central casting as American whites are. Its African setting, too, does not fit the story they wish to tell. The script contradicts their notion of slavery as a uniquely American institution practiced by whites against blacks. In short, it is politically inconvenient.

According to the U.S. State Department's *Country Reports on Human Rights Practices for 2000*, "There continued to be credible reports that government or government-associated forces took children as slaves" in Sudan. "Abductees are subjected to torture and rape, and at times, are killed. These practices have a pronounced racial aspect, as the victims are exclusively black southerners and members of indigenous tribes of the Nuba Mountains."[121] Mauritania has abolished slavery three times, most recently in 1980, yet the slave trade continues in some parts of the country.[122] Vestiges of slavery can be found in Cameroon, Ghana, and Mali as well.[123]

The common denominator among most foreign nations is the debasing of the individual, of which slavery is the most extreme example. Outright slavery, thankfully, is a rarity in the 21st-century world. Occurring quite frequently are small transfers of liberty from the individual to the state that ultimately result in a near total loss of one's freedom. The state becomes the master and the individual its slave. In places such as North Korea, the world's largest concentration camp, this analogy to slavery is certainly valid. Elsewhere, the state's encroachment on individual liberties, although intrusive, does not sink to the level of a slave system. The incentive to work hard, create, or invent, however, is nonexistent when either the government or the slave master gets the reward instead of the individual. This is why oppressive systems, no matter the degree of intrusion, always hamper the creation of wealth. As freedom erodes, prosperity vanishes.

Is America's free-market economy merely different from state-directed economies, or is it better? The answer is in the results. The U.S. economy is the largest in the world. Our gross domestic product (GDP) is nearly twice as large as that of our nearest rival, Japan.[124] The disparity in wealth between the United States and the rest of the world stems from the same cause that makes South Koreans wealthier than North Koreans, Cubans in Miami wealthier than Cubans in Havana, and the inhabitants of Taiwan wealthier than their fellow countrymen in mainland China. It is our freedom that unleashes prosperity just as sure as it is socialism and government interference that create poverty elsewhere in the world.

CONCLUSION

THE PRECEDING SECTIONS have closely examined rarely discussed practices, traditions, and policies found outside our culture. Some of the blemishes of the non-Western world are too obvious for even the most ardent multiculturalist to conceal. While discussions of contemporary chattel slavery or "honor" killings normally occur only below the surface, everyone seems to recognize that nonwesterners are generally more likely to be poor, illiterate, engulfed in war, and prone to outbreaks of disease than their present-day counterparts in the West. We have purposely avoided discussing these drawbacks until this point because they appear to be uncontested. These inadequacies, however, deserve a brief mention.

Most human beings suffer through terrible poverty. There are more than 65 countries with per capita GDPs of less than $1,000. Europe and North America contain only a handful of these nations. The GDP in 43 of these nations is less than $500 per person.[125] War cheapens the lives of too many outside the West. Brutal civil wars that have collectively killed millions of human beings continue in Sudan, Afghanistan, the Democratic Republic of Congo, Algeria, and numerous other hot spots. The educational opportunities open to Americans rarely are open to others. As the earlier statistics on literacy demonstrated, the literacy gender gap is a minor problem compared to the overall tragedy of worldwide illiteracy. Diseases that are rare or nonexistent in America inflict a heavy toll on the Third World. Malaria, for instance, which has been completely eradicated in America, takes the lives of 50,000 Southeast Asians and 1,000,000 Africans annually. The 15,000 AIDS-related deaths that we see in the United States on an annual basis horrify Americans. How, then, do sub-Saharan Africans cope with a syndrome that now leads to the deaths of nearly 2,500,000 Africans annually?[126] Expectedly, people live shorter lives outside the West. The World Health Organization estimates that the average amount of time a person can expect to stay healthy is less than 45 years in 36 countries—all in Africa and Asia. The average American can expect 67 years of good health.[127] The 21st century's Four Horsemen of poverty, war, illiteracy, and disease ride roughshod everywhere—everywhere but in the West.

When we study other cultures, we learn. Primarily, we learn about ourselves. Outside our cultural boundaries, we find people who can't speak freely, elect their own leaders, or join unions. We can. Life for a significant portion of humanity includes female genital mutilation, conversion by the sword, or forced abortions. These practices are nonexistent in America. Leave America's neighborhood, and one encounters women forced to wear masks, trial by ordeal, slavery, and judicial amputation. America is not just different by eschewing these practices. It is better.

Cynics point out that America frequently fails to live up to its lofty ideals. Realists might be wise to respond that this is the result of America actually having high-minded ideals. How would Saudi Arabia violate its ideals? By permitting women to drive or allowing Christians to read the Bible openly? Compare the United States to its ideals, and it will always come up short. Compare America to places that actually exist in the world, and the United States looks rather exemplary. Ironically, multiculturalists, like the protestors at Stanford University, contend that it is our culture that needs to be changed. Attempts to alter the destructive habits of non-Western people, on the other hand, are denounced as cultural imperialism.

Non-Western societies are presented to us not as they are but as Western intellectuals want them to be. It is political expediency and not the truth that motivates the Left's rosy portrayal of the Third World. Frustrated and angry that our culture has rejected their prescriptions for heaven on Earth, intellectuals scour the globe for societies that vindicate their worldview. Like all ideologically blinded searchers, they find what they are looking for. In doing so, they report to simultaneously (1) vindicate their own beliefs by crediting them with producing the ideal societies they present and (2) discredit the West by unfavorably juxtaposing it with the utopia surrounding it. Their caricature of a progressive civilization outside our own stands in sharp contrast to the grim reality of life in the Third World. That the Third World's reality is especially grim for women, minorities, the poor, and other groups that the Left accuses America of waging war on is particularly damning to the credibility of anti-American intellectuals.

A popular perception fostered by elites regards the traditions unique to the West—democracy, freedom, the rule of law, individual rights, religious tolerance—as not unique but universal cross-culturally. Additionally, they insist that there are principles peculiar to civilizations outside our own—matriarch-led societies, sound environmental stewardship, pacifism, economic equality, racial sensitivity—that we would be better off learning from. The premises of these dual contentions are as dangerous as they are untrue. Freedom and democracy are virtually unknown in foreign cultures. War, racism, patriarchy, ecological pollution, and inequality are in fact more common outside Western civilization than inside it.

Theorist Samuel Huntington observes, "Multiculturalism at home threatens the United States and the West; universalism abroad threatens the West and the world. Both deny the uniqueness of Western culture. The global monoculturalists want to make the world like America. The domestic multiculturalists want to make America like the world."[128]

As much as some would like to try, we are virtually powerless to reshape the world in our image. The West's cultural im-

perialism helped rid the world of suttee on the Indian subconti-
nent, cannibalism among the Aztecs, and the veil for some
North Africans, but it failed to erase a thousand other practices
undeserving of humanity's tolerance. In addition, the few gains
that were made came at a terrible price. The toll in human lives
for both the imperial power and those under its dominion was
simply too great to be offset by these minimal advances. If war
and imperialism have but a mixed record in compelling the
vanquished to abandon maladaptive ways of life and adopt
more enlightened ones, there can be little doubt that the idea
that our mere example and moral persuasion will bring about
change in regressive countries is deeply flawed. Just as our own
institutions took thousands of years to develop, the institutions
of other cultures did not turn up overnight. African female genital mutilation, the Hindu caste system, and the Arab world's
enthusiasm for polygamy all pre-date Christianity. What took
millennia to develop will not disappear in one generation.
Doubters may apply their logic to our own civilization. Could
the republican values that began in the Athenian Assembly,
progressed with the Magna Carta, and evolved further with the
Declaration of Independence be universally abandoned in a few
short years? Deeply ingrained practices are difficult to uproot.

We may not be able to change the world. There is something far more important that is within our power to do. We
can preserve our own culture here in America. As this chapter
has shown, the traditions and governments of many foreign nations deserve to expire. Our ability to expedite their demise is
limited. As the following chapter will demonstrate, ours is a nation worth defending. Our ability to strengthen our civilization
is limitless.

CHAPTER 6

AMERICA'S TRUE LEGACY

THE ROMANS "bled us white, the bastards," John Cleese's character "Reg" proclaims in the 1979 Monty Python cult classic *Life of Brian*. "They've taken everything we've owned. And not just from us, from our fathers, and our fathers' fathers." Not to be outdone, a fellow member of the People's Front of Judea, played by Eric Idle, enthusiastically chimes in: "And from our fathers' fathers' fathers. . . . And from our fathers' fathers' fathers' fathers." Restoring order, Cleese asks his Biblical-era followers, "And what have they ever given us in return?"

After a pause, a member of the People's Front of Judea answers Cleese's rhetorical question: "The aqueduct." "Oh yeah, yeah, they did give us that," Cleese quietly acknowledges. "And the sanitation," another mentions. Soon the rank and file of the People's Front of Judea erupt with a series of advances bestowed upon them by the Romans: "the roads," "irrigation," "medicine," "education," "the wine," "public baths." Eric Idle's character notes, "And it's safe to walk in the streets at night now, Reg." Francis, played by Michael Palin, responds, "Yeah, they certainly know how to keep order. Let's face it, they're the only ones who could in a place like this."

Exasperated, Cleese asks, "Alright, but apart from the sanitation, the medicine, education, wine, public order, irrigation, roads, the fresh water system, and public health, what have the Romans ever done for us?"[1]

America's haters face many of the same obstacles encountered by Monty Python's cartoonish fanatics. How does one make something look bad that is responsible for so much good? Reconciling anti-Americanism with the reality that surrounds us is an unenviable task. Despite American responsibility for so much of what we value in the world, knee-jerk condemnations of the United States continue unabated.

Sounding eerily similar to John Cleese's Reg, American al-Qaeda enlistee John Walker Lindh e-mailed his mother in February 2000: "I really don't know what your big attachment to America is all about. What has America ever done for anybody?"[2]

The question reveals more about Lindh than it does about America. No one would bitterly ask, for instance, what has Mongolia ever done for anybody. Only countries that have actually bettered our lot are the subject of such questions. Lindh's query is a tacit acknowledgment that he knows America has done quite a bit, only he is bothered by this because it conflicts with his deeply felt convictions. Thus, he conjures up such a question, the premise of which belies what he knows to be true.

Lindh, of course, is not the only one asking such questions these days. His disdain echoes the sentiments of countless alienated Americans. The ridiculous premise of his rhetorical question does not absolve patriotic Americans from the responsibility of answering it. So, what *has* America ever done for anybody?

ANSWERING JOHN WALKER LINDH

ON THE BALANCE sheet of history, the United States of America is very much in the black. No country has enriched humanity in so many diverse ways. Like an observer standing too close to a painting to see the big picture amidst all the dots,

Americans are often the first to overlook their country's contributions to a better world.

The quality of life for nearly all six billion people on the planet would be unimaginably worse if not for the ingenuity of the American mind. Thomas Edison gave the world electric light, motion pictures, the phonograph, the alkaline storage battery, the mimeograph machine, and thousands of other inventions that enhance the lives of just about every living person.[3] New Yorker Willis Haviland Carrier invented modern air-conditioning.[4] The DuPont Company introduced us to synthetic rubber.[5] Immigrant Alexander Graham Bell's telephone revolutionized the way we communicate.[6] Al Gore may not have invented the Internet, but his fellow countrymen working for the Department of Defense did.[7] The television, the laser, the video cassette recorder, nylon, the computer, the supercomputer, and the personal computer were all spawned by Americans.[8] When America creates, all humanity benefits.

Great courage and daring have put Americans at the forefront of exploration. From Charles Lindbergh's triumphant touchdown on the outskirts of Paris, to William Peary and Matthew Henson's perilous trek to the North Pole, to Chuck Yeager's cracking of the speed of sound, to Neil Armstrong's giant leap for mankind, Americans have stretched the boundaries of human accomplishment. The fearlessness of American adventurers has made the impossible possible. The imagination of American scientists has likewise made the unknown known. Discoveries as varied as Pluto, DNA, atomic energy, and the mapping of the human genome are American achievements.[9]

The world is entertained, for better or worse, by movies, music, sports, and television shows made in the United States. America is the birthplace of jazz, country, the blues, rock and roll, and rap. Homegrown sports such as football, basketball, baseball, skateboarding, and surfing are wildly popular outside the United States. The world's most popular movies and television shows are produced in Hollywood. Critics may lament the low-brow content of much of American entertainment, but they cannot deny its popularity. People who are free to choose what they listen to or watch choose to be entertained by Americans.

Americans have successfully undertaken amazing feats of engineering and construction that have dramatically changed our world. The United States boasted the world's first, and for many years the world's largest, skyscrapers. This revolutionary practice of building vertically instead of horizontally forever altered cities worldwide. Two miles from the Empire State Building, the Brooklyn Bridge sits atop the East River. The celebrated span did so much more than merely connect Brooklyn and Manhattan. By pioneering the use of steel wires, John A. Roebling, the bridge's engineer, extended the bridge until it was twice the length of any existing suspension bridge. Roebling, who was killed during construction, and his son and successor, Washington Roebling, who was paralyzed from the bends during construction, paved the way for all the massive suspension bridges we see today. In the early years of the 20th century, American brainpower joined two oceans. The Panama Canal shortened shipping and travel routes by 7,000 miles. The passage from the Atlantic to the Pacific stands as arguably the most awesome engineering marvel ever. Shortly after the completion of the canal, America embarked on a feat within its own borders nearly as remarkable. The 70-story-high, quarter-mile-wide Hoover Dam, twice as large as any dam that had previously been built, harnessed the power that carved the Grand Canyon. The newly created 115-mile-long Lake Mead supplied water (enough for 5,000 gallons for every human being) to the parched inhabitants of an arid West. The tamed fury of the Colorado River provided clean energy for millions of people. A few decades later, the federal government launched the interstate highway system. In the spirit of the 19th century's transcontinental railroads, the 43,000 miles of highway led to a transportation revolution.[10] Today, America is the leading player in the construction of an international space station. One can only dream of the astonishing projects the future holds.

Unlike the dreaded Romans in *Life of Brian*, America has used its unmatched military power to liberate the oppressed rather than to claim dominion over others. America's armed forces created a nation based on liberty, freed the slaves, helped defeat the Nazis, transformed imperial Japan into a modern republic, and tore down the Iron Curtain without firing a shot. For six decades, we have been the preeminent military power on the globe. A rational look at history, as well as the contemporary world, finds much to be grateful for in America's dominance. If America had lost World War II, the Korean War, the Cold War, or the Persian Gulf War, would the world be better or worse? The alternatives to American hegemony are scary. What country would use the power we possess in a more enlightened manner? China? Iran? France? From ancient Rome to the British Empire, powerful countries have traditionally used their might to claim dominion over others. America charts a different course. Despite 60 years of military superiority, our territory has not expanded even by an inch. That the most powerful country in the world is content to rule only itself is truly a novelty in the annals of history. Our armies march not for empire, conquest, or colonies but in defense of liberty—even when the liberty we are defending is not our own.

America's military power is surpassed only by its economic power. Our gross domestic product (GDP) hovers near the $10 trillion mark. The combined GDP of our three closest economic rivals—Japan, Germany, and the United Kingdom—barely exceeds our nation's wealth.[11] In most countries, our "poor" would be considered quite rich. The republic's wealth did not occur by accident. The rule of law, patent and copyright protection, and a restrained government are a few of the traditions that accelerated the nation's prosperity. Elsewhere, individual success results in reward for the state. Thus, the incentive to pursue success is weak. Here, people receive the reward for their own labor and creativity. Therefore, the pursuit of success is widespread. America generates the products much of humanity buys, the food they eat, and the jobs in which they work. Take this one country out of the economic equation, and the world's misery would increase exponentially. We are the sun around which the world economy revolves.

With our great wealth comes great generosity. In 2000, Americans gave more than $200 billion to charity. As a percentage of GDP, what we give exceeds the amount donated in other industrialized nations. In absolute terms, the amount Americans give to charity dwarfs the dollar amounts donated in other nations.[12] In addition to the vast amounts we voluntarily give, our government doles out massive amounts of our money to foreign nations. Our latest foreign appropriations budget, which details only two-thirds of what our government spends on projects outside the United States, allots $15 billion to other countries and international institutions. Israel gets $3 billion, Egypt $2 billion, and Pakistan $1 billion. The World Bank received more than $1 billion. Nearly $500 million went to the global fight against AIDS. Hundreds of millions target tuberculosis, malaria, and polio.[13] Not included in recent foreign operations budgets are the billions diverted from the Department of Defense budget to peacekeeping, the $18 billion, multiyear allotment to the International Monetary Fund in 1999, and additional billions of debt forgiveness to impoverished countries.[14] Americans make up less than 5% of the world's population yet fund 25% of the budget of the United Nations.[15] From the Marshall Plan to relief aid for survivors of Hurricane Mitch, Americans are the first to bail out the rest of the world. Torched American flags and demands for more money are frequently the "thank-you" we receive.

For the emigrant seeking to escape oppression or find a better life, America continues to be the place to go. No country has opened its arms to the immigrant as America has. We now take in more newcomers than we did at any point in our history, including the years between 1820 and 1930, when we absorbed 60% of the world's immigrants.[16] Poles, Egyptians, Koreans, and Sri Lankans, for example, can come to this country and become Americans. An American reversing the immigrant's path would be laughed at in his adopted homeland if he referred to himself as a Pole, Egyptian, Korean, or Sri Lankan. America separates itself from almost every country on the face of the earth by basing itself on an idea—freedom—and not a nationality or a religion. What Pedro Martinez, Louis B. Mayer, and Andrew Carnegie could not accomplish in the land of their birth, they could here. The world is better for them. Had they stayed at home and not come to this country, their positive impact on the world would have been negated. Only in America could their talents have been utilized to the maximum effect.

The American founding ushered in an age of self-government that continues to this day. Our Founding Fathers were quite aware of the stakes in their bold venture in liberty. Alexander Hamilton realized in *Federalist* 1, "It has been frequently remarked that it seems to have been reserved to the people of this country, by their conduct and example, to decide the important question, whether societies of men are really capable or not of establishing good government from reflection and choice, or whether they are forever destined to depend for their political constitutions on accident and force."[17] The founders' wisdom ensured that a government of "reflection and choice" triumphed not just in America but in other nations worthy of such an endeavor. The ideals of the American founding became contagious. Our example served to topple regimes far from our shores. Even in our present age, democratic symbolism is synonymous with American symbolism. In Tiananmen Square, activists hoisted a crude replica of the Statue of Liberty; elsewhere, pro-democracy writers invoke the words of the Declaration of Independence. America is responsible for setting the trend of self-government in motion. This is certainly one of the greatest bequests America gave to the world.

When a cure for AIDS is found, what country will its discoverers hail from? When modern medicine is able to heal all cancer victims, which country's scientists will pioneer the advancement? When the aged are rescued from Alzheimer's disease, what nation are their saviors likely to call home? If past performance is any guide for the future, Americans will likely discover cures or vaccines for at least one of these diseases, if not all three.

Prior to the 1950s, polio afflicted millions of people worldwide, including America's longest-serving president. The outbreak of 1916 alone left 27,000 Americans disabled and 9,000 dead. Today, only a scant number of westerners contract the disease every decade. The world has Jonas Salk to thank for producing the first vaccine against the crippling malady.[18] The story of polio's eradication is a story that thankfully repeats it-

self in the history of U.S. medical science. Tuberculosis similarly laid waste to massive portions of humanity. Like polio,
the disease has been tamed in the West and in any other part of
the world where the populace makes a concerted effort to
eradicate it. An immigrant to the United States won the Nobel
Prize for developing the first antibiotic to successfully treat the
disease.[19] Americans discovered the vaccines for pneumonia,
hepatitis B, and yellow fever.[20] We developed the successful
treatment for gout and discovered the preventative measures
used against goiter.[21] American scientists pioneered the use of
modern chemotherapy.[22] Americans invented the MRI (medical resonance imaging), the pacemaker, and the CAT (com-
puted axial tomography) scan.[23] The first successful implant of
an artificial heart, as well as the first kidney transplant, took
place in the United States.[24] So dominant is the United States
in the field of medicine that between 1943 and 2002, Americans
won the Nobel Prize outright or held a share in the award 45
out of 60 years.[25]

Life expectancy has risen dramatically around the world
over the course of the past century. More than any other nation, the United States deserves the credit for this. It is no exaggeration to credit American medical advances with saving
hundreds of millions of lives.

Alright, but apart from the telephone; the Internet; the
computer; the television; air-conditioning; the laser; serving as
a place of refuge for immigrants; vaccines for polio, tuberculosis, hepatitis B, pneumonia, and yellow fever; generous allot-
ments of foreign aid; nearly all popular entertainment;
basketball; baseball; surfing; football; the lives of its servicemen
defending the freedoms of non-Americans; the example of self-
government; economic prosperity; a more enlightened world

order; the Panama Canal; the discovery of DNA; and other medical, scientific, and technological advances, what has America ever done for anyone?

America has its own People's Front of Judea. They're called the Left. Unlike Monty Python's fictional extremists, America's reflexive critics stubbornly refuse to concede the great contributions our country has made for the betterment of humanity. Instead, they are monomaniacally transfixed on the negative.

"The American flag is nothing but a symbol of hate and should be used for toilet paper for all I care," remarked a speaker at a Brown University rally following September 11.[26] "We should have read the books and understood / That America is no damn good," rapper Sister Souljah crudely rhymed.[27] "America is a nation of niggers," former congressman Ron Dellums once pronounced. "If you are black, you're a nigger. If you are an amputee, you're a nigger. Blind people, women, students, the handicapped, radical environmentalists, poor whites, those too far to the left are all niggers."[28] A group of Reagan-era flag burners chanted, "America, the red, white and blue, we spit on you."[29]

In the face of what we know about America, the Left's tired critique seems the product more of a pathological condition than of rational thinking. It deserves to be greeted in the same manner as Monty Python's People's Front of Judea skit—with laughter.

One can debate, for instance, whether America's generous military, aid, immigration, and foreign policies have been good for America. To hold that they harm the rest of mankind is preposterous. The Left's willful ignorance of this country's medical, technological, engineering, and scientific advances similarly perplexes. "Americans need to face the truth about themselves,"

Jeane Kirkpatrick once remarked, "no matter how pleasant it is."[30]

ACKNOWLEDGED SHORTCOMINGS

"HE IS A lover of his country," Frederick Douglass observed, "who rebukes and does not excuse its sins."[31] Let no one be deluded by America's wonderful achievements to conclude that the nation is without stain. Nor should we confuse the critic who seeks to cure some great national ailment with the unthinking ideologue who comes to his positions solely by determining what opposes America's interests.

America's shortcomings are many. Rampant drug use, crime, and sexual promiscuity plague society. Compared to other industrialized societies, America is quite violent, boasting some 20,000 murders annually. Fueling such problems is the decline of the American family. Divorce is said to affect nearly half of all marriages. Almost a third of babies come into the world without a father present in the home. Another third of all children conceived are killed in the womb.[32]

Other flaws manifest themselves with more subtlety. Despite producing many great military, political, and business leaders, America has conspicuously produced no Shakespeare or Rembrandt. Foreigners decry our pop culture for exporting sexually degrading, violent, and decadent movies, music, and television shows—and they are right. Our cultural contributions are more Madonna than Mozart, more Danielle Steele than Cervantes. Strip malls, vast concrete pastures, and neon billboards pollute the natural beauty of the land. The capitalist culture that produces great riches leaves too little time for family, community, and leisure. Until September 11, society seemed to lionize the famous rather than the virtuous. Clearly, we still have a way to go.

Pointing out such drawbacks hardly impugns one's patriotism, although ignoring them might. Political leaders, writers, artists, and others often attempt to highlight our problems in the hopes of bettering the nation. Most of these critiques fall into one of two camps: liberal or conservative.

"Liberal," the astute reader understands, is not synonymous with leftist. Noam Chomsky and Dick Gephardt do not occupy the same space on the ideological spectrum. Differences concern not just temperament but ideology. Love of country inspires the liberal's program for America. Leftists, on the other hand, generally view "Amerika" as so inherently corrupt as to be beyond repair.

Modern liberalism, its opponents are wont to point out, is merely a collection of unrelated special interests. At first glance, this may seem accurate. Environmentalists, gun control advocates, supporters of racial preferences, homosexuals, abortion proponents, and anti–death penalty activists promote a diverse set of interests. On further inspection, however, one does find a common thread throughout much of modern liberalism.

The liberal critique generally focuses on issues involving inequality. "No one deserves his greater natural capacity nor merits a favorable starting place in society," philosopher John Rawls opines. "The basic structure can be arranged so that these contingencies work for the good of the least fortunate."[33] Liberals lower on the intellectual food chain than the brilliant professor more or less devour the ideas inherent in Rawls's theory of justice. Lamenting tens of millions of Americans without medical insurance, Hillary Clinton's ambitious health care plan sought in vain to transfer resources from the well-off to the uninsured through a universal government program. Democratic officeholders generally view the tax code as a redistribution mechanism to correct the gulf between the haves and the have-nots. Gay rights, hate crimes legislation, and racial preferences similarly use the law to aid groups perceived to be at a disadvantage in our society.

The conservative critique centers for the most part on moral decline. In *Slouching Towards Gomorrah*, Judge Robert Bork bemoans, "there are aspects of almost every branch of our culture that are worse than ever before and ... the rot is spreading."[34] Vice President Dan Quayle waged a lonely crusade for family values. In his famous speech at 1992's Republican National Convention, Pat Buchanan declared "a cultural war as critical to the kind of nation we shall be as the Cold War itself, for this war is for the soul of America."[35] Each of these cultural critics decries the recent and dramatic rise in abortion, promiscuous sexuality, single-parent families, and vulgar popular entertainment. Recent conservative reform attempts include abolishing the tax code's marriage penalty, boycotts of Disney and Time Warner over offensive entertainment, faith-based charities as a replacement for government welfare programs, legislation outlawing partial-birth abortions, the Defense of Marriage Act, restoring prayer in schools, and state campaigns against no-fault divorce.

Since the moral decline has been accelerated by questionable court decisions, the conservative concern for immorality interlocks with its critique of the judiciary. Under the liberal reading of the Constitution, the Second and Tenth Amendments disappear; the Fourth Amendment suddenly includes a right to "privacy" protecting sodomy, abortion, and assisted suicide; the First Amendment's prohibition of congressional legislation establishing a religion morphs into a ban on all religious activity within any institution remotely connected to any government, including state and local; and noncommercial activities that the court seeks to regulate now become interstate commerce. Liberal judges ignore what the Constitution says and instead rely on what they wish it says. Thus, an appointed bench arrogates to itself the legislative function from democratically elected representatives. By claiming an infinite malleability for the Constitution, the courts in fact disregard the legal document. The judicial usurpation of lawmaking and the courts' disregard for the Constitution have led serious conservatives to ponder "whether we have reached the point where conscientious citizens can no longer give moral assent to the existing regime."[36]

These are strong words, but even their authors want a better America, not no America. So at least in this sense, even many of the most extreme liberal and conservative critiques of the United States fall within the bounds of mainstream discourse. The proponents of such change want reform, not revolution. Thus, they seek not to destroy America but to elevate it. Whether any of the policies offered by liberal and conservative critics will actually improve the nation is open to debate. What is important for the purposes of this book is recognizing the distinction between legitimate criticism of America and knee-jerk anti-Americanism. One aims to improve the nation; the other hopes for its demise.

Only weaklings suffer no criticism, an old adage asserts. America's strength enables it to withstand scrutiny. Indeed, it is often criticism that enables a nation to grow stronger. Yet just as domestic critics have the freedom to level verbal barrages at their country, citizens have the right—some would say the responsibility—to respond when such charges are unfounded. Only a sophist defends the cynic's right to condemn and then cries censorship when the naysayer's arguments are themselves critiqued. Specious arguments sometimes require no response to invalidate them. The vociferousness with which the Left alleges that the land of the free is a big sham, for instance, serves as its own refutation.

Tolerating dissent stands as one of America's longest and proudest traditions. During his presidency, Thomas Jefferson received a foreign visitor who expressed alarm over a scathing newspaper article libeling the esteemed Virginian. Picking the slanderous article up from the third president's desk, the foreigner asked, "Why do you not hang the man?" "Put the paper in your pocket," an amused Jefferson replied, "and on your return to your country, if any one doubts the freedom of our press, show it to him, and tell him where you found it."[37]

Just as Jefferson's aloofness to a dirt-dealer's slander undermined the wordsmith's biased appraisal, America's official policy of tolerance toward denunciations of it often disproves the charges of those sniping at it.

CONCEIVED IN LIBERTY

"THE AMERICANS OF the United States must inevitably become one of the greatest nations in the world," Tocqueville predicted 170 years ago.[38] Time has vindicated the French traveler's prophecy.

But what accounts for America's greatness? Why do we excel while so many others struggle? The wisdom embedded in America's founding separates the United States from all other nations. The Founding Fathers had the benefit of thousands of years of history to base their program on. All of human history had been their laboratory of trial and error. The founders took what worked, discarded what did not, and applied the lessons to the new nation.

The result was something lasting and good. The government the founders put in place has served the public well for more than two centuries. Its longevity is all the more remarkable considering the relatively short existence of our nation. Elsewhere, national constitutions are often ignored, and their life spans are generally fleeting. Thailand's constitution is five years old. Russia will soon celebrate the 10th anniversary of its constitution. Nigeria's constitution dates back to 1999, Colombia's to 1991, South Korea's to 1988, and Spain's to 1978. By contrast, the document crafted by James Madison, John Dickinson, and dozens of other statesmen in the hot Philadelphia summer of 1787 still governs our political affairs more than 200 years later.

The Founding Fathers set us in the right direction—while almost everyone else was traveling in the wrong direction—in four important areas. First, they established political institutions that diffused power, acknowledged basic rights, and implemented self-government. Second, the generation that initiated a tax rebellion against England embraced an economic system that limited state encroachment in the market. Third, religion, released from the stifling grip of the state so that it might spring organically from the people, served as an indispensable aid to liberty (which itself is not enough to make a great society). Finally, the founders embarked on a foreign policy that rebuffed international entanglements and empire in favor of the pursuit of national interest. The common denominator uniting each of the four spheres—political, economic, religious, and foreign—was a desire to restrain the power of government.

The War for Independence gave revolution a good name for once. Unlike the French, Haitian, and Russian Revolutions, the American Revolution did not trade one oppressor for another, more invidious oppressor. It inaugurated something nearly unheard of in the late 18th century and still quite rare today: self-government. Nowhere else on earth in 1787 did so large a portion of a populace have a say in electing their government than in the United States of America.

In the modern mind, terms such as "republic," "democracy," and "self-government" evoke no distinctions. The educated mind of the late 18th century saw things differently. Democracy meant chaos—rule by the mob. Thus, the Constitution instituted safeguards against the tyranny of numerical majorities. These safeguards include the Supreme Court, the electoral college, the Senate, the filibuster, supermajorities for constitutional amendments, a bicameral legislature, and the presidential veto.

The Bill of Rights serves as the most significant check on mob rule. Too jealous of their liberties to have them voted away, the anti-Federalists demanded protections against government encroachments in writing. These inscribed rights included trial by jury; the right to keep and bear arms; freedom of religion, speech, assembly, and the press; and security against uncompensated property seizures. The notion of rights, like that of self-government, remains quite foreign to a large portion of humanity.

Tocqueville observed, "the prominent feature of the administration in the United States is its excessive decentralization."[39] Decentralization was the result of federalism, a system devised largely because of the Founding Fathers' suspicion of power concentrated in the hands of the few. James Madison wrote that the states were each to be "considered as a sovereign body" that was "independent of all others." "In this relation, then, the new Constitution will, if established, be a *federal*, and not a *national* constitution."[40] Federalism ensured that a monopoly of power could never exist. It thus shunned national cookie-cutter approaches to local issues. The founders recognized that one size does not fit all. In a country as geographically immense as the United States, states rather than the nation could more effectively tackle most issues. Therefore, the national government's powers were strictly defined. Defense, coining money, imposing uniform duties, and issuing patents were among the powers granted to the United States. The states retained all that they did not voluntarily give up to the national government. The founders codified this philosophy in the Tenth Amendment, which states, "The powers not delegated to the United States by the Constitution, nor prohibited by it to the states, are reserved to the states respectively, or to the people."[41]

The framers of the Constitution ensured through a system of checks and balances that power unwisely or unjustly used could be blocked. Unenlightened legislation, for instance, could be defeated by either house of Congress, vetoed by the president, or, if unconstitutional, struck down by the Supreme Court. A president pursuing an unauthorized course could be impeached or defunded by Congress; the Supreme Court could strike down his actions. If the executive and the legislative were unhappy with the judiciary, the two branches could seek to amend the Constitution, impeach a justice, or display more thought in selecting future nominees.

Just as federalism is no longer federalism when one body usurps power from another, checks and balances cease to work when one branch of government usurps the functions of another. "The courts must declare the sense of the law; and if they should be disposed to exercise WILL instead of JUDGMENT, the consequence would equally be the substitution of their pleasure to that of the legislative body," Hamilton points out in *Federalist* 78.[42] Along the same lines, he further warns, "No legislative act, therefore, contrary to the Constitution, can be valid. To deny this, would be to affirm, that the deputy is greater than his principal; that the servant is above his master; that the representatives of the people are superior to the people themselves; that men acting by virtue of powers, may do not only what their powers do not authorize, but what they forbid."[43] Our system works, Hamilton seems to say, but only when you play by the rules. Just as a baseball game might become unplayable if umpires demanded at-bats or the home team imposed their interpretation of the rule book, things fall apart when branches of government overstep their defined functions or when judges discard the actual Constitution in favor of a Freudian interpretation of it. As George Wythe, one of the few men both to sign the Declaration of Independence and to serve as a delegate to the Constitutional Convention, put it, "not men but laws should be sovereign."[44]

"The great art of government is not to govern too much," Constitutional Convention delegate Charles Cotesworth Pinckney observed.[45] The South Carolinian's maxim is the embodiment of the second pillar upon which the founders based their new society. It followed that a group that steadfastly guarded religious, political, and press freedoms would also value economic freedom. The proper function of government was to protect liberty, not to infringe on it. A tradition of economic liberty is the second major reason for America's present greatness.

Excessive taxation threatens liberty, the founders acknowledged. British abuses, such as the Stamp Act, sparked George Washington to hold that Parliament had "no more right to put their hands into my pocket without my consent, than I have to put into yours for money."[46] Washington's contemporaries shared his healthy contempt for taxation, which manifested itself in the Constitution's proscription of direct taxes. The constitutional order professed that citizens, through their own consumption, regulated the amount of taxes they paid to the federal government. Not until the Sixteenth Amendment permanently legalized the income tax in 1913 did this change. The framers meshed principles of liberty with utility in their opposition to intrusive taxation. Long before the tax cuts of Calvin Coolidge, John F. Kennedy, and Ronald Reagan enlarged tax revenue, the framers knew that high tax rates paradoxically diminished government coffers. *Federalist* 21 imparts,

> It is a signal advantage of taxes on articles of consumption, that they contain in their own nature a security against excess. They prescribe their own limit; which cannot be exceeded without defeating the end proposed,—that is, an extension of the revenue. When applied to this object, the saying is as just as it is witty, that, "in political arithmetic, two and two do not always make four." If duties are too high, they lessen the consumption; the collection is eluded; and the product to the treasury is not so great as when they are confined within proper and moderate bounds.[47]

With the Constitution limiting the role of the state to a few defined areas, the national government had no pressing need for exorbitant amounts of money. The framers generally exhibited skepticism of government's ability to solve our problems. Jefferson maintained, "the maintenance of the poor, which being merely a matter of charity, cannot be deemed expended in the administration of government."[48] William Patterson worried of an electorate that would vote themselves their neighbors' money, thereby creating "a set of drones or of idle extravagant wretches [who] live upon the earnings of others."[49] Benjamin Franklin remarked, "In my youth I traveled much, and I observed in different countries, that the more public provisions were made for the poor, the less they provided for themselves, and of course became poorer. And, on the contrary, the less was done for them, the more they did for themselves, and became richer."[50]

Equality of condition, the founders recognized, could be achieved only by treating people unequally. This ran counter to the spirit of true equality, which they regarded as equality of opportunity. "Theoretic politicians, who have patronized this species of government [democracy], have erroneously supposed that by reducing mankind to a perfect equality in their political rights, they would, at the same time, be perfectly equalized and assimilated in their possessions, their opinions, and their passions," James Madison asserted.[51] "Inequality," Caleb Strong of Massachusetts believed, "arises from the nature of things, and not from any defect in the form of administration of government. All that the best government can do is prevent that inequality which fraud, oppression, or violence would produce."[52] Clearly, equality of results was not their bag.

"[T]here is no country in the world where the Christian religion retains a greater influence over the souls of men than in America," Tocqueville observed.[53] Even today, America ranks first in churchgoing among First World nations.[54] Religion is an essential component of liberty. Freedom without virtue is useless. Freedom presupposes the freedom to do bad as well as good. In itself, it is insufficient. Liberty refrains from degenerating into chaos only when the people exercising that liberty are morally equipped to make the right choices. The founders understood this.

Religion occupied a central position in the lives of the men and women who made up the founding generation. Of the more than 100 delegates to Virginia's State Constitutional Convention, all were vestrymen but a lonely trio.[55] M. E. Bradford points out that of the 55 delegates to the Constitutional Convention, at least 50 were members of orthodox Christian churches.[56] The signers of the Declaration of Independence, which included preacher John Witherspoon and such Puritans as Roger Sherman and Samuel Adams, were no less pious.

"Of all the dispositions and habits which lead to political prosperity, Religion and morality are indispensable supports," Washington noted. The celebrated general doubted the idea that morality could be achieved independently of religion. "Let it simply be asked," he continued, "where is the security for property, for reputation, for life, if the sense of religious obligation *desert* the oaths, which are the instruments of investigation in Courts of Justice?"[57]

Even the Founding Fathers we least associate with religion believed it necessary for a free society. Franklin proposed that the Constitutional Convention pause in prayer, which others opposed out of a fear of creating the impression that things were going poorly.[58] "Can the liberties of a nation be thought secure," Jefferson asked, "when we have removed their only firm basis, a conviction in the minds of the people that these liberties are of the gift of God?"[59] While Jefferson and Franklin were not exactly 18th-century versions of Pat Robertson, they were not 18th-century forebears of Madalyn Murray O'Hair, either.

With freedom comes responsibility. Religion informs that responsibility. "Thus, while the law permits the Americans to do what they please," Tocqueville observed, "religion prevents them from conceiving, and forbids them to commit, what is rash or unjust."[60] Religion serves order more effectively than all the laws and policemen combined. "Despotism may govern without faith," the Frenchman pointed out, "but liberty cannot."[61]

The fourth pillar holding up the nation the founders constructed is a foreign policy that encouraged our relations with foreigners to involve commerce rather than war. To this end, the Constitution designated the branch of the federal government most representative of the people, rather than a solitary man or a cabal, to decide questions of war. Washington's "Farewell Address" advice to "steer clear of permanent Alliances" best exemplifies the founding generation's thoughts on foreign affairs.

"The Nation, which indulges towards another an habitual hatred, or an habitual fondness, is in some degree a slave," the father of our country pointed out. "It is a slave to its animosity or to its affection, either of which is sufficient to lead it astray from its duty and its interest."[62]

Almost a decade earlier, "Publius" anticipated Washington's counsel.* "Admitting that we ought to try the novel and absurd experiment in politics of tying up the hands of government from offensive war founded upon reasons of the state," *Federalist* 34 hypothesized, "yet certainly we ought not to disable it from guarding the community against the ambition or enmity of other nations."[63] To have peace, the aphorism goes, prepare for war. The men who built America believed this.

---

*"Publius," in this case, was Alexander Hamilton. The fact that he anticipated Washington's words a decade later is not surprising. Washington, after all, selected Hamilton to write his undelivered but tremendously influential "Farewell Address."

They also believed that our peace should be disturbed only when our interests were at stake.

Venture into the world in search of monsters to destroy, and you will find them—in abundance. Allow a solitary ruler's ego to push a whole people into war, and a nation will sacrifice its sons for frivolous undertakings. Interlock your national destiny with the travails of foreign governments, and uncontrollable events rather than elected representatives will determine war and peace. Well schooled in the history of Europe, the founders sought to avoid the senseless wars of the Old World, where covert agreements and kings' egos thrust whole nations into bloody conflicts. A foreign policy based on the capricious whims of a leader, the desire to right every wrong in the world, or the fine print of secret alliances was not fit for a free, independent, and self-governing people.

Men fought and died for the principles handed down to us by the Founding Fathers. When the signers of the Declaration of Independence pledged their lives, fortunes, and sacred honor, they meant it. The wealthy Robert Morris, whose personal funds subsidized the Revolution, found himself in a debtor's prison shortly after the war. The British ransacked Richard Stockton's home and took him prisoner. He died a beggar. South Carolina's Thomas Hayward and Georgia's George Walton were shot in battle and taken prisoner by the redcoats. New York's Francis Lewis experienced the destruction of his home; the British imprisoned his wife for two years without a bed or a change of clothes. After the Crown took over Thomas Nelson's estate, the Virginia militia leader unflinchingly shelled his own home.[64] These men who valiantly affixed their names to the Declaration of Independence sacrificed everything to establish a nation based on truly great principles—self-government, economic liberty, religious freedom, and independence in foreign affairs. Do we honor their self-abnegation today? Do we heed the wise counsel of our Founding Fathers? Do the principles they handed down to us still guide our nation?

Just as America's greatness can be explained largely by the unique principles embedded in its founding, many of this nation's current problems are the direct result of our leaders straying from the path blazed by the Founding Fathers. "We all want progress," C. S. Lewis remarked. "But progress means getting nearer to the place where you want to be. And if you have taken a wrong turning, then to go forward does not get you any nearer. If you're on the wrong road, progress means doing an about-turn and walking back to the right road; and in that case the man who turns back soonest is the most progressive man."[65] As the Egyptians, Romans, and British learned, golden ages do not last forever. If America hopes to hold on to its greatness, it would be wise for Americans to reflect on from where that greatness derives.

"Clearly," writes Stan Evans in *The Theme Is Freedom*, "our freedoms didn't simply happen; they were the result of deliberate precautions and provisos, acts of statecraft which it behooves us to study and remember. If we want to grow orchids instead of weeds, it is well to know what kind of climate, soil, and nurture are congenial to orchids; ignorance of or indifference to these matters will predictably result in failure. Ignorance of or indifference to the safeguards needed for the growth of liberty will issue in a like result, but with effects more baleful to consider."[66]

WHY THE LEFT HATES AMERICA

So WHY DOES the Left hate America? The answer is that America stands as a massive refutation of every pet theory the Left has ever held.

Capitalism is a failed economic system, the Left incessantly pronounces. How, then, do they explain that the most free-market large nation on earth is also the richest? America, their mantra goes, is a racist country. Yet immigrants of color flock to our shores and borders by the millions instead of spending their lives ruled by people of the same hue or ethnicity. Does the Left dismiss these people as masochists for coming here? The United States, they continue, subjugates women. Nowhere in the world, however, is the status of women as high as it is in America and the West. In most important statistical indicators, American women fare dramatically better than American men. The Left condemns Christianity, the dominant religion in America, as intolerant. In America, and practically every other predominantly Christian nation, for that matter, people can practice any religion they want—even ones that are inherently hostile to Christianity. In nations run by men of other faiths, Christianity's tolerance is not reciprocated. What the Left touts in theory the American experience refutes in practice. For people so passionately attached to theory, this is a bitter pill to swallow. Rather than revise their inept theories, the Left lashes out at the nation that disproves them.

Imagine the perfect country. Next to this nation, America is found wanting. The racial prejudice, pollution, economic exploitation, warfare, and greed that are missing from fantasyland are found without difficulty in America. There are limitations to this form of analysis. Countries don't exist in our imaginations. They exist in the world. The world that surrounds America is not particularly idyllic. When we contrast the United States to its surroundings, it is America that begins to resemble an idealized paradise.

Nearly all governments in Africa, the Middle East, and the Orient deny their citizens the right to choose their own leaders.

Foreign cultures subject women to forced abortions, "honor killings," genital mutilation, polygamy, dowry killings, the veil, and other indignities. Zimbabwe conducts an expropriation campaign that targets whites, Sudan sanctions race-based slavery, and Ethiopia runs concentration camps that house its primary ethnic minority. The majority of humanity lives in nations where the private broadcasting of the news is unlawful. Some governments greedily forbid the private ownership of land, monopolize cash-rich industries, and seize massive portions of their citizens' earnings. Numerous Muslim countries mete out judicial amputation, China conducts administrative sentencing, and Liberia condones trial by ordeal. Constitutions commonly feature prohibitions against various forms of speech. A diverse array of nations ban the Bible, various Islamic states punish apostasy with executions, and China subjects people of faith to imprisonment and death.

America is an island of freedom in an unfree world. Americans can say what they want, worship any god they fancy, and associate with any motley crew they care to. We are free to pursue our own wealth, and as a result, we are quite wealthy. We elect our own leaders. This successful venture in self-government sparked many imitators. We are a haven for the oppressed as no other nation is. No country has ever come close to matching America's generosity. America wields its ferocious sword not for territorial aggrandizement but to defend freedom—helping to defeat the two most murderous forces in the history of man, Nazism and Communism. Anywhere on Earth, whenever someone turns on a light, surfs the Internet, watches television, goes to the movies, or talks on the telephone, America receives a tacit endorsement. American doctors and scientists have shielded mankind from tuberculosis, polio, yellow fever, and numerous other debilitating and deathly illnesses. Humans live happier, healthier, and longer lives because of Americans.

The American story is an uplifting narrative. Act 1 begins with men risking everything, including "our Lives, our Fortunes, and our sacred Honor," to forge a new nation conceived in liberty. One thinks of Washington's men surviving the brutal winter at Valley Forge, Nathan Hale's defiance on the gallows, and the homes of numerous signers of the Declaration of Independence sacked by the British. It is a performance that contains great drama. One cannot help but feel moved by Ukrainian immigrant Selman Waksman meeting a little girl saved from death by his cure for tuberculosis, Cubans rafting to the promised land, American GIs liberating Dachau, or Harriet Tubman transforming slaves into freemen along the Underground Railroad. As word spreads about the greatness of her story, America's cast of characters grows larger. Lady Liberty welcomes the newcomers. These newcomers, like Oscar Meyer, John Jacob Astor, and Albert Einstein, repay her warmth by enriching the performance. The American story challenges the imagination: sibling bicycle repairmen in North Carolina emancipating humanity from the oppressive force of gravity, American ingenuity uniting two oceans in Panama, the Wizard of Menlo Park channeling the illuminating power of the sun through electricity, and a people rising to a slain president's challenge by landing a man on the moon. Leading roles abound. The only stage large enough to hold America's great men is the world. Alexander Graham Bell put a telephone in every home, Henry Ford put a car in every driveway, and Bill Gates put a computer in every office. Martin Luther King dreamed of a more racially tolerant world. Ronald Reagan exhorted the Soviets to tear down the Berlin Wall. The American story is filled with action: Union and Confederate soldiers sacrificing all at Gettysburg, Marines planting the flag atop Mt. Suribachi, and New York City firemen knowingly rushing to their deaths in the Twin Towers to save the lives of total strangers.

The story that is America is truly amazing. The greatest part of the American epic is that its most glorious scenes have yet to be acted out.

"To make us love our country," Edmund Burke famously wrote, "our country ought to be lovely."[67] Americans love their country not only because America is their country. Our country is loved because she is lovely.

NOTES

Introduction

1. Quoted in Gorton Carruth and Eugene Ehrlich, ed., *The Giant Book of American Quotations* (New York: Random House, 1988), p. 424.
2. Katha Pollitt, "Put Out No Flags," *The Nation*, October 8, 2001, p. 9.
3. Quoted in Marc Levin, "Bell Hooks Spews Anti-American Tirade in Commencement Speech at Southwestern University in Georgetown, TX," June 7, 2002, www.frontpagemag.com /guestcolumnists2002/levin06-07-02.htm, accessed on June 7, 2002.
4. Lisa Mann, "America Is Not a Nation of Innocents," *Old Gold and Black*, September 13, 2001, p. 10. Jennie Viera, "America Not Blameless," *Colorado Daily*, September 17, 2001, p. 11.
5. James Barron, "Professor 'Sorry' for Pentagon Remark," *Daily Lobo*, September 24, 2001, p. 1.
6. Chris Tisch, "Man Held in Flag Burnings, Break-Ins," *Clearwater Times*, October 20, 2001, p. 1. William Levesque, "Flag-Burning Teen Sentenced to Probation," *Largo Times*, March 27, 2002, p. 1.
7. Daniel Hernandez, "Shouting for Mumia," *Daily Californian*, September 28, 2000, p. 1. Robert Stacey McCain, " 'Cop Killer' Author Says Protesters Strengthen His Message," *Washington Times*, October 2, 2000, p. 3. To listen to my speech, and the mob shouting me down, visit the link on Accuracy in Academia's Web site to the audio of the Berkeley lecture (www.academia .org/audio/d_flynn.html).
8. Benjamin Lowe, "Pro-Affirmative Action Students Hold Protests," *Columbia Spectator*, November 16, 1998, p. 1.

Mia-Margaret Laabs, "Conference Prompts Protest, Debate," *Columbia Spectator*, November 16, 1998, p. 1. "Columbia Censors AIA Conference," *Campus Report*, December 1998, p. 1.

9. For a description of the wild occurrences at the Black Panthers' 35-year anniversary conference, see Dan Flynn, "Black Panthers Hold Reunion at UDC," *Campus Report*, May 2002, p. 1.

10. Dominique Huff, "Angry Students Rally Against College Republicans," *The Signal*, February 19, 2002, p. 1. Chris Chow, "AIA Pamphlets Stolen from College Republicans at Georgia State," *Campus Report*, March 2002, p. 3. See also *Hannity & Colmes*, Fox News Channel, March 4, 2002.

11. The attacks occurred on First Street in Washington, DC, on February 28, 2000. While my attackers escaped arrest for the assaults, close to 200 protestors were arrested that day.

12. Quoted in Carruth and Ehrlich, ed., *The Giant Book of American Quotations*, p. 422.

Chapter 1

1. Peter Kilborn, "Fellow Americans Opening Hearts, Wallets, and Veins," *New York Times*, September 13, 2001, p. 19.

2. Tamar Lewin, "Companies Pledge $100 Million in Relief," *New York Times*, September 15, 2001, p. 13.

3. Michael Janofsky, "People in Need, and the Gift of Blood," *New York Times*, September 13, 2001, p. 19.

4. "The World Is Transfixed by America's Tragedy," *USA Today*, September 12, 2001, p. 13.

5. Cited in "Special Dispatch 275," The Middle East Media Research Institute, September 25, 2001, www.memri.org/sd/SP27501.html, accessed on January 10, 2002.

6. Quoted in Lance Morrow, "Who's More Arrogant?" *Time*, December 10, 2001, p. 122.

7. Quoted in "Special Dispatch 274," The Middle East Media Research Institute, September 21, 2001, www.memri.org/sd/SP27401.html, accessed on January 10, 2002, and "Special Dispatch 281," The Middle East Media Research Institute, October 4, 2001, www.memri.org/sd/SP28101.html, accessed on January 10, 2002.

8. Quoted in Brink Lindsey, "Terrorism's Fellow Travelers," *Cato Policy Report*, November/December 2001, p. 11.

9. Peter O'Neil, "Feminists Anti-U.S. Speech Causes Uproar," *Vancouver Sun*, October 2, 2001, p. 1.

10. Joshua Greene, "Forget the Media and See the Truth," *Daily Athenaeum*, September 13, 2001, p. 4.

11. Christopher Hacker, "'Why' Is the Biggest Question," *Badger Herald*, September 13, 2001, p. 5.

12. David Barsamian, quoted in Jessika Fruchter, "Peace Community Speaks Out Against War," *Colorado Daily*, September 18, 2001, p. 4.

13. Adam S. Kirby, "College Republicans Barred from Holding Memorial Event," *Marquette Tribune*, September 12, 2001, p. 1.

14. "State University Library Bans American Pride Stickers" (Associated Press State and Local Wire), September 18, 2001.

15. Tracey Lomrantz, "Smeaton Calls Removal of Flag a Mistake," *The Brown and White*, September 17, 2001, p. 1.

16. Tony Francetic, "University May Be Infringing on Students' Rights," *Central Michigan Life*, October 10, 2001, p. 1.

17. Kristina Davis, "American Flag Flies in Sahaurto Market Again," September 21, 2001, www.asuwebdevil.com/main.cfm?includ=detail&storyid=98629, accessed on May 2, 2002.

18. Emilie Astell, "Flag Causes Ruckus at Holy Cross," *Worcester Telegram and Gazette*, September 28, 2001, p. B1.

19. Tom Gerety, "A Point Is Made About Free Speech," *Boston Globe*, October 30, 2001, p. 19.

20. Bill Israel, "A Policy of Neglect and Cowardice, a Pay-Off of Death," *Massachusetts Daily Collegian*, September 13, 2001, p. 6.

21. Zander Dryer and Matthew Ferraro, "Where Does America Go from Here?" *Yale Herald*, September 14, 2001, p. 3.

22. Haunani-Kay Trask, quoted in Pat Omandam, "U.S. Bears Sole Blame for September 11, Trask Says," October 18, 2001, www.starbulletin.com/2001/10/18/news/story3.html, accessed on May 2, 2002.

23. Robert Jensen, "U.S. Just as Guilty of Committing Own Violent Acts," *Houston Chronicle*, September 14, 2001, p. 33.

24. Report to author from American University student Benjamin Wetmore, September, 24, 2001. Wetmore attended Kuznick's class.

25. James Barron, "Professor 'Sorry' for Pentagon Remark," *Daily Lobo*, September 24, 2001, p. 1.
26. Peter Beinart, "Talk Show," *New Republic*, October 22, 2001, p. 6.
27. Author interview of Kenneth Hearlson, November 16, 2001; see also William Lobdell, "Teacher's Terrorism Remarks Stir Academic Freedom Debate," *Los Angeles Times*, September 30, 2001, p. 3.
28. Author interview of Bob Dees, November 16, 2001.
29. Author interview of Kenneth Hearlson, November 16, 2001; see also William Lobdell, "Professor at Center of Debate Reinstated," *Los Angeles Times*, December 12, 2001, p. B6.
30. William Lobdell, "Academics and Muslims Await Results of Probe," *Los Angeles Times*, November 26, 2001, p. 3.
31. "Duke University," October 24, 2001, www.thefire.org/issues /terror.php3, accessed on May 1, 2002.
32. "UNC–Wilmington Shames Itself Yet Again" (press release), Foundation for Individual Rights in Education, December 20, 2001 (contact: Thor Halvorson); e-mail exchange printed on the Web site of the Foundation for Individual Rights in Education, www.thefire.org/issues/rosa.php3, accessed on January 10, 2002.
33. Lisa Mann, "America Is Not a Nation of Innocents," *Old Gold and Black*, September 13, 2001, p. 10.
34. Eve Lotter, "A New Movement Emerges Against War, Violence," *Daily Californian*, September 18, 2001, p. 1.
35. Joshua Greene, "Forget the Media and See the Truth," *Daily Athenaeum*, September 13, 2001, p. 4.
36. Kathryn Duke, "American Flag Provokes Frightening Nationalism," *Duke Chronicle*, September 19, 2001, p. 18.
37. Nuno Andrade, "Take a Look in the Mirror, America, and Ask Why," September 14, 2001, www.nyunews.com/getstory.php ?id=20001798, accessed on May 2, 2002.
38. Jennie Viera, "America Not Blameless," *Colorado Daily*, September 17, 2001, p. 11.
39. Author interview of Zewdalem Kebede, October 27, 2001.
40. Jason Williams, "Student: Attack Praised," *Daily Aztec*, October 17, 2001, p. 1.
41. Author interview of Zewdalem Kebede, October 27, 2001.
42. Williams, "Student," p. 1.
43. Ibid.

44. Christopher Chow, "Tufts 'Non-Violence' Activists Attack Patriotic Student," *Campus Report*, December 2001, p. 1.
45. Ibid.
46. Sara Russo, "Hate Crimes Against Muslim Student at Arizona State a Hoax," *Campus Report*, November 2001, p. 7.
47. Monica Alonzo-Dunsmoor, "ASU Assault Called Hate Crime," September 26, 2001, www.arizonarepublic.com/special44/articles/0926hate26.html, accessed on May 2, 2002.
48. Lisa Chiu, "ASU Adds Patrols After Attacks," *Arizona Republic*, September 27, 2001, p. B1. Among other items, the article notes that 48 international students, mostly Middle Easterners, had dropped out since the attacks.
49. Lisa Chiu, "Student May Face Charges in Hoax," October 2, 2001, www.arizonarepublic.com/special44/articles/1002student 02 .html, accessed on May 2, 2002.
50. "ASU Student Charged with False Reporting over Hate Crime Report," October 11, 2001, www.arizonarepublic.com/special44 /articles/1012Indict-ON.html, accessed on May 2, 2002.
51. "Faked Attacks at ASU Deserve Real Punishment," *Arizona Republic*, October 2, 2001, p. B8.
52. "ASU Student Charged with False Reporting of Hate Crime," www.arizonarepublic.com/special44/articles/1012Indict-ON .html, accessed on May 2, 2002.
53. Eric Ostrem, "Crowd Occupies Daily Californian Office over Controversial Cartoon," *Daily Californian*, September 19, 2001, p. 1, and "Crowd Decries Lack of Apology, Daily Cal Web Site Hacked Into," *Daily Californian*, September 20, 2001, p. 1.
54. "End States Who Sponsor Terrorism" (advertisement paid for by the Ayn Rand Institute), *New York Times*, October 2, 2001, p. 20.
55. Cyrus Farivar, "Daily Cals Stolen, Replaced with Protestor Fliers," *Daily Californian*, October 25, 2001, p. 1.
56. Quoted in Brink Lindsey, "Terrorism's Fellow Travelers," *Cato Policy Report*, November/December 2001, p. 1.
57. Dennis Chaptman, "Madison Schools' Pledge Ban Sparks Fury; Hundreds Protest Decision to Allow Only Anthem," *Milwaukee Journal Sentinel*, October 10, 2001, p. 1.
58. "Long May It Wave," *Denver Post*, November 6, 2001, p. B8.
59. Jennifer Mack, "Teacher Accused of Burning Flag in Classroom," September 26, 2001, beta.kpix.com/news/local/20.../Teacher

_Accused_of_Burning_Flag_in_Classroom.htm accessed on September 27, 2001.

60. Michael Park, "As Usual, Berkeley Dances to a Different Drum," October 17, 2001, www.foxnews.com/story/0,2933,36630,00, accessed on November 1, 2001.

61. Quoted in Dave Sommers, "Lethal Lesson," *The Trentonian*, November 16, 2001, p. 1.

62. "Speaking Her Mind Has Won Barbara Lee Thousands in Donations" (Associated Press State and Local Wire), February 3, 2002.

63. Quoted in Stephen Dalton, "It's No Walk in the Park," *Times 2* (*The Times* of London), January 21, 2002, pp. 16–17, and "Director Altman: 'Americans Are Full of It!'" January 22, 2002, www.newsmax.com/archive/print/shtml?a=2002/1/22/91248, accessed on January 23, 2002.

64. Quoted in David Bamber and Chris Hastings, "Bobby Fischer Speaks Out to Applaud Trade Center Attacks," *The Telegraph*, December 2, 2001, p. 17.

65. Evan Thomas, "A Long, Strange Trip to the Taliban," *Newsweek*, December 17, 2001, pp. 30–36.

66. Speech by William Jefferson Clinton, November 7, 2001, Georgetown University, Washington, DC.

67. A Nexis search turned up many examples of Turkish government officials denying the Armenian genocide. Examples include "Turkey Cornered in Armenian Allegations," *Turkish Daily News*, February 5, 2001; Antoine Terjanian, "Turkish Embassy Falsifying History," *Ottawa Citizen*, June 11, 2001, p. 11; and "Cay: Armenian Genocide Allegations Aim to Block Turkey's Future," *Turkish Daily News*, May 19, 2001.

68. See Gavan Davis, *Prisoners of the Japanese: POWs of World War II in the Pacific* (New York: William Morrow, 1994), pp. 24–25; see also Arthur M. Schlesinger, Jr., *The Disuniting of America: Reflections on a Multicultural Society* (New York: W. W. Norton, 1998), p. 56.

69. For a discussion of the millions of killings committed by the Soviet government, see Stephane Courtois, Nicolas Werth, Jean-Louis Panne, et al., *The Black Book of Communism: Crimes, Terror, Repression* (Cambridge, MA: Harvard University Press, 1999), pp. 1–268.

70. Walt Kelly, "Pogo" (comic), April 22, 1971.

Chapter 2

1. Theodore Draper, *The Roots of American Communism* (Chicago: Ivan R. Dee, 1985), pp. 190, 273.

2. Stephane Courtois, Nicolas Werth, Jean-Louis Panne, et al., *The Black Book of Communism: Terror, Crimes, Repression* (Cambridge, MA: Harvard University Press, 1999), p. 4.

3. Ibid., p. 471.

4. Ibid., p. 88.

5. Quoted in ibid., p. 420.

6. Ibid., p. 603.

7. Cited in Draper, *The Roots of American Communism*, p. 53.

8. Cited in ibid., p. 274.

9. Richard Gid Powers, *Not Without Honor: The History of American Anti-Communism* (New York: The Free Press, 1995), p. 89.

10. Daniel J. Flynn, "The Canonization of W. E. B. Du Bois," *The New Criterion*, April 1996, pp. 79–80.

11. Quoted in Paul Hollander, *Political Pilgrims: Travels of Western Intellectuals to the Soviet Union, China, and Cuba* (New York: Oxford University Press, 1981), p. 64.

12. John Earl Haynes and Harvey Klehr, *Venona: Decoding Soviet Espionage in America* (New Haven, CT: Yale University Press, 1999), p. 9.

13. Alger Hiss is featured in a lone translated spy cable, Venona #1822, Washington to Moscow, March 30, 1945. Harry Dexter White appears in numerous cables, including Venona #1388-9, New York to Moscow, October 1, 1944, and Venona #1119-21, August 4–5, 1944. Lauchlin Currie makes numerous appearances in Venona as well, including Venona #928, New York to Moscow, June 30, 1943, and Venona #1634, New York to Moscow, November 20, 1944.

14. Robert Louis Benson and Michael Warner, eds., *Venona: Soviet Espionage and the American Response, 1939–1957* (Washington, DC: National Security Agency and Central Intelligence Agency, 1996), pp. xiv, xv.

15. U.S. Senate Committee on Government Operations, "Transfer of Occupation Currency Plates—Espionage Phase," December 15, 1953.

16. Haynes and Klehr, *Venona*, pp. 295–303, 307–311.

17. Kenneth Campbell, *Moscow's Words, Western Voices* (Washington, DC: Accuracy in Media, 1994), pp. 74–79.

18. Michael Straight, *After Long Silence* (New York: W. W. Norton, 1983).

19. Venona #1433-5, New York to Moscow, October 10, 1944, and Venona #1506, New York to Moscow, October 23, 1944.

20. Campbell, *Moscow's Words, Western Voices*, pp. 7–43.

21. Quoted in "Hollywood Ignores Real Blacklist," *The AIM Report*, December-B 1997, p. 1.

22. Harvey Klehr, John Earl Haynes, and Kyrill Anderson, *The Soviet World of American Communism* (New Haven, CT: Yale University Press, 1998), p. 72.

23. Kenneth Lloyd Billingsley, *Hollywood Party: How Communism Seduced the American Film Industry in the 1930s and 1940s* (Rocklin, CA: Prima Forum, 1998), pp. 76–77.

24. Quoted in Billingsley, *Hollywood Party*, pp. 47–48.

25. Klehr et al., *The Soviet World of American Communism*, p. 53.

26. Powers, *Not Without Honor*, p. 188.

27. Ellen Schrecker, *Many Are the Crimes: McCarthyism in America* (Boston: Little, Brown, 1998), p. 184.

28. Powers, *Not Without Honor*, pp. 176–177.

29. Allen Weinstein and Alexander Vassiliev, *The Haunted Wood: Soviet Espionage in America—the Stalin Era* (New York: Random House, 1999), pp. 140–150.

30. Ronald Radosh, "The Two Evils," *New Republic*, May 11, 1998, p. 42.

31. Billingsley, *Hollywood Party*, p. 93.

32. "Hollywood Ignores Real Blacklist," p. 2.

33. Billingsley, *Hollywood Party*, p. 94.

34. Quoted in ibid., p. 237.

35. Schrecker, *Many Are the Crimes*, p. 181.

36. Quoted in Billingsley, *Hollywood Party*, p. 52.

37. Klehr et al., *The Soviet World of American Communism*, p. 325.

38. Ibid., pp. 213–215.

39. Herbert Romerstein and Eric Breindel, *The Venona Secrets: Exposing Soviet Espionage and America's Traitors* (Washington, DC: Regnery, 2000), p. 12.

40. Klehr et al., *The Secret World of American Communism*, pp. 142–143.

41. Ibid., pp. 151–187.
42. Ibid., p. 129.
43. Ibid., p. 144.
44. Ibid., pp. 113, 147–163.
45. Quoted in Patrick J. Buchanan, *The Death of the West: How Dying Populations and Immigrant Invasions Imperil Our Country and Civilization* (New York: St. Martin's Press, 2002), p. 73.
46. T. W. Adorno, Else Frenkel-Brunswik, Daniel J. Levinson, and R. Nevitt Sanford, *The Authoritarian Personality* (New York: Harper and Brothers, 1950), p. 10.
47. Ibid., p. 656.
48. Ibid., p. 142.
49. The statement used for both the conservatism scale and the fascism scale was "The businessman and the manufacturer are much more important to society than the artist and the professor." Ibid., p. 254.
50. Martin Jay, *The Dialectical Imagination: A History of the Frankfurt School and the Institute of Social Research—1923–1949* (Berkeley and Los Angeles: University of California Press, 1973), p. 225.
51. Quoted in ibid., p. 228.
52. Adorno et al., *The Authoritarian Personality*, pp. 147, 720, 722.
53. Herbert Marcuse, *Eros and Civilization: A Philosophical Inquiry into Freud* (Boston: Beacon Press, 1966), p. 45.
54. Robert Paul Wolff, Barrington Moore, Jr., and Herbert Marcuse, *A Critique of Pure Tolerance* (Boston: Beacon Press, 1970), p. 117.
55. Ibid., p. 109.
56. Ibid., p. 111.
57. Herbert Marcuse, *One-Dimensional Man: Studies in the Ideology of Advanced Industrial Society* (Boston: Beacon Press, 1967), p. 40.
58. Herbert Marcuse, *An Essay on Liberation* (Boston: Beacon Press, 1971), p. 85.
59. Ibid., p. 86.
60. Herbert Marcuse, *Counter-Revolution and Revolt* (Boston: Beacon Press, 1972), pp. 1, 24–29; Marcuse, *An Essay on Liberation*, p. 60.
61. Marcuse, *One-Dimensional Man*, p. 102.
62. Jay, *The Dialectical Imagination*, p. 4.

63. Harold Jacobs, ed., *Weatherman* (USA: Ramparts Press, 1970), pp. 481, 496–503, 512. For a description of the Pentagon bombing, see Bill Ayers, *Fugitive Days: A Memoir* (Boston: Beacon Press, 2001), pp. 256–263.

64. J. A. Parker, *Angela Davis: The Making of a Revolutionary* (New Rochelle, NY: Arlington House, 1973), pp. 169–170.

65. Quoted in Jay, *The Dialectical Imagination*, p. 279.

66. Quoted in Alvin J. Schmidt, *Under the Influence: How Christianity Transformed Civilization* (Grand Rapids, MI: Zondervan Publishing House, 2001), p. 76.

67. Quoted in Dinesh D'Souza, *What's So Great About America* (Washington, DC: Regnery, 2002), p. 188.

68. Quoted in Dinesh D'Souza, *The End of Racism: Principles for a Multiracial Society* (New York: The Free Press, 1995), p. 146.

69. Margaret Mead, *Coming of Age in Samoa* (New York: William Morrow, 1928), p. xv.

70. Ibid., p. 158.

71. Ibid., p. 216.

72. Ibid., p. 212.

73. Ibid., p. 151.

74. Ibid., p. 105.

75. Ibid., p. 108.

76. Ibid., p. 136.

77. Derek Freeman, *Margaret Mead and Samoa* (Cambridge, MA: Harvard University Press, 1983), p. 204.

78. Ibid., p. 203.

79. Ibid., p. 234.

80. Mead, *Coming of Age in Samoa*, p. 151.

81. Margaret Mead, *Social Organization of Manua* (Honolulu: Bernice P. Bishop Museum, 1969), p. 87.

82. Derek Freeman, *The Fateful Hoaxing of Margaret Mead* (Boulder, CO: Westview Press, 1999), p. 177.

83. Freeman, *Margaret Mead and Samoa*, p. 239.

84. Ibid., p. 104.

85. Ibid., p. 249.

86. Freeman, *The Fateful Hoaxing of Margaret Mead*, p. 187.

87. Freeman, *Margaret Mead and Samoa*, p. 249.

88. Ibid., pp. 248–249.

89. Ibid., p. 249.

90. Freeman, *The Fateful Hoaxing of Margaret Mead*, p. 3.
91. Quoted in "Multiracial Ground Zero Statue Offends Some NYC Firefighters and Families," January 11, 2002, www.foxnews.com /story/0,2933,42799,00.html, accessed on January 12, 2002.
92. Richard Bernstein, *The Dictatorship of Virtue: Multiculturalism and the Battle for America's Future* (New York: Alfred A. Knopf, 1994), p. 4.
93. Alvin J. Schmidt, *The Menace of Multiculturalism: Trojan Horse in America* (Westport, CT: Praeger Publishing, 1997), p. 8.
94. Quoted in Avik S. A. Roy, "Race Studies Trump the Canon," winter 1997, www.yale.edu/lt/archives/v3n2/index.htm, accessed on May 3, 2002.
95. Quoted in George Roche, *The Fall of the Ivory Tower* (Washington, DC: Regnery, 1994), p. 200.
96. Quoted in D'Souza, *What's So Great About America*, p. 38.
97. Quoted in D'Souza, *The End of Racism*, p. 344.
98. Quoted in ibid., p. 346.
99. Ivan Van Sertima, *They Came Before Columbus: The African Presence in Ancient America* (New York: Random House, 1976).
100. Mary Lefkowitz, *Not Out of Africa: How Afrocentrism Became an Excuse to Teach Myth as History* (New York: Basic Books, 1996), p. 137.
101. *African-American Baseline Essays* (Portland, OR: Portland Public Schools, 1987), pp. S51–S54.
102. Peter LaBarbera, "L.A. Educator Asserts Lincoln Had Homosexual Affairs," *Lambda Report*, June 1995, p. 1.
103. William A. Henry, *In Defense of Elitism* (New York: Doubleday, 1994), p. 45.
104. Donald A. Grinde and Bruce Johansen, *Exemplar of Liberty: Native America and the Evolution of Democracy* (Los Angeles: Regents of the University of California, 1991), p. xxiv.
105. Elisabeth Burgos-Debray, ed., *I, Rigoberta Menchu: An Indian Woman in Guatemala*, trans. Ann Wright (New York: Verso, 1998), p. 38; Larry Rother, "Nobel Winner Finds Her Story Challenged," *New York Times*, December 15, 1998, p. 8.
106. For a description of Menchu's brother's death, see Burgos-Debray, ed., *I, Rigoberta Menchu*, pp. 172–181; see also David Stoll, *Rigoberta Menchu and the Story of All Poor Guatemalans* (Boulder, CO: Westview Press, 1999), pp. 69–70.

107. Burgos-Debray, ed., *I, Rigoberta Menchu*, p. 89.
108. Stoll, *Rigoberta Menchu and the Story of All Poor Guatemalans*, pp. 159–166, quote on p. 165.
109. Rother, "Nobel Winner Finds Her Story Challenged," p. 8.
110. Stoll, *Rigoberta Menchu and the Story of All Poor Guatemalans*, p. 163; see also Rother, "Nobel Winner Finds Her Story Challenged," pp. 1, 8.
111. Burgos-Debray, ed., *I, Rigoberta Menchu*, p. 103.
112. Ibid., p. 2.
113. Ibid., pp. 102–116.
114. Stoll, *Rigoberta Menchu and the Story of All Poor Guatemalans*, pp. 29–40.
115. Ibid., p. 32.
116. Robin Wilson, "Anthropologist Challenges Veracity of Multicultural Icon," *Chronicle of Higher Education*, January 15, 1999, p. 14.
117. John A. Peeler, Letter: "'Historical Truth' vs. 'Narrative Truth' in Rigoberta Menchu's Autobiography," *Chronicle of Higher Education*, February 12, 1999, p. B3.
118. David Maeng, "Stanford Grad Doubts Nobel Laureate's Story," *Stanford Review*, February 3, 1999, pp. 4–5, 11.

Chapter 3
1. Based on the author's observations while attending the February 2, 2002, protest of the World Economic Forum in New York City.
2. Author interview of Walter Daum at the protest of the World Economic Forum, New York, February 2, 2002.
3. Author interview of Eric Josephson at the protest of the World Economic Forum, New York, February 2, 2002.
4. Author interview of Phil Houser at the protest of the World Economic Forum, New York, February 2, 2002.
5. Patrick J. Buchanan, *The Death of the West: How Dying Populations and Immigrant Invasions Imperil Our Country and Civilization* (New York: St. Martin's Press, 2002), pp. 130–131.
6. Movimiento Estudiantil Chicano de Aztlán (MEChA), "El Plan de Aztlán," www.gladstone.uoregon.edu/~mecha/plan.html, accessed on April 15, 2002.

7. Russell Means, "For Americans to Live, Europe Must Die" (speech), July 1980, Black Hills, South Dakota, www.russell means.com/speech.html, accessed on April 15, 2002.

8. Ann Carnahan, Sarah Huntley, and Todd Hartman, "147 Arrested at Parade Standoff," *Rocky Mountain News*, October 8, 2000, p. 4.

9. For a view of the Black Panthers from the inside, see David Horowitz, *Radical Son: A Generational Odyssey* (New York: The Free Press, 1997).

10. The Black Panther Party, "The Ten Point Plan," www.black panther.org/TenPoint.htm, accessed on March 20, 2002.

11. "Black Panther Party 35thYear Reunion" (event attended by author), University of the District of Columbia, Washington, DC, April 19, 2002.

12. Richard Locker, "Allegiances Clash During Pledge in House," *The Commercial Appeal*, June 2, 2001, p. B1.

13. Frank Keating, "Freeing Peltier Would Stain Clinton's Legacy," *Wall Street Journal*, December 19, 2000, p. 20.

14. Buchanan, *The Death of the West*, p. 128.

15. Quoted in Michael Medved, *Hollywood vs. America* (New York: Harper Perennial, 1993), p. 216.

16. Chomsky's reaction to the Cambodian genocide is outlined in Paul Johnson, *Intellectuals* (New York: Harper and Row, 1988), pp. 340–341. For Chomsky's U.S.–Nazi conspiracy theory, see Noam Chomsky, *What Uncle Sam Really Wants* (Berkeley, CA: Odonian Press, 1992), pp. 14–19.

17. K. L. Billingsley, "Noam Chomsky, Punk Hero," frontpagemag .com/het/classics/billingsley3-96.htm, accessed on April 9, 2002.

18. "Take the Power Back" (song), Rage Against the Machine, 1992.

19. *National Standards for United States History: Exploring the American Experience* (Los Angeles: National Center for History in the Schools, UCLA, 1995). See also Wilcomb Washburn, "Serious Questions About the *National Standards for United States History*," *Continuity*, spring 1995, pp. 47–56.

20. *National Standards for United States History*, p. 77.

21. Author's observations at "The Promise of Equality and Democracy," National Museum of American History, March 30, 2002.

22. Quoted in Thomas G. West, *Vindicating the Founders: Race, Sex, Class, and Justice in the Origins of America* (Lanham, MD: Rowman & Littlefield, 1997), p. 112.

23. West, *Vindicating the Founders*, pp. 17, 75–77, 113–119.

24. Howard Zinn, *A People's History of the United States, 1492–Present* (New York: Harper Perennial, 1995), p. 614.

25. Gary Crosby Brasor, *Turmoil and Tension at the University of Massachusetts at Amherst: History, Analysis and Recommended Solutions* (Somerville, MA: Massachusetts Association of Scholars, 1994), pp. 44–45.

26. Zinn, *A People's History of the United States*, p. 616.

27. Tamara Race, "Native Americans to Protest Plymouth Walk Again," *The Patriot Ledger*, November 25, 1997, p. 1.

28. Brasor, *Turmoil and Tension at the University of Massachusetts at Amherst*, pp. 57–60.

29. Rod Dreher, "Raise Hell over More Than Flag," *New York Post*, January 18, 2000, p. 22.

30. Connor Cruise O'Brien, *The Long Affair: Thomas Jefferson and the French Revolution* (Chicago: University of Chicago Press, 1996), pp. 301–325.

31. Quoted in Buchanan, *The Death of the West*, p. 161.

32. James Loewen, *Lies My Teacher Told Me: Everything Your American History Textbook Got Wrong* (New York: The New Press, 1995), p. 110.

33. Quoted in David Horowitz, *Uncivil Wars: The Controversy over Reparations for Slavery* (San Francisco: Encounter Books, 2002), p. 132.

34. *African-American Baseline Essays* (Portland, OR: Portland Public Schools, 1987), pp. SS60–SS64.

35. Quoted in ibid., p. 48.

36. Zinn, *A People's History of the United States*, p. 215.

37. Ibid., p. 228.

38. Ibid., p. 232.

39. *National Standards for United States History*, p. 139.

40. Ron Chernow, *Titan: The Life of John D. Rockefeller, Sr.* (New York: Random House, 1999), pp. 241, 314, 487, 569, 618.

41. Ibid., pp. 227, 257–258 (Rockefeller quoted on p. 257).

42. *National Standards for United States History*, pp. 199–204.

43. "The Full Story Should Be Told," *Atlanta Journal and Constitution*, July 12, 1995, p. 12.

44. Gerald Mizejewski, "View from Hiroshima," *Washington Times*, July 8, 1995, p. 1.

45. Laurence Jarvik, "Vets, Historians Rip ABC," *Washington Times*, July 29, 1995, p. 3 (Maddox quoted therein).

46. Author's observations at "A More Perfect Union: Japanese Americans and the United States Constitution," National Museum of American History, March 30, 2002.

47. Paul S. Boyer, Clifford E. Clark, Joseph F. Kett, et al., *The Enduring Vision: A History of the American People, Volume 2* (Lexington, MA: D. C. Heath, 1996), pp. 886, 887.

48. Senator Russell Feingold, "Statement on 'Wartime Treatment of European Americans and Refugees Study Act,'" March 14, 2002; Sarah M. Earle, "Germans, Too, Were Imprisoned in WWII," *Concord Monitor*, January 23, 2000, p. 1.

49. Joseph Fallon, "The Censored History of Internment," *Chronicles*, February 1998, p. 38.

50. Author's observations at "A More Perfect Union."

51. Wendy Koch, "Group Seeks Inquiry into USA's Treatment of Italians During War," *USA Today*, October 27, 1999, p. 15; James Brooke, "After Silence, Italians Recall the Internment," *New York Times*, August 11, 1997, p. 10.

52. Fallon, "The Censored History of Internment," p. 38.

53. Author's observations at "A More Perfect Union."

54. Fallon, "The Censored History of Internment," p. 38.

55. John Earl Haynes and Harvey Klehr, *Venona: Decoding Soviet Espionage in America* (New Haven, CT: Yale University Press, 1999), p. 9.

56. Mary Beth Norton, David M. Katzman, Paul D. Escott, et al., *A People and a Nation: A History of the United States* (New York: Houghton Mifflin, 1998); John M. Blum, William S. McFeely, Edmund Morgan, et al., *The National Experience: A History of the United States* (New York: Harcourt, Brace, Jovanovich, 1993); Boyer et al., *The Enduring Vision*.

57. William Chafe, *The Unfinished Journey: America Since World War II* (New York: Oxford University Press, 1995), pp. 471, 473, 477, 486, 492.

58. Robert L. Bartley, *The Seven Fat Years and How to Do It Again* (New York: The Free Press, 1992), pp. 3–6.

59. Norton et al., *A People and a Nation*, p. 976.

60. Bureau of the Census, *Money Income of Households, Families and Persons: 1990* (Washington, DC: U.S. Government Printing Office, 1991), p. 202. Statistics are in constant 1990 dollars and show, for instance, that the average income of the lowest quintile grew from $6,836 in 1980 to $7,372 in 1989.

61. Blum et al., *The National Experience*, p. 908.

62. David Sacks and Peter Theil, *The Diversity Myth: "Multiculturalism" and the Politics of Intolerance at Stanford* (Oakland, CA: The Independent Institute, 1995), p. 38.

63. J. Ryan Gilfoil, "The *Review* Surveys the Faculty," *Dartmouth Review*, October 24, 1995, p. 1.

64. Tony Mecia, "UNC Professors Lean Toward Political Left," *Daily Tar Heel*, October 28, 1996, p. 1.

65. Bill Scanlon, "One-Party Rules Among CU Profs," *Rocky Mountain News*, April 27, 1997, p. 1.

66. Kenneth Lee, "Where's the Diversity?" *Cornell Review*, September 28, 1995, p. 1.

67. Senate Resolution 106, 104th Congress, January 20, 1995. See also Don Feder, "Shutting Off Flow of Money Leftward Will Level the Field," *Boston Herald*, February 27, 1995, p. 25.

68. Bill McClellan, "WU Law School Bars Grads in Military Jobs from Loan Program," *St. Louis Post-Dispatch*, March 20, 2002, p. B1 (Tokarz quoted therein).

69. Author interview of Tom Fitzpatrick, December 19, 2001. See also Dan Flynn, "Marine Shouted Down at UNLV," *Campus Report*, January 2002, p. 1.

70. "Bin Laden Ties to Harvard," *Harvard Crimson*, September 13, 2001, p. 1. For a discussion of the ban on the ROTC, see Daniel J. Flynn, "The Academy Dishonors ROTC," *Washington Times*, December 8, 1995, p. 23.

71. Both Rutgers and Penn State house Paul Robeson Cultural Centers. The gushing reaction from the singer/actor/athlete over winning the award can be found in Paul Robeson, "Thoughts on Winning the Stalin Peace Prize," January 1953, www.mltranslations.org/Miscellaneous/RobesonSPP.htm, accessed on March 15, 2002.

72. Daniel J. Flynn, "The Canonization of W. E. B. Du Bois," *The New Criterion*, April 1996, pp. 79–80.
73. Joel Kovel currently serves as Alger Hiss Professor of Social Studies at Bard College.
74. William Honan, "Two Scholarships Given New Names After Controversy," *New York Times*, April 12, 1995, p. B11.
75. Peter Collier, "Angela Davis as Tenured Activist," *Washington Times*, April 2, 1995, p. B4.
76. Roger Kimball, *The Long March: How the Cultural Revolution of the 1960s Changed America* (San Francisco: Encounter Books, 2000), pp. 120, 121n.
77. Bill Ayers, *Fugitive Days: A Memoir* (Boston: Beacon Press, 2001).
78. Quoted in Jonah Goldberg, "I'm Not Afraid of Technology," June 7, 2000, www.nationalreview.com/goldberg/goldberg 060700 .html, accessed on April 1, 2002; "Unabomber Lands a Book Deal," Associated Press, February 11, 1999.
79. Daniel J. Flynn, *Cop Killer: How Mumia Abu-Jamal Conned Millions into Believing He Was Framed* (Washington, DC: Accuracy in Academia, 1999).
80. George Orwell, *1984* (New York: Signet Classic, 1983), p. 204.
81. Freedom Forum survey cited in "AIM Gets Donny's Dander Up," *The AIM Report*, June-A 1996, p. 1.
82. Robert Lichter, Stanley Rothman, and Linda Lichter, *The Media Elite* (Bethesda, MD: Alder & Alder, 1986), p. 30.
83. Luntz data cited in Sara Russo, "Bias Revealed Among Ivy League Faculty," *Campus Report*, February 2002, p. 1.
84. Sacks and Theil, *The Diversity Myth*, p. 38; Kenneth Lee, "Where's the Diversity?" *Cornell Review*, September 28, 1995, p. 1; Scanlon, "One-Party Rules Among CU Profs," p. 1.
85. Eric Hoffer, *The True Believer: Thoughts on the Nature of Mass Movements* (New York: Harper and Row, 1951), p. 78.
86. Quoted in Kimball, *The Long March*, p. 128.

Chapter 4

1. V. I. Lenin, *On Youth* (Moscow: Moscow Publishers, 1970), p. 245.
2. Alexis de Tocqueville, *Democracy in America: Volume II* (New York: Vintage Classics, 1990), p. 115.

3. Quoted in Paul Hollander, *Anti-Americanism: Critiques at Home and Abroad, 1965–1990* (New York: Oxford University Press, 1992), pp. 70–71.

4. Christina Hoff Sommers, *Who Stole Feminism? How Women Have Betrayed Women* (New York: Simon and Schuster, 1994), pp. 13–14.

5. Ibid., pp. 11–12.

6. Kelly Oliver, "Keller's Gender/Science System," *Hypatia*, summer 1989, p. 146.

7. Christine Stolba, *Lying in a Room of One's Own: How Women's Studies Textbooks Miseducate Students* (Arlington, VA: Independent Women's Forum, 2002), p. 12.

8. Statistics cited in Andrew Kimbrell, *The Masculine Mystique: The Politics of Masculinity* (New York: Ballantine Books, 1995), pp. 5, 12.

9. Statistics cited in ibid., pp. 10–11.

10. Statistics cited in ibid., p. 6.

11. Centers for Disease Control and Prevention, *National Vital Statistics Report*, July 24, 2000, pp. 26–28.

12. U.S. Census Bureau, "Table A3. People Without Health Insurance for Entire Year by Selected Characteristics: 1999 and 2000," *Health Insurance Coverage: 2000*, January 18, 2002.

13. Christina Hoff Sommers, *The War Against Boys: How Misguided Feminism Is Harming Our Young Men* (New York: Simon and Schuster, 2000), pp. 24–25.

14. U.S. Department of Education, "Total Fall Enrollment in Degree-Granting Institutions, by Attendance Status, Sex of Student, and Control of Institution, 1947–1998," *Digest of Education Statistics 2000* (Washington, DC: U.S. Department of Education, 2000), p. 202.

15. Robert Anderson and Peter DeTurk, "United States Life Tables: 1999," *National Vital Statistics Report*, March 21, 2000, p. 2.

16. Statistics cited in Kimbrell, *The Masculine Mystique*, p. 210.

17. Centers for Disease Control and Prevention, "Table 7. AIDS Cases by Sex, Age at Diagnosis, and Race/Ethnicity, Reported Through June 2001, United States," *HIV/AIDS Surveillance Report*, Midyear 2001 Edition, www.cdc.gov/hiv/stats/hasr1301/table7.htm, accessed on April 20, 2002.

18. Andrew Knestnaut, "Fewer Women Than Men Die of Work-Related Injuries," *Compensation and Working Conditions Online* (U.S. Department of Labor), June 1996, www.bls.gov/opub /cwc/1996/Summer/brief3.htm, accessed on April 20, 2002.

19. John Tierney, "Recycling Is Garbage," *New York Times Magazine*, June 30, 1996, p. 5.

20. Al Gore, *Earth in the Balance: Ecology and the Human Spirit* (Boston: Houghton Mifflin, 1992), p. 325.

21. Joseph L. Bast, Peter J. Hill, and Richard C. Rue, *Eco-Sanity: A Common-Sense Guide to Environmentalism* (Lanham, MD: Madison Books, 1994), pp. 110–116.

22. Paul Ehrlich, *The Population Bomb* (New York: Ballantine Books, 1978), p. xi.

23. Author interview of Kenneth Stewart at Washington, DC, rally, April 20, 2002.

24. James Loewen, *Lies My Teacher Told Me: Everything Your American History Textbook Got Wrong* (New York: The New Press, 1995), p. 256.

25. Maggie Farley, "The City with the Grittiest Air on Earth," *Los Angeles Times*, June 15, 1999, p. 1.

26. "Asia-Inc in a Haze O\over Report That KL Is Third Most Polluted City," *New Straits Times* (Malaysia), October 3, 2000, p. 9.

27. Bast et al., *Eco-Sanity*, p. 11.

28. Ibid., pp. 22–23.

29. Ibid., pp. 15–18.

30. Gregg Easterbrook, "America the O.K.," *New Republic*, January 11, 1998, p. 22.

31. "Los Angeles Officials Want to Turn Wastewater into Drinking Water," April 17, 2000, 10:57 P.M. EST, www.cnn.com/2000 /NATURE/04/17/toilet.to.tap.02, accessed on April 26, 2002.

32. Paul R. Ehrlich and Anne H. Ehrlich, *The Population Explosion* (New York: Simon and Schuster, 1990), p. 162.

33. "The Heidelberg Appeal to Heads of States and Governments" (petition), 1992.

34. David Horowitz, *Uncivil Wars: The Controversy over Reparations for Slavery* (San Francisco: Encounter Books, 2002), p. 111.

35. Dinesh D'Souza, *What's So Great About America* (Washington, DC: Regnery, 2002), pp. 66, 121.

36. *African-American Baseline Essays* (Portland, OR: Portland Public Schools, 1987), p. S-77.

37. Arthur Schlesinger, Jr., *The Disuniting of America: Reflections on a Multicultural Society* (New York: W. W. Norton, 1998), p. 85.

38. David Horowitz, "Black America at War," November 5, 2001, www.frontpagemag.com/horowitzsnotepad/2001/hn11-05-01.htm, accessed on March 2, 2002.

39. Quoted in Roger Kimball, *The Long March: How the Cultural Revolution of the 1960s Changed America* (San Francisco: Encounter Books, 2000), p. 97.

40. Author interview of University of Massachusetts–Amherst student Zachary Spilman, April 29, 2002.

41. Mike Hill, ed., *Whiteness: A Critical Reader* (New York: New York University Press, 1997), p. 347.

42. Remarks by Frank Kellum, "Black Panther 35th Year Reunion" (speech attended by author), University of the District of Columbia, Washington, DC, April 18, 2002.

43. For statistics confirming increased national levels of illegitimacy, drug use, and crime since the 1960s, see William J. Bennett, *The Index of Leading Cultural Indicators: American Society at the End of the Twentieth Century* (New York: Broadway Books, 1999).

44. Remarks by Timothy Jenkins, "Black Panther 35th Year Reunion" (speech attended by author), University of the District of Columbia, Washington, DC, April 18, 2002.

45. U.S. Department of Education, "Enrollment Rates of 18- to 24-Year-Olds in Degree Granting Institutions, by Race: Ethnicity: 1967–1999," *Digest of Education Statistics* (Washington, DC: U.S. Department of Education, 2000), p. 216.

46. For black per capita income levels since 1967, see U.S. Census Bureau, "Table P-1b. Black CPS Population and Per Capita Money Income: 1967–2000," *Historical Income Tables—People*, April 18, 2002, www.census.gov/hhes/income/histinc/p01b.html, accessed on April 27, 2002; for information on other racial groups, see the U.S. Census Bureau's charts on the subject, www.census.gov/hhes/income/histinc/incperdet.html, accessed on April 27, 2002.

47. For black per capita income in the United States, see U.S. Census Bureau, "Table P-1b. Black CPS Population and Per Capita

Money Income: 1967–2000," *Historical Income Tables—People*, April 18, 2002, www.census.gov/hhes/income/histinc/p01b .html, accessed on April 26, 2002; for the per capita incomes of African nations, see Gerald P. O'Driscoll, Kim R. Holmes, and Mary Anastasia O'Grady, *2002 Index of Economic Freedom* (Washington, DC: Heritage Foundation and *Wall Street Journal*, 2001).

48. Author interview of Kenneth Stewart at Washington, DC, rally, April 20, 2002.

49. Author interview of Vincent Hausman at Washington, DC, rally, April 20, 2002.

50. Author interview of Chris Powers at Washington, DC, rally, April 20, 2002.

51. Author interview of Charles Freed at Washington, DC, rally, April 20, 2002.

52. Ibid.

53. Author interview of Beverley Anderson at Washington, DC, rally, April 20, 2002.

54. Author interview of Rachel Garskof-Leiberman at Washington, DC, rally, April 20, 2002.

55. Noam Chomsky, *What Uncle Sam Really Wants* (Berkeley, CA: Odonian Press, 1992), pp. 22–24.

56. Howard Zinn, *A People's History of the United States, 1492–Present* (New York: Harper Perennial, 1995), p. 556.

57. Gore Vidal, "Taking Liberties," *The Guardian*, April 27, 2002, p. 1.

58. Gary Kamiya, "Gore Vidal" (interview), fiot.1accesshost.com /vidal2.html, accessed on May 9, 2002.

59. Author interview of Eric Triffin at Washington, DC, rally, April 20, 2002.

60. Samuel Huntington, *The Clash of Civilizations and the Remaking of World Order* (New York: Simon and Schuster, 1996), p. 91.

61. U.S. Senate, 104th Congress, "Foreign Aid Reduction Act of 1995: Report," June 23, 1995, p. 12. The report notes that from the end of World War II to 1995, the United States handed out $450,000,000,000. Since that time, U.S. foreign aid has hovered around the $20 billion mark annually, making $500,000,000,000 a conservative estimate of the total amount given by the U.S. government since World War II.

62. Larry Nowels, "Appropriations for FY2002: Foreign Operations, Export Financing, and Other Related Programs," Congressional Research Service, February 4, 2002; U.S. Senate, 104th Congress, "Foreign Aid Reduction Act of 1995."

63. Loewen, *Lies My Teacher Told Me*, p. 279.

64. John Fetto, "One Nation," *American Demographics*, March 2002, p. 17.

65. Curt Anderson, "Tax Burden Falls on the Wealthy" (Associated Press wire), April 9, 2002, 2:08 A.M. EST.

66. U.S. Census Bureau, "Table IE-3. Household Shares of Aggregate Income by Fifths of the Income Distribution: 1967 to 2000," *Historical Income Tables—Income Equality*, April 16, 2002, www.census.gov/hhes/income/histinc/ie3.html, accessed on April 26, 2002.

67. U.S. Census Bureau, "Table 3. Household Income Limits by Percentile: 1967–1998," *Income Inequality (1967–1998)*, August 24, 2000. In real, inflation-adjusted, dollars, the average income of the poorest 10% of the population has climbed from $7,324 in 1967 to $9,700 in 1998, www.census.gov/hhes/income/incineq/p60204/6098tb3.html, accessed on April 26, 2002.

68. For the per capita incomes of the nations of the world, see O'Driscoll et al., *2002 Index of Economic Freedom*. The U.S. poor are economically better off than the average person living in every African and South American country and in nearly every Asian country save Japan.

69. Friedrich A. Hayek, *The Constitution of Liberty* (Chicago: University of Chicago Press, 1978), p. 87.

70. U.S. Treasury Department statistics cited in Ed Rubenstein, "Moving Up," *National Review*, August 31, 1992, p. 47.

71. Urban Institute statistics cited in ibid.

72. Wilfred T. Masumura, "Moving Up and Down the Income Ladder" (Washington, DC: U.S. Census Bureau, 1998), pp. 1–4.

73. U.S. Census Bureau, "Dynamics of Economic Well-Being: Poverty, 1993 to 1994," December 13, 2000.

74. "The Four Hundred Richest Americans," September 27, 2001, www.forbes.com/2001/09/27/400.html, accessed on April 25, 2002.

75. "The Forbes 400," *Forbes*, October 8, 2001, pp. 127–298.

76. Niccolo Machiavelli, *The Prince* (VT: Everyman Publishing, 1998), p. 97.

Chapter 5

1. For a discussion of the Stanford controversy, see David Sacks and Peter Theil, *The Diversity Myth: "Multiculturalism" and the Politics of Intolerance at Stanford* (Oakland, CA: The Independent Institute, 1995), pp. 1–4

2. Will Durant, *Our Oriental Heritage* (New York: MJF Books, 1994), pp. 727–729, 780–781.

3. Ibid., p. 180.

4. Robert Edgerton, *Sick Societies: Challenging the Myth of Primitive Harmony* (New York: The Free Press, 1992), p. 143.

5. Durant, *Our Oriental Heritage*, p. 50.

6. Edgerton, *Sick Societies*, p. 82.

7. Ibid., p. 58.

8. Arthur Schlesinger, Jr., *The Disuniting of America: Reflections on a Multicultural Society* (New York: W. W. Norton, 1998), p. 134.

9. Quoted in Arthur Herman, *How the Scots Invented the Modern World* (New York: Crown Publishers, 2001), p. 301.

10. Quoted in Dinesh D'Souza, *The End of Racism: Principles for a Multiracial Society* (New York: The Free Press, 1995), p. 156.

11. Tamara von Fausten, quoted in Henry Salivator, "The Rewriting of Sexual History," www.users.bigpond.com/sarcasmo /hystery.html, accessed on January 9, 2002.

12. U.S. State Department, *Country Reports on Human Rights Practices for 2000* (Washington, DC: U.S. Government Printing Office, 2001), "China," p. 780; "Kenya," p. 339; "India," p. 2245; "Chad," p. 112; "Egypt," p. 1849.

13. In addition to the obvious fact that polygamy exists in the Middle East, *Country Reports on Human Rights Practices for 2000* documents polygamy occurring in scores of African nations, including Botswana (p. 32), Burkina Faso (p. 44), Cameroon (p. 79), the Republic of the Congo (p. 164), Djibouti (p. 201), Equatorial Guinea (p. 213), Gabon (p. 259), Gambia (p. 269), Lesotho (p. 350), Mali (p. 388), Mauritania (p. 401), Mozambique (p. 430), Nigeria (p. 472), Senegal (p. 504), Somalia (p. 535), South Africa (p. 551), Togo (p. 621), Uganda (p. 637), and Zambia (p. 653), among others.

14. Ibid., "India," p. 2245.
15. Information and quote can be found in Nahid Toubia and Susan Izett, *Female Genital Mutilation: An Overview* (Geneva: World Health Organization, 1998).
16. U.S. State Department, *Country Reports on Human Rights Practices for 2000*, "China," pp. 753–755, 778–779.
17. Some examples of countries that apply a lower value to women's testimony can be found in ibid., "Iran," p. 1875; "Jordan," p. 1954; "Kuwait," p. 1971; "Qatar," p. 2069; "Saudi Arabia," p. 2083; "Maldives," p. 2269; "Pakistan," p. 2314.
18. Ibid., "Algeria," p. 1834; "Bahrain," p. 1844; "Egypt," p. 1865; "Jordan," p. 1963; "Morocco," p. 2044; "Oman," p. 2061; "Qatar," p. 2069; "Saudi Arabia," p. 2083; "Syria," p. 2097; "Tunisia," p. 2117; "Maldives," p. 2269; "Djibouti," p. 201; "Bangladesh," p. 2193.
19. Ibid., "Kuwait," p. 1975; "Jordan," p. 1959; "Egypt," p. 1861.
20. Ibid., "Yemen," p. 2150; "Saudi Arabia," p. 2080.
21. Ibid., "Iran," p. 1887; "Saudi Arabia," p. 2076.
22. Quoted in Tarek Al-Issawi, "Saudi Schoolgirls' Fire Deaths Decried," *Washington Times*, March 18, 2002, p. 11.
23. Adrian Karatnycky, ed., *Freedom in the World 2000–2001: The Annual Survey of Political Rights and Civil Liberties* (Piscataway, NJ: Transaction, 2001), p. 589. U.S. State Department, *Country Reports on Human Rights Practices for 2000*, "Iran," p. 1887.
24. U.S. State Department, *Country Reports on Human Rights Practices for 2000*, "Algeria," p. 1831; "Kuwait," p. 1971; "Saudi Arabia," p. 2075; "United Arab Emirates," p. 2123; "Yemen," p. 2150.
25. Ibid., "Algeria," p. 1834; "Egypt," p. 1864; "Kuwait," p. 1978; "Morocco," p. 2045.
26. Ibid., pp. 1864, 2069, 1951, 2149, 1995.
27. Ibid., "Iraq," p. 1905.
28. Ibid., "Pakistan," p. 2288.
29. Paul Marshall, ed., *Religious Freedom in the World: A Global Report on Freedom and Persecution* (Nashville, TN: Broadman and Holman Publishers, 2000), p. 70.
30. U.S. State Department, *Country Reports on Human Rights Practices for 2000*, "Pakistan," p. 2291; "Bangladesh," pp. 2183, 2193.
31. Ibid., "Iraq," p. 1895.

32. Ibid., "Egypt," p. 1864.
33. Ibid., "Bangladesh," pp. 2181, 2193; "Pakistan," p. 2311.
34. Ibid., "India," pp. 2244–2245.
35. Ibid., "South Africa," p. 551; "Lesotho," p. 350; "Cameroon," p. 80; "Republic of Congo," p. 164.
36. Ibid., "Tanzania," p. 605; "Uganda," p. 637; "Zimbabwe," p. 673.
37. Ibid., "Benin," p. 22; "Ethiopia," p. 246.
38. Karatnycky, ed., *Freedom in the World 2000–2001*, pp. 501–505.
39. Ibid., pp. 607–610.
40. Ibid., p. 440.
41. U.S. State Department, *Country Reports on Human Rights Practices for 2000*, "Liberia," p. 365.
42. Karatnycky, ed., *Freedom in the World 2000–2001*, pp. 261, 350.
43. Ibid., pp. 90–93.
44. U.S. State Department, *Country Reports on Human Rights Practices for 2000*, "Sudan," pp. 577–578; "Mauritania," pp. 404–405.
45. Ibid., "Ethiopia," pp. 229, 235.
46. Karatnycky, ed., *Freedom in the World 2000–2001*, p. 270.
47. Ibid., pp. 113–116.
48. Gerald P. O'Driscoll, Kim R. Holmes, and Mary Anastasia O'Grady, *2002 Index of Economic Freedom* (Washington, DC: Heritage Foundation and *Wall Street Journal*, 2001), "Armenia," p. 96; "Azerbaijan," p. 102; "Bahrain," p. 106; "Belarus," p. 112; "Bulgaria," p. 128; "Cuba," p. 168; "Kazakhstan," p. 254; "Kuwait," p. 262; "Kyrgyz Republic," p. 264; "Laos," p. 266; "Mauritius," p. 294; "Mongolia," p. 300; "Nigeria," p. 318; "Tanzania," p. 382; "Turkmenistan," p. 394.
49. U.S. State Department, *Country Reports on Human Rights Practices for 2000*, "Saudi Arabia," pp. 2072–2079.
50. Ibid., "Iran," pp. 1871–1889.
51. Ibid., "Algeria," p. 1830; "Bahrain," p. 1841; "Egypt," p. 1859; "Jordan," p. 1957; "Kuwait," p. 1973; "Oman," p. 2059; "Tunisia," p. 2112; "United Arab Emirates," p. 2125; "Yemen," p. 2144; "Sudan," p. 569; "Bangladesh," p. 2190; "Pakistan," p. 2304.
52. Ibid., "China," pp. 763–774 (quote found therein).
53. Julia Duin, "Three Christians Sentenced to Death," *Washington Times*, January 11, 2002, p. 13; Katherine Arms, "China Gives Jail Term to Bible Courier" (United Press International), January 28, 2002, posted 7:02 A.M. EST.

54. Quoted in Marshall, ed., *Religious Freedom in the World*, p. 12.

55. U.S. State Department, *Country Reports on Human Rights Practices for 2000*, "Mauritania," p. 397; "Qatar," p. 2067; "Comoros," p. 119; "Oman," p. 2059.

56. Ibid., "Laos," pp. 944–945; Marshall, ed., *Religious Freedom in the World*, p. 117.

57. U.S. State Department, *Country Reports on Human Rights Practices for 2000*, "Burma," p. 713; "Bhutan," p. 2206.

58. "Religious Violence Causes 400 Deaths in India" (Associated Press Wire), March 2, 2002.

59. Bob Harvey, "Keeping the Faith," *Ottawa Citizen*, December 22, 2001, p. B1; "Blasts Hit Churches in Indonesia," *Courier Mail*, January 2, 2002, p. 10.

60. Samuel P. Huntington, *The Clash of Civilizations and the Remaking of World Order* (New York: Simon and Schuster, 1996), p. 256.

61. Thomas Jefferson, *Notes on the State of Virginia* (New York: W. W. Norton, 1982), p. 159.

62. U.S. State Department, *Country Reports on Human Rights Practices for 2000*, "Algeria," p. 1829; "Egypt," p. 1858; "Bahrain," p. 1840; "Iran," p. 1878; "Iraq," p. 1901; "Jordan," p. 1956; "Kuwait," p. 1978; "Libya," p. 2002; "Morocco," p. 2032; "Oman," p. 2058; "Saudi Arabia," p. 2077; "Syria," p. 2093; "Yemen," p. 2141; "Maldives," p. 2266; "India," p. 2235; "China," p. 758; "Cameroon," p. 73; "Djibouti," p. 198; "Mauritania," p. 396; "Rwanda," p. 487; "Seychelles," p. 509; "North Korea," p. 920; "Laos," p. 942; "Vietnam," p. 1092; "Turkmenistan," p. 1710; "Burma," p. 709; "Cuba," p. 2514.

63. *Press Freedom Survey 2001* (New York: Freedom House, 2001), p. 25; U.S. State Department, *Country Reports on Human Rights Practices for 2000*, "Kuwait," p. 1972.

64. U.S. State Department, *Country Reports on Human Rights Practices for 2000*, "Senegal," p. 500.

65. Ibid., "Bhutan," p. 2209.

66. *Press Freedom Survey 2001*, p. 12.

67. U.S. State Department, *Country Reports on Human Rights Practices for 2000*, "Seychelles," p. 509.

68. Ibid., "Uruguay," p. 2805.

69. Ibid., "Togo," p. 613.

70. Ibid., "Yemen," p. 2141.
71. Ibid., "Zimbabwe," p. 665.
72. Ibid., "China," p. 740.
73. Ibid., "Libya," pp. 2002–2003.
74. Ibid., "Democratic People's Republic of Korea," pp. 916–918.
75. Ibid., "Iraq," p. 1894.
76. Schlesinger, *The Disuniting of America*, p. 160.
77. Richard Boudreaux, "Russia's Last Free Channel Dealt a Blow," *Los Angeles Times*, January 12, 2002, p. 3; Ben Aris, "Court Closes Russia's Last Independent TV Station," *Daily Telegraph*, January 12, 2002, p. 18.
78. Paul Gottfried, *After Liberalism: Mass Democracy in the Managerial State* (Princeton, NJ: Princeton University Press, 1999), p. 105.
79. *Press Freedom Survey 2001*, p. 22.
80. Schlesinger, *The Disuniting of America*, p. 158.
81. Based on the author's reading of various human rights reports, the countries that conceivably could be characterized as legitimate republics in Africa at the time of this book's publication are Benin, Botswana, Cape Verde, Ghana, Namibia, Mauritius, Sao Tome and Principe, Seychelles, and South Africa. This evaluation obviously includes island nations not technically on the continent. It also generously overlooks such less-than-ideal conditions among the "democratic" countries as government ownership of the major media outlets and the fact that democratically elected governments in several of these nations never have peacefully yielded power to their rivals on the occasion of being voted out of office.
82. U.S. State Department, *Country Reports on Human Rights Practices for 2000*, "Cameroon," pp. 71–77.
83. Ibid., "Tanzania," pp. 593–597, 601.
84. Ibid., "Ivory Coast," pp. 168–185.
85. Ibid., "Ethiopia," pp. 230–239.
86. Churchill made these famous remarks in a speech to the House of Commons on November 11, 1947, quoted in *Oxford Dictionary of Quotations* (New York: Oxford University Press, 1979), p. 150.
87. Dostoyevsky, quoted in Howard Zinn, *A People's History of the United States: 1492–Present* (New York: Harper Perennial, 1995), p. 505.

88. U.S. State Department, *Country Reports on Human Rights Practices for 2000*, "Liberia," p. 356.
89. Ibid., "Saudi Arabia," p. 2073; "Sudan," p. 561; "Nigeria," pp. 456–459.
90. Ibid., "China," p. 750.
91. Ibid., "China," p. 745; "Pakistan," p. 2293; "Nigeria," p. 461; "Cameroon," p. 64; "Democratic Republic of Congo," p. 139; "Somalia," p. 530; "Equatorial Guinea," p. 206.
92. Ibid., "Libya," p. 2001.
93. Ibid., "Democratic People's Republic of Korea," p. 925.
94. Ibid., "Ghana," p. 280.
95. Ibid., "Kenya," p. 325.
96. Ibid., "Niger," p. 448; "Rwanda," p. 480.
97. Ibid., "Uganda," p. 629.
98. Ibid., "Nigeria," p. 460; "Benin," p. 18; "Burkina Faso," p. 38; "Ghana," p. 277; "Madagascar," p. 368.
99. For information on adult-juvenile and coed jails, see ibid., "Central African Republic," p. 94; "Madagascar," p. 368; "Mali," p. 384; "Nigeria," p. 460; "Equatorial Guinea," p. 206.
100. Ibid., "Mozambique," p. 417.
101. Ibid., "Niger," p. 447.
102. Ibid., "Côte D'Ivoire," p. 172.
103. Ibid., "Republic of Congo," p. 158.
104. Ibid., "Tanzania," p. 590; "Benin," p. 17; "Indonesia," p. 866; "Kenya," p. 321.
105. Ibid., "Brazil," pp. 2403–2404.
106. Ibid., "Ecuador," p. 2555.
107. Ibid., "Venezuela," pp. 2810–2812.
108. Ibid., "Argentina," p. 2357.
109. Ibid., "China," pp. 743–751.
110. O'Driscoll et al., *2002 Index of Economic Freedom*, pp. 22–26.
111. See ibid. (Burma, p. 132), (Mozambique, p. 304), (Rwanda, p. 346).
112. Based on author's interpretation of information included on price controls in ibid.
113. Ibid. (Angola, p. 92), (Azerbaijan, p. 102), (Bangladesh, p. 108), (Bosnia-Herzegovina, p. 122), (Burma, p. 132), (China, p. 150), (Republic of Congo, p. 162), (Costa Rica, p. 164), (Cuba, p. 168), (Egypt, p. 182), (Ethiopia, p. 190), (India, p. 228), (Iran, p.

234), (Iraq, p. 236), (Kazakhstan, p. 254), (North Korea, p. 258), (Laos, p. 266), (Libya, p. 274), (Nepal, p. 308), (Qatar, p. 338), (Russia, p. 342), (Sri Lanka, p. 366), (Syria, p. 378), (Tajikistan, p. 380), (Togo, p. 386), (Tunisia, p. 390), (Turkmenistan, p. 394), (Ukraine, p. 398), (Uruguay, p. 408), (Uzbekistan, p. 410), (Vietnam, p. 414), (Yugoslavia, p. 420).

114. Ibid., p. 112.

115. Marshall, ed., *Religious Freedom in the World*, pp. 69–70.

116. Mugabe, quoted in "Charges Dropped Against Alleged Killer of White Zimbabwean Farmer" (Deutsche Presse-Agentur), December 5, 2000, posted at 14:26 CET, and "Zimbabwe Accepts White Farmers Offer of 1 Million Hectares" (Deutsche Presse-Agentur), September 5, 2001, posted at 18:50 CET.

117. Thomas Sowell, *Migrations and Cultures: A World View* (New York: Basic Books, 1996), pp. 320–322.

118. O'Driscoll et al., *2002 Index of Economic Freedom*, pp. 21–26.

119. U.S. State Department, *Country Reports on Human Rights Practices for 2000*, "Saudi Arabia," p. 2084; "Equatorial Guinea," p. 214; "Sudan," p. 576; "Egypt," p. 1868; "China," p. 787; "North Korea," p. 926; "Cuba," p. 2524; "Iraq," p. 1908; "Libya," p. 2005; "Oman," p. 2062; "United Arab Emirates," p. 2129; "Bhutan," p. 2211.

120. Ibid., "China," p. 787.

121. Ibid., "Sudan," pp. 577–578.

122. Ibid., "Mauritania," pp. 404–405.

123. Ibid., "Cameroon," pp. 60, 82; "Ghana," pp. 289, 293; "Mali," p. 390.

124. The latest figures available rank the U.S. GDP number one at $8.9 trillion and Japan's GDP number two at $5.5 trillion. This information can be found in O'Driscoll et al., *2002 Index of Economic Freedom*, pp. 247, 403.

125. Information on the low GDPs of non-Western countries can be found in ibid. Of European and North American nations, Moldova, Ukraine, and Albania all have per capita GDPs of less than $1,000.

126. World Health Organization, Global Burden of Disease Project 2000: "Estimates of Number of Deaths by Sex, Cause, and WHO Region, Version 1 Estimates for 2000," www .who.int/whosis/menu.cfm?path=whosis,burden,burden_gbd

2000,burden_gbd2000_region&language=english, accessed on January 31, 2002.

127. *The World Health Report 2000* (Geneva: World Health Organization, 2000), pp. 178–183.

128. Huntington, *The Clash of Civilizations and the Remaking of World Order*, p. 318.

Chapter 6

1. *Life of Brian* (film), John Goldstone, producer (Handmade Films, 1979).

2. "Lindh's E-Mail Hostile to U.S.," *Newsday*, February 8, 2002, p. 7.

3. National Inventors Hall of Fame, "Thomas Alva Edison," www.invent.org/hall_of_fame/50.html, accessed on April 18, 2002.

4. National Inventors Hall of Fame, "Willis Haviland Carrier," www.invent.org/hall_of_fame/29.html, accessed on April 18, 2002.

5. National Inventors Hall of Fame, "Wallace Hume Carothers," www.invent.org/hall_of_fame/28.html, accessed on April 18, 2002; National Inventors Hall of Fame, "Julius Nieuwland," www.invent.org/hall_of_fame/111.html, accessed on April 18, 2002.

6. Trevor I. Williams, *The History of Invention* (New York: Facts on File Publications, 1987), pp. 234–235.

7. Thom Stark, "They Might Be Giants," *Boardwatch Magazine*, December 2000, pp. 112–131.

8. Williams, *The History of Invention*, pp. 267, 272–273, 300–306.

9. For a discussion of the completion of the human genome project, see Frederic Golden and Michael D. Lemerick, "The Race Is Over," *Time*, July 3, 2000, pp. 18–23. For a discussion of the discovery of Pluto, see Patrick Moore, "Traveller, Poet, and Misfit of Mars," *Times Higher Education Supplement*, September 21, 2001, p. 35.

10. "Superstructures: Thinking Big," David Darlow and Stephen H. Schwartz, producers (The Learning Channel, 2002).

11. Gerald O'Driscoll, Kim R. Holmes, and Mary Anastasia O'Grady, *2002 Index of Economic Freedom* (Washington, DC: Heritage Foundation and *Wall Street Journal*, 2001).

12. Melissa S. Brown, ed., *Giving USA 2001: The Annual Report on Philanthropy* (Indianapolis: AAFRC Trust for Philanthropy, 2001), pp. 138–143.

13. Larry Nowels, "Appropriations for FY2002: Foreign Operations, Export Financing, and Other Related Programs," Congressional Research Service, February 4, 2002.

14. Ibid.; U.S. Department of Treasury, "U.S. Debt Reduction Activities FY 1990 Through FY 1999," February 2000. The report documents that during the 1990s, the United States relieved more than $14 billion in debts owed by several dozen nations. The reduction of these debts preceded the "Jubilee 2000" campaign seeking to forgive billions in Third World debt.

15. "Facts About the United Nations," www.un.org/News/facts /setting.htm, accessed on May 10, 2002.

16. Center for Immigration Studies, "History," www.cis.org/topics /history.html, accessed on April 18, 2002; Encyclopedia.com, "Immigration in the United States," www.encyclopedia .com/html/section/immigrat_immigrationintheunitedstates .asp, accessed on April 18, 2002.

17. Alexander Hamilton, James Madison, and John Jay, *The Federalist* (New York: Barnes & Noble Books, 1996), p. 89.

18. M. Lawrence Podolsky, *Cures out of Chaos: How Unexpected Discoveries Led to Breakthroughs in Medicine and Health* (Amsterdam: Harwood Academic Publishers, 1997), p. 250–252.

19. Ibid., p. 216.

20. Ibid., pp. 165–172; Ron Chernow, *Titan: The Life of John D. Rockefeller, Sr.* (New York: Random House, 1999), p. 569; National Inventors Hall of Fame, "Irving Millman," www .invent.org/hall_of_fame/103.html, accessed on April 18, 2002; National Inventors Hall of Fame, "Baruch Blumberg," www .invent.org/hall_of_fame/17.html, accessed on April 18, 2002.

21. Podolsky, *Cures out of Chaos*, pp. 57–64, 217–218, 278.

22. Ibid., pp. 275–278.

23. National Inventors Hall of Fame, "Raymond V. Damadian," www.invent.org/hall_of_fame/36.html, accessed on April 18, 2002; National Inventors Hall of Fame, "Wilson Greatbatch," www.invent.org/hall_of_fame/70.html, accessed on April 18, 2002; National Inventors Hall of Fame, "Robert S. Ledley,"

www.invent.org/hall_of_fame/95.html, accessed on April 18, 2002.

24. Williams, *The History of Invention*, p. 284.

25. Nobel e-Museum, "The Nobel Prize in Medicine-Laureates," www.nobel.se/medicine/laureates/index.html, accessed on April 18, 2002.

26. Peter Zedrin, quoted in Andy Golodny, "Students, Profs Walk out of Class to Protest Air Strikes," *Brown Daily Herald*, October 10, 2001, p. 1.

27. Quoted in Michael Medved, *Hollywood vs. America* (New York: Harper Perennial, 1993), p. 217.

28. Quoted in Paul Hollander, *Anti-Americanism: Critiques at Home and Abroad, 1965–1990* (New York: Oxford University Press, 1992), p. 66.

29. Quoted in Robert Bork, *Slouching Towards Gomorrah: Modern Liberalism and American Decline* (New York: ReganBooks, 1996), p. 99.

30. Quoted in Dinesh D'Souza, *What's So Great About America* (Washington, DC: Regnery, 2002), p. 181.

31. Quoted in James Loewen, *Lies My Teacher Told Me: Everything Your American History Textbook Got Wrong* (New York: The New Press, 1995), p. 306.

32. For the statistics cited in this section, see William J. Bennett, *The Index of Leading Cultural Indicators: American Society at the End of the Twentieth Century* (New York: Broadway Books, 1999), pp. 17, 53, 59, 69, 82.

33. John Rawls, *A Theory of Justice* (Cambridge, MA: Harvard University Press, 1971), p. 102.

34. Bork, *Slouching Towards Gomorrah*, p. 2.

35. Patrick Buchanan, speech at the Republican National Convention, Houston, TX, August 17, 1992.

36. "The End of Democracy? The Judicial Usurpation of Politics," *First Things*, November 1996, p. 18.

37. Quoted in B. J. Lossing, *Lives of the Signers of the Declaration of Independence* (Aledo, TX: WallBuilder Press, 1998), p. 183n.

38. Alexis de Tocqueville, *Democracy in America: Volume 1* (New York: Vintage Classics, 1990), p. 403.

39. Ibid., pp. 82–83.

40. Hamilton et al., *The Federalist*, p. 283.

41. "Amendment X," The Constitution of the United States of America.
42. Hamilton et al., *The Federalist*, p. 493.
43. Ibid., p. 492.
44. M. E. Bradford, *Founding Fathers: Brief Lives of the Framers of the United States Constitution* (Lawrence: University Press of Kansas, 1990), p. 158.
45. Ibid., p. 196.
46. Ibid., p. 128.
47. Hamilton et al., *The Federalist*, p. 190.
48. Thomas Jefferson, *Notes on the State of Virginia* (New York: W. W. Norton, 1982), p. 173.
49. Bradford, *Founding Fathers*, p. 58.
50. Quoted in Thomas G. West, *Vindicating the Founders: Race, Sex, Class, and Justice in the Origins of America* (Lanham, MD: Rowman & Littlefield, 1997), p. 135.
51. Hamilton et al., *The Federalist*, p. 133.
52. Bradford, *Founding Fathers*, p. 13.
53. Tocqueville, *Democracy in America: Volume 1*, p. 304.
54. Cited in D'Souza, *What's So Great About America*, p. 145.
55. Paul Johnson, *A History of the American People* (New York: HarperCollins, 1997), p. 207.
56. Bradford, *Founding Fathers*, p. xvi.
57. George Washington, "Farewell Address," September 19, 1796.
58. M. Stanton Evans, *The Theme Is Freedom: Religion, Politics, and the American Tradition* (Washington, DC: Regnery, 1994), p. 274.
59. Quoted in ibid., p. 35.
60. Tocqueville, *Democracy in America: Volume 1*, p. 305.
61. Ibid., p. 307.
62. Washington, "Farewell Address."
63. Hamilton et al., *The Federalist*, p. 250.
64. Lossing, *Lives of the Signers of the Declaration of Independence*.
65. C. S. Lewis, *Mere Christianity* (Glasgow: Fount, 1997), p. 23.
66. Evans, *The Theme Is Freedom*, p. 9.
67. Edmund Burke, *Reflections on the Revolution in France*, edited by J. C. D. Clark (Stanford, CA: Stanford University Press, 2001), p. 241.

INDEX